Essential Data Skills for Business and Management

Editors

Steve Hurd

Jean Mangan

Statistics for Education

Published by Statistics for Education
5 Bridge Street
Bishops Stortford
CM23 2JU

Telephone   01279 652183
Internet   http://www.statsed.com
e-mail statsed@dial.pipex.com

© 2001 Statistics for Education

ISBN 1 872849 83 0

Produced in collaboration with:
Office for National Statistics
Room B1/09
1 Drummond Gate
London, SW1V 2QQ

Internet: http://www.statistics.gov.uk

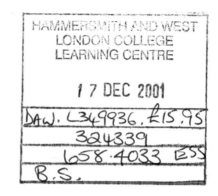

Data tables and Chapter 2 have been published with the permission of the Office for National Statistics on behalf of the controller of Her Majesty's Stationery Office © Crown Copyright 2000.

Design and typesetting by Patrick Armstrong, Book Production Services, London
Printed and bound in Great Britain by MPG Books Ltd.
Cover design by Michelle Franco, Office for National Statistics

Contents

Introduction 1

1   The use of statistics in business 5
    Ian McClean

2   Understanding national statistics 21
    Helen Shanks

3   Trends and fluctuations 39
    Steve Hurd

4   Market segments 55
    Barry Harrison

5   Analysing costs and prices 69
    Julian Gough

6   Demand forecasting 87
    Shabbar Jaffry and Frank Asche

7   The economy and business 99
    Professor Nigel Healey

8   National accounts and economic forecasts 113
    Martin Weale

9   Using economic data: a multinational perspective 127
    Donald Hepburn

10 Exports, imports and exchange rates 139
    Jean Mangan and Ian Jackson

    Data appendix 151

Acknowledgements

The editors are grateful to a number of people who have helped in the preparation of this publication. From the Office for National Statistics (Communication Division): Sally Mogford was instrumental in initiating the publication, and Kevin McHale, Tim Bishop, Morag Watson-Laight have been assiduous referees and proof readers. Alistair Dawson of Staffordshire University has cast a detailed and critical eye over the whole manuscript. Jill Leyland, from the Society of Business Economists and the World Gold Council, provided invaluable assistance during the planning stages of the publication, as did Roger Watson of Statistics for Education.

Introduction

Statistical data are a valuable business resource. What is surprising is that many firms fail to appreciate just how much external data exist to aid them in their day-today decisions and how relatively inexpensive they are. Nevertheless, whenever firms ponder their performance in different spheres it is difficult to avoid using the sorts of external benchmarks that published statistics provide.

Some of the many questions where widely available published data can provide valuable insights are:

- How does our performance compare with that of our industry? How are movements in the economy affecting our industry?

- Are our cost changes in line with similar businesses? Are our raw material and wage costs in line with the norms for our industry?

- How do our price changes compare with price trends for our sector? How do they compare with the prices in the wider economy?

- What do we know about our performance in different market segments? What is happening to the age, sex, income and regional composition of our markets? How should this affect our marketing and distribution strategies?

- How are we doing in relation to our competitors abroad? How well are we penetrating foreign markets compared to similar businesses? Are foreign firms breaking into our home market? What factors affect our competitiveness? How will we be affected by changes in interest rates and exchange rates?

- What do the economic forecasts predict is likely to happen to economic growth and inflation? Have we taken account of these predictions in our production and investment planning? Will we need to adjust our levels of employment? What about our prices?

The book concentrates particularly on how official government data can help to answer questions such as the ones above. *National Statistics* is the specialist agency responsible for the publication and dissemination of official statistics. Although an arm of government, it is constitutionally independent, and has responsibility for ensuring the quality and integrity of official statistics. Commitment in the UK to data as a public good guarantees that business and other users are supplied with a wealth of high quality and relatively inexpensive statistics on the economy as a whole and on individual sectors.

Essential Data Skills for Business and Management provides readers with:

- Information on useful statistics from inexpensive official sources;

- A guide to finding the most appropriate data for different purposes;

- An understanding of commonly used statistical definitions and measurement conventions;

- Calculation and graphing techniques enabling data to be presented effectively;

- Advice on how to use data intelligently to inform business decision-making.

This is an introductory book written by experienced business professionals and academics. It assumes no prior knowledge of statistical methods. The book has been written for people who need to use data as part of their day-to-day work in business and commerce. It is relevant to all of the main areas of business, including market research, production planning, costing and finance, human resource management and business strategy areas. This material will also be invaluable for B.A. and M.B.A. students of Business and Management undertaking data handling courses and project work.

What follows is a brief sketch of the content of each of the chapters.

In Chapter 1 Ian McClean provides an overview of the use of statistics in business. He starts from the premise that statistics are one of the most important information flows available to management, and surveys their role in strategic planning, research and development, production and distribution and marketing. The chapter explains how a firm might estimate the size of its market, and assess how well it is doing in relation to the market as a whole using such data sources as *PRODCOM* and the *Index of Production*. The use of official statistics in an indirect manner to produce business estimates of target variables is also discussed.

In the second chapter Helen Shanks explains how official statistics are obtained, and what is done to make them more useful to data consumers. The chapter provides an essential explanation of the rationale for the UK National Accounts as presented in the *Blue Book* and *UK Economic Accounts* publications. It also describes the different forms in which the data are presented, including the differences between current and constant price measures, the calculation and use of index numbers and the process of seasonally adjusting data.

Chapter 3 focuses on time-series data. Steve Hurd begins by describing some of the main sources of time-series. The material in Chapter 2 is extended to further explore nominal and real expenditures, and discuss ways to identify and describe patterns in time-series data, using the *Monthly Digest of Statistics*. Numerical examples are presented showing how to make sense of data in the form of index numbers, growth rates and logarithmic series. The chapter ends by discussing techniques for fitting trends to data series.

Barry Harrison discusses the use of cross-sectional data in Chapter 4. He begins by explaining the different ways of defining market segments. There is discussion of the use of cross-sectional data on age groups, gender, incomes and regional characteristics. The chapter introduces a number of standard sources of cross-sectional data, including the Family Expenditure Survey, the General Household Survey, *Social Trends* and *Regional Trends*.

In Chapter 5 Julian Gough explains how firms can use published data to help them gain a perspective on their costs and prices. He explains how to analyse the dynamic movement of costs and prices over time, including how to create an index of costs and to compare various cost components with industry and economy-wide indices published in *Economic Trends* and the *Monthly Digest of Statistics*. The chapter discusses the use of price deflators and goes on to discuss alternative approaches to pricing.

The subject of Chapter 6 is demand forecasting. Using data from the *National Statistics* web site, Shabbar Jaffry and Frank Asche provide a step-by-step guide to constructing a model of demand and estimating its equation using the multiple regression procedure in the *Excel* spreadsheet. They explain how the estimated equation can be interpreted and how to use it to forecast future demand, using alternative assumptions about the movement of key variables. The chapter ends by explaining how to monitor the performance of a forecast.

In Chapter 7 Nigel Healey explains the importance to firms of understanding the macro-economic environment of business. He surveys the meanings and measurement of economic growth, aggregate demand, unemployment, wage inflation, inflation, interest rates, the current balance of payments and exchange rates. While showing how data from *Economic Trends* and *Financial Statistics* can be used to track these variables, the chapter emphasises the importance of viewing the UK in a wider European context, by using such publications as *European Economy*.

Martin Weale provides essential background to understanding macroeconomic forecasting in Chapter 8. Much of the chapter is devoted to developing an appreciation of the underlying variables that form the basis of any forecast. These include the various elements of the national accounts that make up the Gross Domestic Product, and the composition of the sectoral accounts. There is further discussion of the distinction between real and nominal values. The chapter ends by presenting a *National Institute for Economic and Social Research* forecast, and discussing forecast uncertainty.

In Chapter 9 Donald Hepburn presents a business economist's perspective on the use of statistical data in the context of a multinational enterprise. With reference to the strategic policy issues facing multinational business, he discusses the use of national and international data from *International Financial Statistics (IMF)*, the *World Bank* (web site), *Economic Outlook (OECD)*, *Family Expenditure Survey (NS)* and various forecasting organisations. The chapter emphasises the need for firms to understand the economic and political climate in which they operate, and the role that judgement plays in the use of data.

In the final chapter of the book, Jean Mangan and Ian Jackson concentrate on trade and exchange rates. They begin by considering the questions that are important to firms whether they are trading in international markets, or simply competing with imports in the home market. There is a discussion of how benchmarks of performance can be established

using published data from the *Monthly Review of External Trade Statistics*, *UK Trade in Goods Analysed in Terms of Industries*, *UK Balance of Payments (the Pink Book)* and the *World Bank* (web site). The chapter moves on to an examination of the effects of exchange rate changes and the determinants of international competitiveness.

The book includes a Data Appendix. This constitutes an introductory guide to national government and other sources of business data. It explains how to navigate the *National Statistics* web site, in order to find and down load data. There is a list of some of the most useful *National Statistics* publications and also of other sources mentioned within the text.

The book has an accompanying data CD-ROM and workbook. These are designed to allow readers to practice some of the techniques and investigations introduced in the individual chapters, and to become familiar with working with official data in an electronic format. The data files are provided in two alternative formats for the *Secos* data handling and Microsoft *Excel* programs.

Essential Data Skills for Business and Management will be updated on a regular basis, and the publishers are anxious that the content should be continually refined to meet the changing needs of users. To this end we would welcome suggestions from readers on how to improve the publication. Please contact:

Statistics for Education
5 Bridge Street
Bishops Stortford
CM23 2JU
Tel 01279 652182 (or 01782 750338)
e-mail: statsed@dial.pipex.com

Steve Hurd and Jean Mangan
December, 2000

1 The Use Of Statistics In Business

Ian Maclean, Managing Director, Business and Trade Statistics Ltd

FOCUS QUESTIONS

- What are the main sources of business statistics?
- In what areas of business decision making are statistics important?

- What type of information is most useful to firms?
- How can firms make full use of official statistics from government sources?
- How can firms use official data to derive estimates of non-published variables?

INTRODUCTION

Information is at the heart of management decisions and statistics are one of the most important elements in the information flows available to management. In terms of classical economics a company brings together three elements: land, labour and capital. In the early 20th century a fourth element was added – organisation. Today information is very definitely not only the fifth element, but also the one that binds all the others together.

Management information can conveniently be divided into internal and external. The data generated internally to control the company and the data derived externally that positions a company in its market environment.

Expenditure on management information is vast. Externally, business information is a multi-billion pound market. Internally, up to ten per cent of a typical firm's turnover is allocated to collecting and analysing information. Statistics only form part of this information flow, but a very important part. The last fifty years has seen an internal management information revolution with the

transition from purely financial accounting to highly detailed management accounts that measure all aspects of a company's operations – research and development, production, sales, advertising, direct mail, exhibitions. All are subject to detailed analysis – what they cost, what revenue they generate, and the effect on profits. This vast flow of information is enshrined in budgets and plans for every part of the company. The use of external data lags behind. Companies still tend to measure their performance by internal accounting ratios – profit on sales, profit on investment, profit per employee, profit on shareholders funds. Few follow through to the most objective of all measurements – the extent to which a company has taken advantage of the opportunities open to it. This leads to the key question that this chapter seeks to answer,

Has the company out performed or under performed the market?

This question breaks down into several sub-questions, which underlie competitiveness. They are developed in the following paragraphs where we consider:

- the characteristics of the demand for business statistics;
- the types of decision for which those statistics are used;
- the information required to underpin decisions;
- the role of official statistics and the methods by which those statistics can be made more relevant by utilising internal company data.

CHARACTERISTICS

A number of aspects of information are worth noting in passing before we consider decisions in depth. These fall into two main categories, variations between sectors and the importance of the decision under consideration, but there are also other factors to consider.

Variations between sectors

There are sectors in which external information flows are an essential part of the day-to-day operations and profitability. For stockbrokers and commodity traders, external information is one of their main *factors of production*, so expenditure on market information is high. In the fast moving consumer goods sector advertising and sales promotion is a major expenditure item, and market research an essential part of monitoring the effectiveness of that expenditure in terms of its impact on market share. The majority of firms in manufacturing industry however operate in small markets which cannot justify routine high levels of expenditure on market information, so are dependent on low cost sources such as official statistics.

Importance of the decision

The importance of the decision strongly influences the price that business is prepared to pay for information. When a company is considering acquisitions, major research and development, large new capital investments, new markets or whether to bow out of old, then large sums can be spent on specially commissioned market research (budgets of £100 thousand plus are not uncommon). At

the other end of the scale there is a very wide range of line-management decisions affecting the company's response to short-term changes in the market that need access to low-cost external information if those decisions are not to made just on hunch or guess work.

High or low level information ?

The most useful data has the attributes of being both relevant and timely. The more carefully targeted and up-to-date the higher the value of the data concerned, for example:

- The UK product report – called the *PRODCOM* series, from National Statistics is in reasonable detail as it covers almost 5,000 products. The data is collected annually and published almost a year later, so it is only useful to firms wishing to make comparisons with past performance. It is however relatively inexpensive.
- Commercially produced reports which bring together available published information on a sector plus a limited amount of new research and analysis, typically cost around £200.
- Multi-client reports, which research the market in-depth - costing £2000 upwards. These reports highlight the individual markets served by the company and provide the basis for direct actionable management decisions.
- Retail audits cost around £20,000. These provide specific brand market share information, normally by the end of the month following that to which the data relates.
- Panel studies on buying intentions can be as expensive as £100,000 or more. They are highly product and market specific, providing advance warning of likely movements in sales levels.

The external trade statistics are a good example of the graduation in price as the data becomes more specific:

- Trade statistics based on the Harmonised System collected by Customs and Excise cost about £1 per product code. They are excellent value for money, provided the classification fits the market definition. There are over 10,000 product headings so there is a good chance of achieving a reasonable fit, but it is frustrating if the product you are researching is grouped under 'other', the catch all heading that picks up all those products that are not specifically listed.

- Moving annual totals based on Customs data cost £25 per product. This report provides the same product detail as above but instead of just the current month's data provides an indication of market trends.
- Services based on ships' manifests, which provide the name of the exporter and the importer, ports of loading and discharge, the name of the ship and details of the cargo cost £200 per product. These are highly product specific right down to brand names and are published monthly within a month of collection.

Horses for Courses
Different types of decision require different types of information. The broadly based long-term strategic plan undertaken by a large company will rely heavily on the same type of macroeconomic information used by Government. ICI, for example, in deciding which sectors of the market to stay in and from which to withdraw will consider broad economic and social trends as well as specific information about its own industry and products. Should the company stay in fertilizers, man-made fibres, basic chemicals, speciality chemicals as well as pharmaceuticals? Where should the company operate? Globalisation is a term now very much in fashion, as companies have the freedom to set up production plants or source their inputs throughout the world. These major decisions are made at board level and will be based on very extensive research and analysis, but for every member of the board involved in major strategic decisions there are hundreds of individual product and marketing

managers making day-to-day decisions who require detailed information about their market niche or segment in order to react in time to market movements.

The various types of decision are discussed below.

BUSINESS DECISIONS
Statistics are not required for their own sake but as an aid to decision making. What products should a firm be developing, what capital investment is required to increase capacity or to reduce costs, what production levels should be scheduled, how many employees should be taken on or sacked, what is our market share and how do we protect/improve it, what markets should we be attacking with what resources, what should be the level of exports and which countries should we concentrate on? Are imports a threat? The list goes on and on! But the key issues may be conveniently grouped under those relating to planning and those for performance measurement.

Planning
Timescales may vary from months or even weeks for a trader importing the latest novelty, to decades for public utilities such as water and electricity considering major capital investments in new power stations and reservoirs. The decision areas include:

- strategic or long-term planning;
- research and development;
- production and distribution;
- marketing.

Each of these raises distinct questions.

Strategic Planning
What direction should the company take in the longer term: stay in the same sector, expand into new sectors, withdraw from an existing sector, spread into other countries for production or sourcing, develop by acquisition or internal growth?

Research and Development

The modification of existing products, development of new products and similar decisions for production methods, represent a major expenditure. Where are the existing products in their life cycle? What new products are required to sustain company growth and profitability? Are major changes needed in production methods to reduce costs and ensure competitiveness?

Production and Distribution

How large should the firm become? Where should it locate? Should it have one production and distribution unit or several? Are the economies of scale significant? Plant size and capacity utilisation, production scheduling and levels of stocks and work in progress, warehousing and transport policy, all exercise a critical influence on profitability and the survival of the company in a competitive market environment.

Marketing

Marketing plans occur at several levels, from the overall plan that allocates resources between the different elements of promotional activity – the sales force, advertising, exhibitions – to the individual plan for each of these elements, e.g. how many sales persons are required? What level of experience must they have? How should they be organised – by region, by industry or by size of customer? Should they be product or market specialists or generalists? A full-scale marketing plan is a very comprehensive document.

Performance Evaluation and Monitoring

The overall marketing plan has one over-riding aim – to ensure that the company exploits to the full the opportunities open to it. The key management question to answer is not how well the company is doing historically in terms of growth or turnover, return on capital, improvements in productivity, or any of the other standard management accounting measurements, but how well the company has performed in relation to the opportunities

open to it. Inflation has complicated comparisons, as it is perfectly possible to show an annual increase in turnover, yet to be losing market share. There is a need to establish the external yardsticks against which the actual performance of the company can be measured, including:

* Is the company gaining or losing market share?
* Is it responding to the changing patterns of the market?
* Is import penetration rising and where is the danger coming from?
* Where are the export opportunities?

The identification of these opportunities introduces another important concept – market segmentation. Markets rarely exist as massive concentrations. A typical situation facing most companies is that the market is divided up by product type, by end-user sector, by region, and by customer size. Each of these segments can be expanding or declining at a different rate. Each can require a different marketing approach. This is developed in the next section and in Chapter 4.

INFORMATION REQUIREMENTS

The information required to place the company in its market environment, whether for planning both in the long or short term or monitoring performance, can be classified under five main headings:

1. market size;
2. market structure;
3. market trends;
4. factors influencing market share;
5. company information.

Market Size

Before the size of a market can be determined it is necessary to determine what is meant by the market. The market for electric motors, for instance, is made up of an enormous size variation from small fractional horse-power motors used in hand tools and washing machines up to the huge motors, of several thousand horse-power, used for steel rolling mills. Then there is the much higher standard of design and production required for flameproof motors for hazardous installations such as chemical plants. These different types of electric motor have such widely different marketing characteristics that effectively they form entirely different markets.

Having defined the market in product terms, it is still necessary to consider the extent to which that market is accessible and profitable to the company. Some of the factors that reduce the total available market are tied suppliers, reciprocal-purchasing arrangements and long-term contracts. In terms of profitability, regional factors may restrict the market to the economic distribution radius around a given plant or depot. The difficulties of selling into certain end-user industries may limit the market, and the wide variation in customer size may also restrict the market to the size range the company can deal with efficiently. These factors are discussed in more detail in the section on Market Structure.

Market Structure

Industrial markets are characterised by a high degree of segmentation and each different segment exercises a different influence on product requirements, marketing approach and growth potential.

The principal areas of segmentation are by:

- application;
- user industry;
- region;
- size of customer;
- channel of distribution.

Applications

A recurring feature in many markets is that companies which have produced and sold a product for many decades are still not certain about the exact uses to which their product is put by their customers. If all the various applications for the product were equally subject to the same external influences there would be no problem, but frequently they are differently affected. For example, dissolved acetylene as a fuel gas is used for welding and cutting metal. As a welding gas it has no real competition, as a cutting gas it is in direct competition with propane. Propane is much cheaper so has steadily eroded the acetylene market for metal cutting but left the welding market intact.

The application of the product also influences the marketing approach. Carbon dioxide, for example, can be used as an inert gas for welding, to carbonate beer and soft drinks, or, in solid or liquid form, as a refrigerant. As a carbonating agent in beverages, it is essential that the gas should be odourless and tasteless, whereas no-one would complain of the tainting of a metal shaft that had been shrunk fit into place with the use of liquid CO_2.

User Industries

Industries grow and decline at different rates so it is important that the relative share of each end-user industry within the total market is known. Industries also exhibit very different purchasing characteristics. New industries tending to be more willing to deal with new suppliers and to use more sophisticated techniques in selecting their supplier.

Few companies only supply one single product and because most companies have a different range of products, very different marketing situations can develop between different end-user industries. To take another example from the industrial gases market, engineering and brewing are among the industries to which carbon dioxide is sold. At one time there were only two suppliers – Distillers and Air Products. Distillers with their base in whisky and other spirits naturally had a strong position in the brewing industry, but carbon dioxide was the only major product they supplied to the engineering industry. Air Products, on the other hand, while only supplying carbon dioxide to the brewing industry, marketed a whole range of other industrial gases to engineering.

Regions

Just as industries grow and decline at different rates, so there is a substantial difference in the growth rates of the different regions of Britain. This factor is of even greater importance for exports when consideration is given to the relative movements of the economies of different countries. Regional patterns also affect customer supplier relationships; just as the older industries tend to be more conservative and loyal in their attitude to suppliers, so the more rural areas of the country tend to show greater loyalty, often expressed to a representative rather than to a company.

Size of Customer

In developing a market plan it is normal practise to analyse the market in terms of customer size, the 80/20 rule – 80 per cent of demand from 20 per cent of the customers is a well-known feature of most markets. In the case of consumer goods, market research companies have invested heavily in methods of identifying and targeting heavy product users. In business-to-business markets the variation

in customer size is much more pronounced and justifies a high level of research to establish the patterns appropriate to each market served by the company.

A typical customer breakdown is shown in Table 1.1 below:

The identification of customer size is not straight forward as it is not always directly associated with the actual size of the firm. The largest companies buy many products in small quantities, especially when purchasing is de-centralised to the branch factory or depot.

The importance of the size of customer breakdown lies in the fact that there is a size limit below which it is uneconomic to deal directly with a customer for a variety of reasons.

To take sales costs as an example, on the basis of £20 for a sales call, and a call order ratio of one in ten, the cost of a sales call per order is of the order of £200. If the profit margin on sales is 20 per cent, then the company could not make a profit on any firm which places an order for less than £1,000. These are not standard figures, but similar ones can be established for any firm. Only part of the market is worth dealing with through the sales force, and it is one of the roles of marketing research to identify the 'significant customer' element, and to show how many companies there are above and below this line

Table 1.1 *Customer breakdown*

Annual size of purchases £'000	Customers Number	%	Total Purchases £'000	%	Average customer size £'000
Over 100	4	1	1,200	18	300
51 – 100	20	2	1,400	21	70
26 – 50	50	6	1,750	26	35
11 – 25	100	11	1,500	22	15
1 – 10	200	23	800	12	4
Less than 1	500	57	100	1	0.2
TOTAL	874	100	6,750	100	8

of significance, and what this means in terms of sales.

Several other factors need to be taken into account, the cost of the salesman's visit is only one element; other costs include the servicing of customers and invoicing. As a result of these calculations, turnover and employment figures will emerge which will provide a cut-off point in terms of the size of customer that the company can afford to deal with directly. This is not to suggest that small customers are unprofitable. All markets are potentially profitable, but only if their characteristics are recognised and the appropriate organisation set up to deal with them. For small orders the answer may be distributors, agents or some form of postal selling. The Internet will result in far reaching changes and it is no surprise that it is the business-to-business sector that is the most rapidly expanding part of Internet sales.

The size of company analysis is also highly relevant in terms of the size and calibre of the sales force. The link between the number of customers and the number of salesmen is dependent on the number of customers and the frequency of call, the frequency of call in turn being dependent on the size of the customer, large customers being called on more often than small. It is also normal practice to allocate the large accounts to the more experienced and successful salesmen, so a size of customer analysis provides guidelines for

the composition as well as the size of the sales force.

Trends

There are two main elements that influence the rate of expansion or contraction of a market:

- the growth or decline of the end-user sectors into which the product is sold;
- the technical, economic and social changes that are taking place that may affect the demand for the product in these sectors.

Forecasting based on the extrapolation of past trends does to some extent include the effects of both these elements but the forecasting model can be significantly improved if there is a clear understanding of the forces at work in the market. Just what is it that is causing the market to grow or decline, and how do these factors inter-relate? Again, market segmentation is a key to that understanding.

A company making numerically-controlled metal-forming machine tools may be classified to manufacturing industry, more exactly to mechanical engineering, then machine tools but, as Table 1.2 shows, the factors influencing the demand for individual products within a product group can vary widely. There is no way you can follow the trend in demand for an individual machine tool's classification by reference to the index of output for machine tools in total, let alone the overall index of

Table 1.2 *Index of production change by market sector*

SIC*	Sector	1991	1992
	All Manufacturing Industries	100	96
29	Machinery and Domestic Appliances	100	93
29.4	Machine Tools	100	80
29.401	Metal Working Machine Tools	100	75
29.402113	NC Metal Forming	100	160
29.403131	Non-Precision Grinders	100	48

*The standard industrial classification (SIC) is a 5 digit hierarchical nomenclature which has been extended to 8 digits for the PRODCOM series. All products are classified to one of these 8 digit headings.
Source: National Statistics, *PRODCOM* and Machine Tool Trades Association

production. Each product effectively is operating in a micro-marketing climate. Regions of a country can also show similar variations in market conditions. The closing of a steel mill in South Wales has very extensive knock on effects on local markets. Staying with the weather analogy, a weather forecast for the whole of Europe – *generally fine* – is not much help when you are setting out for a day's walking. You need the local forecast.

Market Share

The size of a market and the structure of a market are largely outside the control of an individual company, but the share of the market held by the company is strongly influenced by the energy, enterprise and expenditure displayed by the company in comparison to its competitors.

Given the size of the 'available' market, the principal forces at work are:

- the loyalty of customers to their existing suppliers;
- the needs of the customer and the degree of satisfaction felt by the customer with the products and service of suppliers;
- the extent to which suppliers are getting through to the right levels of purchasing responsibility within the customer company;
- the effectiveness of the various forms of communication between the supplier and customers;
- the activity of competitors. All of the information relating to a customer-supplier relationship needs to be expressed against the background of the competitive climate within the sector.

Company Information

In the business-to-business market, the final aim of the planning process is to secure the sale of a product or service to a 'customer' company. The marketing plan, therefore, must not only describe the market in terms of the numbers of customers by size, industry or region, but must also list those customer companies by name and describe them as fully as possible in terms of turnover, product range, profitability, and credit rating. Similar information is required for competitors in order to prepare the appropriate plans for meeting the competition.

THE ROLE OF OFFICIAL STATISTICS

The information required for the full marketing plan and budget is brought together from a wide range of sources, both internal and external: existing company records, the experience of the sales force, the media in its various forms – technical journals, conference papers, and market research. For many companies official statistics form a relatively small and neglected part of the total information flow, but where the official statistics are applicable they represent one of the most valuable and lowest cost sources of information.

Taking each of the information requirement sectors in turn:

- market size;
- market structure;
- market trends;
- factors influencing market share;
- company information.

Market Size

There are three alternatives:

- Information is already collected in exactly the form required.
- Statistics are available but out of date.
- No figures exist but information on market size may be deduced from other statistics.

Existing Data

The PRODCOM series published by National Statistics gives the output in volume and value for some 5,000 products. PRODCOM is the result of an EU directive covering all member states. The data is collected on an annual basis and published with a lag of about one year. Service statistics are also available under broad aggregates.

The external trade figures are also a valuable series to firms. They are published with only a short lag and are highly disaggregated. Import and export data is available for 10,000 separate products classified to the Combined Nomenclature, an eight digit classification that is common for all countries of the European Community and based on a six digit classification covering 6,000 products – the Harmonised System, which is a world standard to which all countries subscribe.

One of the advantages of the PRODCOM system is that the product output classifications align closely to the Combined Nomenclature, so that it is possible to calculate UK apparent consumption – production minus exports, plus imports.

Updating

The PRODCOM data can be updated by the monthly index of production but this is only a very rough and ready approach as there are only just over 300 industries in the index and individual products can move very differently from the industry average. See Table 1.2.

Derived Data

If there is no direct source of information it may be possible to calculate market size by establishing the relationship with a statistical series for which there is up to date, frequent and detailed information. It was possible to determine the market for dissolved acetylene, a product for which there are no official statistics, by utilising internal company data. There is a strong link between the usage of dissolved acetylene per employee in different industries. Utilising internal company data (in the absence of such data market research can be used to establish the factors) a consumption factor per employee per industry can be established. This can then be applied to the national employment statistics on an industry sector basis. See Table 1.3 below.

Where the employment method is invalid, there may be a relationship between the

---

Table 1.3 *Estimating the market for dissolved acetylene(DA) in 1997*

SIC	Industry	Employment			DA Consumption* Millions cu. feet	
		Known '000	Total '000	Known %	Known	Total
24	Chemicals	43.0	269	16	2.2	13.7
27	Metals	62.5	139	45	24.6	54.7
28	Fabricated Metal Products	136.0	400	34	54.3	159.6
29	Machinery & Equipment	49.6	405	12	7.1	59.3
31	Electrical Machinery	19.7	197	10	2.7	27.4
34	Motor Vehicle	48.4	121	40	2.9	72.3
35	Other Transport Equipment	52.5	164	32	2.2	68.4
	Total	**	**	**	95.9	456.1

*Figures have been altered to avoid disclosing confidential data. ** totals not relevant.

Sources: The table was derived by analysing existing sales reports and customer records. Each customer for which acetylene consumption was available was listed under the appropriate industry heading. The employment figure relevant to that company was then identified (from directories and sales records), totalled by industry and compared with the total employment for that industrial sector taken from the annual labour returns published by National Statistics.

product being researched and another for which information is available. Taking the acetylene example again, acetylene is used in conjunction with oxygen, the total market for oxygen was known. From internal company data is was possible to establish a relationship between oxygen sales and acetylene sales, so from there on only simple arithmetic was required to estimate the size of the acetylene market.

The employment figures that have already been referred to are the most universal official statistical series available for modification, but a review of the output of the government statistical services throws up a wide variety of other usable statistical series for all major industries.

Market Structure

Structural information is rarely available for detailed product market sectors but is readily available at the SIC level, both in terms of regions and the number and size of companies.

As with estimating market size, the data can be significantly improved through establishing a relationship between the market under review and the appropriate available statistical series. In this example – determining the regional breakdown of the market for oxygen, the oxygen consumption factor per employee for each industry heading can be established from internal company data and then applied to the employment data for that industry in each region. It is a similar approach to Table 1.3 but extended to provide a regional analysis of a market in Table 1.4 and with variations to the breakdown of the market by size of company in Table 1.5.

A further development of the size-of-company analysis approach is to consider the market in terms of significant customers. In most marketing situations there will be size groups of customer that the company wants to deal with direct, and sizes that are too small; using this approach it is possible to identify

Table 1.4 *Estimating size of regional and industrial sector markets in 1997*

SIC		Per Capita Oxygen Consumption	Employment Regions		Oxygen Demand Standard cu. feet/Month 000s	
		Scf/MONTH	London*	Total UK	London*	Total UK
24	Chemicals	25	15	250	0.4	6.3
27	Metals	300	3	132	0.9	39.6
28	Fabricated Metal Products	100	18	424	1.8	42.4
29	Machinery & Equipment	40	14	398	0.6	15.9
34	Motor Vehicle	70	12	225	0.8	15.8
35	Other Transport Equipment	150	3	154	0.5	23.1
Total		**	**	**	5.0***	143.1**

Scf = standard cubic feet
* Only one region shown in table
** Total for those columns are not relevant
*** Figures have been changed to prevent disclosure. Actual market size is confidential as there are less than 3 suppliers.

Sources: Per capita consumption per industry - company data
Employment – National Statistics, *Annual Employment Report*

exactly the number of companies above the significant size level. In the example shown in Table 1.5, the objective is to identify the customers for liquid oxygen. The market for oxygen is divided into two parts: gaseous oxygen supplied compressed in cylinders and liquid oxygen supplied in insulated tanks. The former is very much more cumbersome and labour intensive and therefore more expensive to supply.

The supply in liquid form, however, is not economic below about 10,000 standard cubic feet per month. The aim is to establish a method of utilising official statistics from the *Size Analysis of UK Business* to identify the number of companies available for the liquid oxygen market. The results are shown in Table 1.5.

The importance of this approach is clearly demonstrated by the fact that the 5,285 establishments in the machinery sector yield only 160 companies as potential customers for liquid oxygen.

Trends in the Market

Given a reasonable time series, there is an embarrassment of choice of forecasting methods available at the touch of a key. All standard forecasting techniques balance the various factors influencing a trend. In order to understand the way the market is moving, however, it is sometimes sensible to consider those factors independently.

For manufacturing industry two of the most important factors are:

- changes in the output of the user industry sectors;
- changes in the use made of the product for technological or economic reasons.

Identifying the relative importance of these two factors is critical for a real understanding of the forces at work in the market. The approach is to:

1. Establish over a period of historical time, say the last five years, what the growth of product sales would have been had they kept pace with the growth or decline in the market.
2. Compare the estimated figure for the market at the end of the five-year period with the actual result. The difference, being due to technical or economic changes affecting the way in which the product is used in the

Table 1.5 Market analysis by size of significant customers in machinery sector

| Industry | SIC | Significant Customers | | | |
		Oxygen Usage per Employee scf/Month*	Minimum Employment	No. Employing over the Minimum	Total no. of companies in industry sector
Agricultural Machinery	2932	50	200	5	1305
Special Purpose Machinery	2956	20	500	5	1920
Contractors Plant	2952	200	50	65	435
Mechanical Handling Plant	2922	150	100	85	1605
TOTAL	-	-	-	160	5285

*Figures changed to avoid disclosure of confidential information.

Sources. Oxygen usage per employee per industry from company data.
Size of company data from National Statistics, *PA1003 Size Analysis of UK Business.*

market. This difference can now be expressed as a percentage change factor, which can be applied to forecasts of the growth/decline of the user industries. The market sector approach is critical as frequently there are significant differences in the way the product is used in each sector.

Table 1.6 below illustrates both the results and the method.

The value of calculating the technical and economic change function (TECF) for each industrial sector, rather than for the market in total, is well illustrated by Table 1.6 as the technological change has been far more significant in some sectors than others. In the

example shown above there is a significant substitution of hydraulic motors for electric motors in the mechanical handling and contractors plant industries, whereas sectors such as pumps are relatively unaffected.

The machine tool sector is of particular interest as the available company intelligence did not identify the falling techno-economic demand and was missed by a market research survey. It is only after calculating the TECF and then going back to the key respondents and asking them to explain the divergence between predicted and actual purchases that it could be discovered that the composition of machine tool output had changed. There has been a shift to a higher proportion of numerically controlled machine tools which

Table 1.6 *Calculating the technical and economic change function for electric motors of 1 horse power and over, 1990-95*

Machinery Sector	Column 1 Electric Motor Demand in 1990 £M	Column 2 Index of Sector Output 1995 (1990=100)	Column 3 Demand Projection for 1995 £M	Column 4 Actual Demand 1995 £M	Column 5 Five year TECF*
Machine Tools	4.5	88	4.0	3.2	-20%
Pumps	3.8	99	3.8	3.6	-3%
Compressors	2.4	99	2.4	2.2	-8%
Textile Machinery	2.3	82	2.7	2.5	-7%
Contractors Plant	1.9	90	1.7	1.1	-35%
Mec. Handling	3.8	86	3.3	2.2	-33%
Other Machinery	4.8	80	3.8	3.4	-11%
Users	8.3	110	9.1	8.9	-2%
TOTAL	**31.8**	-	**30.8**	**27.1**	**-12%**

*TECF = the technical and economic change factor.
The sources and various stages in the procedure are:

1. Estimate demand for product in each market sector in the base year through market research or company data – Column 1
2. Enter the index of sector output in Column 2 from the National Statistics, *Index of Production*
3. Calculate the projected change in demand based on the change in the index of production – Column 3 = Column 1 x Column 2 ÷ 100
4. Estimate demand in current year through market research or company data – Column 4
5. Calculate the economic change function – Column 5. This is the difference between Columns 3 and 4 expressed as a percentage of Column 3.

have a much higher unit value. The result is that the index of output, which is based on turnover, had not fallen as much as the number of machine tools, and it is the number of tools that determines the demand for electric motors.

Factors Influencing Market Share

The assessment of factors influencing competition is largely derived from company intelligence and market research, but official statistics can assist in several ways:

* directly to measure changes in market share
* to help assess competitiveness
* to provide a basis for market research field work.

Measuring Changes in Market Share

The PRODCOM series provides a direct measure of market share for the 5,000 products for which statistics are collected. Some of the products have quarterly data available, but for the majority it is only annual. The PRODCOM series is not the only source of product details. The Department of the Environment, Transport and the Regions (DETR) also collects quarterly information on the output of building and construction materials. Exporters and importers are more fortunate as the trade statistics are collected monthly.

Assessing Competitiveness

In the context of competition the NS *Index of Production* can be utilised to provide up-to-date monthly indicators of change in a company's competitive position. Comparisons with the total Index of Production will frequently be very wide of the mark because the company does not serve the total market. The company needs to calculate what has happened to its own sectors in proportion to their importance to the company

Table 1.7 below illustrates how the company market profile throws up the gap between actual performance against the market

Table 1.7 *Company market profile*

S.I.C.	Industry	Column 1 Sector Importance In base year %	Column 2 Industry Growth* over last 5 years %	Column 3 Increase in company sales over last 5 years %
331	Agricultural Machinery	10	25	13
335	Textile Machinery	10	27	13
336	Contractors Plant	5	54	8
337	Mech. Handling Plant	15	24	19
339/1	Mining Machinery	25	4	26
339/5	Pumps and values	25	16	29
339/5	Compressors	10	32	13
TOTAL		**100**	**26**	**21**

* Based upon National Statistics, *Index of Production*.

Source and Method
The calculations are derived from
* an analysis of existing company sales classified to each of the industrial sectors that form the market
* the importance of each sector is calculated (Column 1) (here the figures are made up)
* the growth of each industry sector over the last five years (Column 2)
* the actual change in company sales to that sector over the period (Column 3)

movement. In this example the company's growth has been 21 per cent over the past five years (Column 3), compared with the 26 per cent increase for its market (Column 2). So the company has lost market position.

This approach can be used on a regular monthly basis to ensure that timely warning is given of any gaps between the company performance and market movement expectation, as in Figure 1.1 below.

Figure 1.1 *Comparing company sales and market movement*

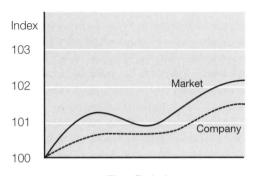

Source: Index of Growth of Market
Index of Growth of Company Sales

Assisting Market Research

Official statistics can help to determine market share but do not cover the factors influencing competition. That is essentially the role of market research. Official statistics however can play an important role in market research survey planning, as Table 1.8 below shows. Sampling is an essential element in market research and official statistics can help in defining the population from which the sample is drawn. Let us suppose that the aim is to determine the number of interviews required to provide a high degree of coverage of each of twelve industry end user sectors. Out of 3,258 enterprises, 115 accounted for 70 per cent of sales, and the 81 firms selected for interview were responsible for two-thirds of the output of the firms that formed the market. This approach can be used to calculate the total market from the survey data as grossing up factors can be established.

Company Information

Although official statistics are useful for many aspects of business decision making, in two particular areas they are indispensable: company accounts and industry lists.

Table 1.8 *Identification of sample for a survey in the food processing industry*

	Large Firms				
	No. of Enterprises	No. of Establishments	% of gross output	Total no. of Enterprises	Sample size
Biscuits	5	25	68	78	4
Bacon Curing and Meat Products	21	93	65	651	16
Milk Products	7	79	60	301	7
Sugar	4	28	96	19	3
Grain Milling	7	87	61	408	5
Cocoa, Chocolate and Sugar Confec.	11	54	70	454	8
Fruit and Vegetable Products	12	76	65	313	8
Animal and Poultry Food	10	73	55	541	6
Margarine	4	5	82	20	2
Starch and Miscellaneous Foods	10	30	58	217	6
Brewing and Malting	14	258	70	96	10
Spirit Distilling	10	87	92	60	6
TOTAL	**115**	**895**	**70**	**3258**	**81**

Source: NS, *Census of Production*

Company Accounts

Companies are required by law to lodge with Companies House detailed accounts covering turnover, profits, investment, etc. Various commercial organisations, such as Inter-Company Comparisons (ICC), produce reports with a whole set of ratios which provide a real insight into the health and performance of a company. Individual company reports are available cheaply from Companies House at Cardiff.

Industry Lists

The ultimate justification for marketing plans is a successful sale to a customer and the sales force is always eternally grateful for potential customer lists, preferably with an indication of likely demand.

National Statistics maintains the *Interdepartmental Business Register* – a complete record of who manufactures what product. There are many countries in the world that do make such registers available but in the United Kingdom the publication of company names based on the register is held to contravene the 1948 Statistics of Trade Act. There have been various suggestions that the Acts could be amended but it is not high on the government's legislative agenda. There has been a compromise. The firms responding to statistical enquiries are asked for permission to include their name in an industry directory. NS publish such a directory, which contains some 70% of company names. (30% of companies did not tick the box giving permission!) What we are seeking however is not an industry but a product directory – based on the 5000 Prodcom classifications not just the 300 SIC headings. Interestingly the names and addresses of importers into the United Kingdom are available monthly under the full tariff code classification (over 10,000 individual products). This was the result of a special legislation in 1989, so perhaps there is hope that it may eventually be extended to production.

Conclusion

The government spends over £200 million annually on collecting statistics, which are largely made available to users at the marginal cost of publication. The Government absorbs the collection costs. The economic and business statistics are the responsibility mainly of National Statistics. All government departments collect statistics – health, education etc, which can assist in assessing those markets. The cost to the users of official statistics is only a fraction of the cost of market research so it makes eminent sense to check them out first. In this context it is essential to look beyond the raw data. Finding something exactly right is a matter of chance. What we have tried to do in this chapter is to encourage the approach that seeks to utilise whatever official statistics are available and convert them into relevant data. Applying initiative and imagination can unlock a virtual Aladdin's cave of valuable market intelligence at a fraction of the cost of private collection.

2 National Statistics in the UK

Helen Shanks, Head of National Accounts Training, Office for National Statistics

FOCUS QUESTIONS

- What do we mean by National Statistics?
- What sort of data are included?
- How is the collection of National Statistics related to our understanding of the national economy?

- What do we need to know about methods and conventions of measurement and presentation?
- What is done to make the statistics more useful?
- How can we obtain relevant National Statistics?

INTRODUCTION TO NATIONAL STATISTICS

This chapter takes a closer look at where official statistics in the UK come from and the processes used to bring the statistics together for publication. A brief description of the framework for National Statistics – which ensures the quality and independence of official statistics - is provided before the focus moves to the economy and some of the main economic statistics frequently used in business and management.

The areas covered by National Statistics include:

- the national or economic accounts – which includes Gross Domestic Product (GDP) and the Balance of Payments;
- prices and measures of inflation – for example the Retail Price Index (RPI);
- short-term indicators like the Indices of Production (IOP) and Retail Sales Index;

- regional accounts, which break down GDP and household income and expenditure by region;
- at a more detailed level, information on commerce and industry – for example specific areas of industry like manufacturing and retailing.

National Statistics themselves are a subset of official statistics produced in the UK, which are used to provide an accurate, up-to-date, comprehensive and meaningful picture of the economy and society to support the formulation and monitoring of economic and social policies by government at all levels.

Their aim is to:

- inform the Parliaments and Assemblies and the citizen about the state of the nation and provide a window on the work and performance of government, allowing the impact of government policies and actions to be assessed;

- provide business with a statistical service which promotes the efficient functioning of commerce and industry;
- provide researchers, analysts and other customers with a statistical service that assists their work and studies;
- promote these aims within the UK, the European Union and internationally and provide a statistical service to meet European Union and international requirements.

The statistics produced and analysed within the framework cover all areas of UK national life under the following themes:

- Agriculture
- Commerce and industry
- Crime and justice
- Economy
- Education and training
- Health and care
- Labour market
- Natural and built environment
- Population and migration
- Social and welfare
- Transport and tourism
- Other

A comprehensive list of National Statistics can be found on the National Statistics website at *http://www.statistics.gov.uk.*

THE ECONOMY AND THE ECONOMIC ACCOUNTING FRAMEWORK

For the purposes of this book the main themes of interest are the economy, commerce and industry, and the labour market. Figures on the economy cover: annual and quarterly information on the national accounts (which can be likened to the accounts of UK Plc), monthly figures on prices and inflation, monthly and quarterly figures on the Trade Balance and Balance of Payments respectively, and indicators like the Retail Sales Index.

To make the best of this information – and other data series on the economy – it is necessary to take a little time to understand more about what we are measuring and how we estimate and present these series.

There is no agreed definition of the economy. Economists seem to be happier to define economics rather than the economy. Some possible definitions include:

The collection of institutions and people who combine together to produce, buy, sell and use goods and services.

or

The production, distribution and exchange of goods and services.

On any one day there are billions of transactions involving individuals and businesses who buy things, sell things, lend money, donate to charity, pay taxes and so on. The economic or national accounts bring together and present this myriad of information in a framework that helps make sense of all of this complexity. The way that this is done is by grouping together similar things in the economy. So, for example, we may group together all taxes paid by corporations or all wages earned by individuals. In this way we get a set of statistics that are designed to help economists and others who are trying to interpret the movements in the economy.

Within the national accounts we start by identifying and grouping together the participants in the economy and the economic transactions which they undertake.

Participants in the Economy

The participants are collections of people or 'institutions' who take part in economic activity. National accountants group together similar types of institutions (into institutional sectors) to put a structure on the accounts and to provide a framework for analysis. The simplest way of grouping is:

- **Households** Individuals, households and so on who consume goods and services, work, get paid, pay taxes.
- **Corporations** Any organisation that produces a good or service for sale.
- **Government** Public administration and government departments.
- **The rest of the world** Anyone not resident in the UK.

Almost anything can be made to fit into this broad classification although a more refined approach is needed when we compile the national accounts.

Economic Transactions

The participants in the economy are involved in the many transactions or economic exchanges that take place on a daily basis. For example, people and households receive wages and buy things, companies export goods, government levies taxes and overseas companies set up subsidiary companies in the UK. National accountants aim to group together these transactions. One, almost exhaustive, grouping is as follows:

- **Transactions in products** are transactions relating to the origin and use of goods and services. These include: domestic output (what is produced in the UK), imports (spending on foreign goods and services by people in the UK) and intermediate consumption (things bought for use in the production process which are used up, or transformed, in that process - for example raw materials). They are usually classified into *household consumption expenditure* (current spending by individuals and households), *government consumption expenditure* (current spending by central or local government), *fixed capital formation* (companies and government buying capital goods – for example a piece of machinery or computer system) and *exports* (spending on UK goods and services by people in other countries).

- **Distributive transactions** are transactions by which the income generated by production is distributed. These include *compensation of employees* (mainly wages and salaries but includes, for example, bonuses, pension contributions paid by employers and any payments in kind), and *operating surplus* (what corporations have left after paying their employees). This money is then redistributed in the form of, for example, taxes (paid by corporations and households), social security contributions, income support payments, subsidies and interest payments.

- **Financial transactions** include the acquisition of *financial assets* (someone owes me something) or incurring a *financial liability* (I owe someone something) which includes: putting money in a bank or building society account, buying foreign currency or a company issuing shares.

The different transactions are grouped together and displayed in various *accounts*, which are designed to give information in a form useful to users of the accounts. One of the most commonly used measures or groupings wihin the accounts is known as **Gross Domestic Product** or **GDP**. GDP is often referred to as the summary measure of activity in the economy, as it estimates the size of production or output in the economy in a number of different ways.

Probably the easiest way to represent the economy and how the national accounts, and so GDP, measure the economic activity that takes place is to look at the simplified picture below.

Gross Domestic Product

Output method

Corporations produce an output of goods and services. For each corporation the difference between the value of this output and its intermediate consumption (the value of the goods and services – or raw materials – used up in the production of this output) is its gross value added. This represents the 'value added' to the raw materials in transforming them into an output. This provides us with the first approach to measuring Gross Domestic Product. Here GDP equals the sum of each individual producer's gross value added, which is the same as the final output of finished goods and services produced in the economy. This approach is known as the output or production approach to measuring GDP.

Income method
This gross value added is then distributed. It is distributed as compensation of employees or operating surplus (loosely 'profit') to the producer (who as individuals are also part of the household sector, hence the direction of the arrow). Summing these figures provides another way to measure Gross Domestic Product. The total of these factor incomes gives the income approach to measuring GDP. (These incomes can then be analysed to see how they are distributed or redistributed further, for example through taxation and benefits or through the payment and receipt of dividends and interest).

Expenditure method
We can also look at the spending on the finished goods and services in the economy. When goods or services are sold for the last time, their price reflects the value added at each stage of production. So if we sum together all of the spending of the final buyers – household consumption, government consumption, exports and investment expenditure (i.e. expenditure on capital goods which is funded by savings) - and remove imports, we have another measurement of GDP. This is the expenditure approach to measuring GDP.

In the UK, all three approaches are used to produce a single estimate of GDP.

The sequence of accounts
The national accounts start with the current accounts, followed by the accumulation accounts and then the balance sheets.

The **current accounts** begin with the production of goods and services, before moving on to look at how the income from production is generated, distributed and then used. After this the **accumulation accounts** look at the acquisition of physical assets (capital expenditure) and financial assets (which can be used to finance this capital expenditure). The **balance sheets** then show the value of the holding of assets in the economy.

The key strength of an accounting system is that is has certain checks and balances built in. The crosschecking is highly developed and gives us useful information in the compilation of the accounts.

KEY ECONOMIC SERIES AND INDICATORS AVAILABLE FOR ANALYSIS
The national accounts obviously provide a range of indicators and economic series of use to analysts and in business. For example, the different approaches to the measurement of Gross Domestic Product each provide information for different analyses of the economy.

The output approach provides information on the output in the economy which can be split by institutional sector or by industry. The industry to which a producing unit is allocated depends on the classification of the units main product according to the *Standard Industrial Classification (SIC) 1992*. The income approach provides detailed information on the incomes earned by the household and corporate sectors and by industry. The expenditure approach details the expenditure of the different sectors, as well as providing information on the different goods and services purchased.

Other important series are:

Box 2.1

GDP - Gross Domestic Product
What do the words actually mean?

Product: Production or final output.

Domestic: The production has taken place on UK domestic territory.

Gross: An estimate for *capital consumption* has not been removed from the
                       figures.

*During the production process some of the capital goods (for example
the plant and machinery) will have been, quite literally, worn away.
However, although, value added equals output less intermediate
consumption, intermediate consumption does not include an estimate
for this capital consumption or depreciation. So, because we have not
taken anything out to represent this capital consumption, an
economy's GDP will be bigger than it's true or 'net' domestic product
(NDP), which is measured net of capital consumption.*

*Difficulties in estimating this capital consumption mean that, although
estimates of NDP are made available, the gross measure, GDP, is
usually preferred.*

Market prices and basic prices

GDP is valued in two ways in the UK: market (also known as purchasers' prices) and basic
prices.

   Market prices are the prices actually paid by the purchaser for goods and services,
including transport costs, trade margins and taxes. **Basic prices** reflect the amount received
by the producer, and therefore exclude these items.

GDP at market prices = GDP at basic prices

                         + Transport prices paid separately

                         + Non deductible taxes on expenditure

                         - Subsidies received

The expenditure analysis of GDP also includes taxes and subsidies, so is available at both
basic prices and market prices.

- **Gross National Product** or **National Income** is GDP plus the net property income from the rest of the world. **Net property income** is a measure designed to capture UK residents' earnings in the rest of the world whilst excluding those UK earnings that end up being paid to the rest of the world. As a result net property income includes the rent dividends and interest received by domestic residents from overseas but excludes rent, dividends and interest paid to non-residents.
- **The Balance of Payments** is the difference between all money coming into a country and the money going out. It includes trade, property income flows and other transfers. It goes wider than the trade balance, which is the difference between exports and imports of goods and services.
- **The saving ratio** is normally calculated for the household sector. It is the ratio of saving to disposable income expressed as a percentage.
- **Real household disposable income** is a measure of the purchasing power of households calculated by adjusting households' disposable income to remove the effect of inflation.
- **Net lending/borrowing of companies** has been highlighted as a key measure of companies' activities – showing whether they are borrowing money or have cash to spare.
- **Prices and measures of inflation** including the Retail Prices Index, the Harmonised Index of Consumer Prices and the Producer Prices Index are detailed below.

MEASURING THE ECONOMY IN PRACTICE

The measures described above allow us to make comparisons within the economy between the different sectors and the different transactions (e.g. the role of the government, our transactions with the rest of the world, how and where company profits are changing,

which industries are leading growth within the economy, and what household are spending on what). We also want to make comparisons between different national economies and, of course, we want to make comparisons of these variables over *time* (e.g. the structure of the economy, the distribution of wealth, the growth of the output of individual industries within the economy and the growth in the whole economy).

Current and constant prices

As a result we need to be able to measure and monitor both *how prices are changing* and *how the economy is growing*. This involves bringing together information in a range of different formats that allow comparisons to be made.

To illustrate let us look at the trends of UK GDP (see Figure 2.2). Looking at *current price GDP* it is hard to tell how quickly the economy is growing because current price figures measure value. The prices are current prices because, for each year, they use that year's prices. This series shows how both the price and quantity (or volume) has changed over time. Without further information it is difficult to know whether the UK economy is growing (i.e. whether volumes are growing) or not.

However, by using the prices of one particular year – here 1995 – it is possible to isolate the changing quantities and see more clearly how the economy is growing. This *constant price* series tells us quite a different (and a much more informative) story.

Probably the most widely used measure of activity in the economy revolves around the information contained in the constant price graph. Most commentaries talk about how the economy has *grown* compared to the latest quarter and the same quarter a year ago. In general these commentaries will be referring to the growth in GDP at *constant market prices*. The rate at which the *volume* of output in the economy is growing. Price movements in the economy – the other half of the picture – are also a very important area in their own right and we will return to them later.

Figure 2.2 *GDP in both current and constant prices*

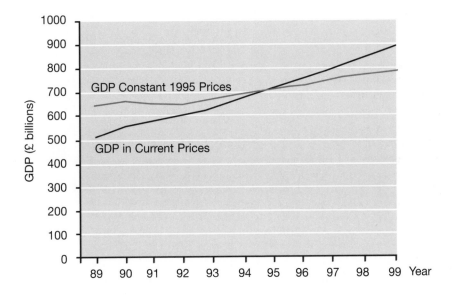

Source: NS, Monthly Digest of Statistics

The information is used to make comparisons in the *short term*: growth in the economy over the last year, growth in consumer's expenditure, or the change in output of a particular industry within the economy, or change in prices (e.g. retail and wholesale prices) over the same period.

Growth in the *longer term* is not quite as straightforward as movements in the relative prices of goods and services begin to influence how and where the economy grows: Prices and quantities cannot be separated neatly into two different effects. This fact influences our approach to measuring growth.

There are two main approaches to measuring growth or the change in volume. They are:

• Constant prices
• Index numbers

Estimation of volumes using index numbers

Index numbers are generally used to measure the changes in some heterogeneous aggregate (i.e. they are used to measure the change in a group of different things, like the change in the volume of production in the UK or the change in the price of a basket of goods). But before getting too bogged down in the definition of an index number, we will create a very simple index number.

Look at my consumption of apples below:

Time	Apples
Period 0	*50*
Period 1	*60*

If we want to compare apple consumption in periods 0 and 1 (assuming no change in the quality of the apples) we can create an index by first expressing period 1 as 100 (to get 100 all we have done is divide the number by itself and multiply by 100) and we compare period 1 to period 0 by dividing it by the figure in period 0 (always divide by the number you want to compare with) and then multiplying by 100.

Box 2.2

What are current prices?

- They measure value.
- For each time period they use prices in that time period.
- They show how prices multiplied by quantities (i.e. values) change overtime.

What are constant prices?

- They measure volume.
- They use the prices of one particular year (the base).
- By removing the effects of price movements, changes in the volume purchased can be clearly seen.

Time	Apples	Calculation	Index
Period 0	50	50/50 * 100	100
Period 1	60	60/50 * 100	120

Here the index number makes it very straightforward to compare consumption in the two periods.

Two or more commodities

Now let us say I started eating pears as well as apples and wanted to create an index number showing my total fruit consumption. How do I add up apples and pears? How many apples are equivalent to how many pears? How do we compare the value of pears and apples?

The most effective way to compare apples and pears is through the price. As I cannot directly add apples and pears, if I want to compare the volume of my consumption in periods 0 and 1, I have to settle for a comparison of the value of consumption in the two periods. By fixing the price in one period we can focus on the volumes.

Using the data and method shown in Table 2.1, we are able to work out an index that allows me to compare fruit consumption in the two periods. Consumption has risen by 20% since period 0.

The resulting index – calculated using the prices in period 0 - is given by:

370/280 * 100 = 132.1

This is called a **base weighted** or a **Laspeyre's index.** It is interpreted as measuring the percentage change in the total value of fruit consumption holding the prices at their level in period 0 (the base period). The index fixes the prices so that we can remove the effect of the change in prices. By using period 0 prices, we can compare period 0 and periods 1 by isolating the volume or quantity changes that we are interested in comparing. If we had data available for period 2, or 3 we would calculate the relevant index number by using the prices in period 0 and making the same comparison.

However, if relative prices have changed since the base period we could be giving too much weight to those items now relatively more expensive and too little to those that are now relatively less expensive. This happens because in reality consumers are likely to replace some of the product which is now relatively more expensive with a product which is relatively less expensive. The resulting index is therefore likely to be slightly higher than would actually be observed.

This interaction between prices and quantities over time makes it very hard to achieve a perfect measure of the changing volumes. However it is generally accepted that base-weighted index numbers, provide a straightforward approach that is easy to apply and understand in practice, and when updated (rebased) regularly, can provide a suitably accurate measurement of growth in the longer term. Rebasing is described in more detail below.

Table 2.1 *Constructing a base weighted (Laspeyre's) index*

	Period 0 (Base period)			Period 1 (Next period)	
	Quantity (q0)	Price (p0)	Value (p0 x q0)	Quantity (q1)	Value (p0 x q1)
Apples	20	10	200	25	250
Pears	10	8	80	15	120
Total at Period 0 prices			280		370
Index of consumption			100		132.1

Estimation of volumes using constant prices

Another approach to the estimation of volumes is through the calculation of **constant price series**. By holding prices constant – expressing a series in the prices prevailing in one time period (say 1995) – we can focus on the changing volumes.

There are three methods of obtaining constant price series: revaluation, deflation and volume extrapolation. In general the best method of estimating volume change is to remove the effect of changing prices by dividing the current price series by *an appropriate price index* which is representative of the general price movements in that series. This process is known as **deflation** and the price index used is known as the **deflator**.

Where t denotes the current time period and 0 the base period we can show how this works as follows:

Current value = price x quantity
i.e. $CP_t = P_t * Q_t$

So, by dividing through by the price series (P_t/P_0) we obtain a constant price series.

Constant value = $\dfrac{P_t Q_t}{P_t/P_0} = P_0 \times Q_t$

The **revaluation** method of calculating a constant price series requires separate information on the base price (the P_0) and the quantities (the Q_t's) for each individual commodity in the series. For example for a series on beer we would need separate information, for price and quantity, for each type of beer, in all of the different forms in which it is sold. This level of detail is really only available for those commodities on which excise duty is paid.

The third and last method of constant price calculation relies on using **volume extrapolation** that is, bringing together the current prices in the base period with information on how the quantities (the Q_t's) are changing.

From the constant price series it is possible to create a base weighted volume index - simply divide the constant price by the value in the base period.

From theory to practice

So how do we measure and present estimates of GDP in the UK? As mentioned in the earlier section, theoretically there are three ways of approaching the measurement of GDP. These are as the sum of value added in the economy, as the total of the incomes generated and as the expenditure on goods and services produced.

The income approach: The incomes generated by production go in the form of gross operating surplus (profits) and compensation of employees (income from employment plus pension, other benefits and bonuses). This approach provides data in current price terms. Table 1.2 of the UK *National Accounts Blue Book* (see Data appendix) shows the different categories of incomes that are used.

The expenditure approach: GDP is also the total of spending on goods and services for final use. The main categories of spending are households' final consumption, government final consumption, exports, gross domestic fixed capital formation, changes in inventories and acquisitions less disposals of valuables. Each of these may include spending on goods that have been imported so imports need to be removed.

The expenditure analysis is constructed at both *current and constant prices* enabling comparison over time of both values and volumes of types of expenditure. The constant price series are, for the most part, obtained by using the deflation method described above and as such are 'base weighted'.

The production or output approach: In theory this last approach to measuring GDP is to use the sum of gross value added (output less intermediate consumption) for all producing institutions within the economy. So, to obtain figures at *constant prices*, the value of output and intermediate consumption would need to be deflated separately in a process known as double deflation. However in the UK, this theoretical approach has not been used. There are a number of reasons for this. But, in particular, estimates of intermediate consumption are not available on a quarterly basis and, at the moment, it is also difficult to produce an appropriate deflator for intermediate consumption.

In practice the UK's approach is designed to produce a quick and reliable indicator of the *changes* of the volume of GDP each quarter. This approach is based on the assumption that, in the short term, the ratio of gross output to

value added (or net output) is constant (i.e. they will grow at the same rate). In a stable economy like the UK's this assumption is regarded as valid. The approach is followed for the production industries, in the monthly Index of Production, and for the services industries within GDP. Estimates of the change in real output within the Index of Production are approximated by, for example, deflated turnover. For some service industries more direct measures such as, for example, the number of passenger kilometres travelled on the railways are needed. These detailed industry estimates are presented as a series of base weighted index numbers all equal to 100 in the base year. To obtain GDP, the indices are then 'weighted together' using the contribution of the industry to output in the base year (i.e. the relative value of that industries output as a proportion of the total).

The base year and rebasing

As already mentioned, in order to measure economic growth accurately, the interaction between the price and quantities of goods and services needs to be kept up-to-date. To demonstrate this let us suppose that the published data on the national accounts is presented with 1995 identified as the 'base year', the year in whose prices constant price series are expressed, or the year in which the volume indices are equal to 100. So, if 1995 is the base year, the volumes will be valued and aggregated using the price structure prevailing in 1995.

Because the relative prices of goods change over time, these weights will not be representative of time period much before or after 1995. As a result the base weights need to be updated – or **rebased** - at intervals to ensure that they remain representative. Historically, in the UK, this has generally happened every five years. However when we rebase we do not carry the new price structure all the way back to the beginning of the series. This would not make sense as the new 'base' or price structure would be unlikely to be representative of previous time periods.

Table 2.2 illustrates how the structure of the economy, and so the relative importance of each industry (in parts per 1000), compared in 1956 and 1995.

It is worth pointing out that, although the weight of a particular sector may have declined in parts per thousand, this does not mean that the sector has declined in size. For example the output index (1995=100) for agriculture and fishing was 44.5 in 1956 and 100 in 1995 - although it has come to represent a smaller proportion of the total economy it has continued to grow in size (see Figure 2.3).

To bring the data on different price bases together we overlap successive price bases by one year - the link year - where the series are calculated on both price bases. So, for each of the earlier price sets we can convert the values to that of the next base year using the ratio for the link year. We **rereference** the data so that, superficially, it looks as though it is all on the same base.

The effect of this process is to preserve the growth rates for those years calculated on earlier price bases. For example the growth rates between 1986 and 1994 have been calculated on the 1990 price base, the price base representative in this time period: Rereferencing onto a 1995 base will not have altered these growth rates. A further consequence is that there will, almost certainly, not be additivity in the series before the last link year. This *loss of additivity* can be a problem for users who expect the published

components to add up to totals or who want to create their own 'aggregates'. However by preserving the price structures (good) the growth rates are preserved (good), but at the expense of additivity before the last link year.

Because of the increasing speed of change in the structure of the economy, the base period is unlikely to be representative for long: The further from the base period we get, the less appropriate the structures are for the calculation of growth rates (and so the less accurate the calculated growth rates). As a result, in the near future, the UK will begin rebasing every year as opposed to every five years. This process is known as **annual chainlinking**.

Prices and measures of inflation

Having looked at some of the measures of how the economy is growing it is also clear that there will be measures of how prices are changing in the economy. There are a number of series which, as well as being important indicators in their own right, provide detailed price indices which are used as deflators in many areas of the national accounts. Consumer prices – the Retail Price Index and the Harmonised Index of Consumer Prices – focus on the prices affecting households, the Producer Price Indices and the Corporate Services Price Indices focus on prices affecting the manufacturing, production and service industries, and the Final Expenditure Prices index looks more widely at changing prices in

Table 2.2 *The changing structure of the economy*

	1956	1995
Agriculture and Fishing	61	18
Manufacturing	413	266
Construction	62	52
Services	464	664
Total	1000	1000

* Services include distribution, transport, financial services, public administration and other services.

Source: NS, Monthly Digest of Statistics

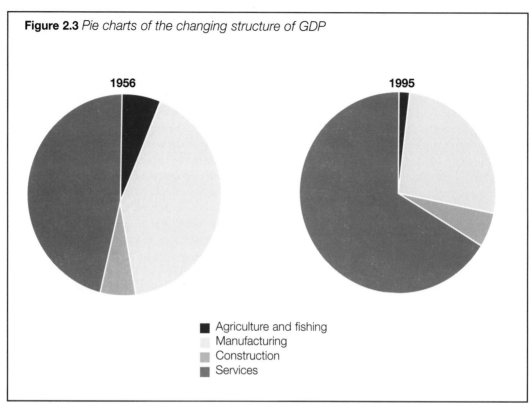

Figure 2.3 *Pie charts of the changing structure of GDP*

1956

1995

■ Agriculture and fishing
  Manufacturing
  Construction
■ Services

the whole economy. These index number series will be looked at in turn below.

The Retail Prices Index

The Retail Prices Index - the RPI - is the main domestic measure of inflation in the UK. It measures the average change from month to month in the prices of goods and services bought by most households in the United Kingdom. The spending pattern on which the index is based is revised each year, mainly using information from the *Family Expenditure Survey*. So that this spending pattern is representative of the majority of households, the expenditure of certain higher income households, and of pensioner households mainly dependent on state pensions, is excluded. The resulting index is an annually chain-linked Laspeyres index (it is a base weighted index updated on an annual basis).

The index is compiled using a large and representative selection of more than 600 separate goods and services. Price movements of 500 of these goods and services are regularly measured in 146 areas throughout the country with the remaining 100 collected centrally. This results in some 130,000 separate price quotations being used each month to compile the index.

As well as the headline 'all items RPI', many other RPI series are available. For example, the *RPI all items excluding mortgage interest payments* (RPIX) and the *RPI all items excluding mortgage interest payments and indirect taxes* (RPIY) are published alongside the index numbers for many of the individual goods and services like, bread, fruit and vegetables and housing.

The index is given in full in *Consumer Price Indices (MM23)* (see Data appendix) and a complete explanation of methodology used in compiling the Retail Prices Index is given in the *RPI Technical Manual*, published by The Stationery Office (TSO).

The Harmonised Index of Consumer Inflation: The HICP

The HICP - launched in 1997 – has been developed to provide a comparable measure of inflation for Member States of the European Union (a requirement of the Maastrict treaty). Like the RPI this index is published monthly and measures the average change from month to month in the prices of goods and services bought by households in the European Union.

Whilst the coverage and methodology of the HICP is similar to that for the RPI it does differ in a number of ways. For example the HICP includes airfares and boats, which are not included in the RPI, but excludes a number of RPI series; in particular those relating to owner occupied housing costs. In addition the weights in the HICP are based on the expenditure by foreign visitors to the UK, as well as all of the resident private and institutional households. Further details can be found in a series of articles in *Economic Trends* dated March 1998, December 1998 and March 2000.

Producer Price Indices: The PPIs

The PPIs are a series of monthly indicators that measure the change in the price of goods bought and sold by UK manufacturers. Like the consumer price index numbers they also work on the 'basket of goods concept'. A wide selection of representative goods is selected and the prices of these goods are then collected each month. The movements in these prices are weighted to reflect the relative importance of the products in the base year. The resulting index numbers (base weighted Laspeyres) are calculated and available for groups of commodities and materials for broad sectors of the manufacturing industry.

The input PPIs measure changes in the prices of materials and fuel bought by manufacturers for processing. These cover raw materials like rubber and cocoa, and also intermediate goods for use in the production process, for example steel and electrical components purchased by car manufacturers

The output PPIs indicate changes in the prices manufacturers charge for goods as they leave the factory gate. These should be net of VAT and after any discounts, and reflect the cost of recoverable overheads such as the cost of materials, salaries and wages, as well as profit margins.

At present some 3,700 manufacturing companies provide 9000 price quotations on a wide range of home produced products and imported commodities. In addition some prices are obtained from administrative sources. These raw price quotes are converted into a basic set of about 1,000 price indices from which broader series are built up to reflect the price trends of manufacturing input and output across whole sectors of industry. The industrial classification used to classify the industry groups is the *1992 Standard Industrial Classification* (SIC).

PPIs have a range of uses. They are used by government to monitor and measure inflation, and they are used to obtain other national statistics. In particular the Index of Production, and so estimates of GDP, use PPIs to deflate values to obtain constant price series. In addition, and importantly for the purposes of this book, PPIs – either 'off the shelf' or 'tailor made' by request – are used extensively by industry. For example many detailed PPIs are used in price variation clauses in trading contracts or for internal cost accounting. Some PPIs are compiled for stocks and fixed assets held by various industries. These help company accountants to revalue assets from historic to replacement cost terms.

Producer prices for imports and exports are also available. The import PPIs are economic indicators that measure changes in the prices of goods and raw materials imported by UK manufacturers. They are a key component of the input price indices. Export price indices are set up to measure changes in the prices in goods manufactured in the UK for export. Export and import prices are also used in the calculation of the UK balance of payments.

Corporate Services Price Indices (CSPIs)

The Corporate Services Price Indices (CSPIs) development programme was initiated in 1993 to plug the gaps in UK service prices. Indices are being developed to cover the prices of services sold by businesses to business and other non-private customers (including customers in government). An article setting out the development plans was published in the July 2000 edition of *Economic Trends*.

The Final Expenditure Prices Index (FEPI)

The Final Expenditure Prices Index (FEPI) is an experimental price index published monthly in *Economic Trends*. The FEPI provides a more comprehensive measure of inflation than price indices like the RPI or the PPI because it captures inflationary pressures impacting on the whole economy. The index is still being developed by National Statistics and, subject to the satisfactory completion of a number of methodological developments, is planned for publication as a mainstream economic indicator from March 2002.

The FEPI covers all final expenditure in the economy and its coverage broadly mirrors the expenditure measure of Gross Domestic Product (GDP). The FEPI consists of: the Index of Consumer Prices (ICP) with coverage corresponding to households final consumption expenditure, the Index of Investment Prices (IIP) with coverage corresponding to Gross Fixed Capital Formation, and the Index of Government Prices (IGP) with coverage corresponding to Government final consumption expenditure. A range of price indicators, including indices from the RPI and PPI, import deflators, average house price indicators and average earnings indicators, are used in the construction of the index.

OVERVIEW OF THE DATA SOURCES AND THE DATA COLLECTION PROCESS

National Statistics obtains its data in two main ways. Many data are derived from *administrative systems*. Examples of these include the UK's trade in goods with non-EC countries, the Inland Revenue's systems for PAYE and taxation of companies' profits, and the numbers claiming unemployment benefit and social security benefit. The data are relatively cheap and timely, but are governed by *administrative* rather than statistical needs. This means that changes in the working of the system, such as changes in the entitlement to a social security benefit, can lead to discontinuities in the statistical series. However, because of the large quantities of administrative data available, these data sources do have powerful applications. For example the large volumes of information on the claimant count can provide a wealth of detail on the age and gender of those claiming unemployment benefit in a particular area of the UK.

National Statistics also carries out *statistical surveys*, such as the *Labour Force Survey* and a large number of business surveys (for example the *Annual Business Survey* or the *Retail Sales Inquiry*). Surveys of people, businesses or other organisations are designed specifically to give relevant and reliable statistics, and to provide a snapshot of a topic at any one particular time.

The national accounts are built up from a variety of data sources, combining the most appropriate administrative and survey based information available. As a user of the data it is useful to have an idea about these stages and what they involve. These are outlined below with the process of seasonal adjustment and data quality also described for completeness.

Making survey data useable

Obviously by the time survey data are published in their final form – giving information on, say, industry output– they will have gone through a number of processing stages. The flow chart in Figure 2.4 provides a simplified summary of the common stages frequently involved in the collection, processing and publication of survey data.

Figure 2.4 *Processing survey data*

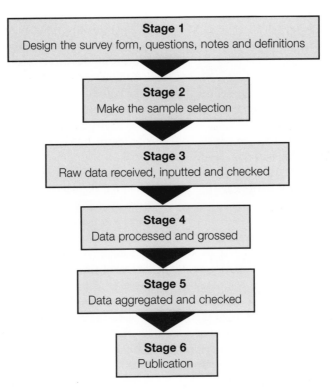

Stage 1
Design the survey form, questions, notes and definitions

Stage 2
Make the sample selection

Stage 3
Raw data received, inputted and checked

Stage 4
Data processed and grossed

Stage 5
Data aggregated and checked

Stage 6
Publication

Stage 1: The survey form

At the first stage in the process – which for an annual inquiry is likely to begin about a year before the form is actually to be sent out – the form itself has to be designed. It is important that the questions are clearly worded and that the notes and definitions ensure that the information collected is what was intended. For example, for national accounts purposes, the definition of a company's profits is slightly different to what the company itself would define as profits and so it is important to specify exactly what is required.

Stage 2: Selecting the sample

The second stage is the design of the sample of households or businesses to which the forms will be sent. Stratified random sampling is used with the size of the sample decided, in the main, by statistical theory. For some business inquiries, where a few companies account for most of the industry output, all of these larger contributors are likely to be included within the sample with a smaller proportion of the smaller contributors being sampled. Because of the requirement to minimise the burden on suppliers, in particular small businesses, some reselection may have to take place. The collection of survey information for National Statistics is recognised to place a burden on those asked to supply the information: a burden which can be felt acutely by small businesses. As a result, as part of a wider commitment, National Statistics undertake that small businesses can only receive a specific number of forms within a set time period. Once the selection is made the forms will then be sent out at the end of the time period being surveyed.

Stage 3: Raw data received, inputted and checked

The third stage is the inputting and checking

of the information returned on the completed forms. This checking procedure will ensure, not just that the information has been transferred without error, but that the data itself seems valid. This validation takes into consideration:

- data for an earlier time period submitted by the company, for example the figures reported in the previous year;
- any related data reported by the same company;
- the figures reported by other companies of a similar size within that particular industry.

Stage 4: Data processed and grossed

After the sample data are checked and inputted, the data can then be used to provide estimates for the whole industry. For example, the estimate of the turnover for a particular industry will be inferred from the figures on turnover returned by the companies in the sample. As a result each industry estimate has an associated 'sample error' because a different sample, if selected, would give rise to a slightly different estimate. The sampling and grossing procedures are designed to ensure that this error is within defined limits. However, in practice, the exact size of the statistical error can be difficult to pinpoint because of the need to adjust the sample selection (to ensure that individual businesses are not overburdened) and the fact that the industry population will vary continuously throughout the period under investigation.

Stage 5: Data aggregated and checked

Once estimates have been obtained the series are, where necessary, seasonally adjusted and then aggregated into component series depending on different uses to which they are put. Additional checking takes place against related estimates and aggregates. For example because the estimates in the economic accounts, say GDP, can be estimated in a number of different ways and are part of the same framework, they should be presenting a

coherent picture of the economy. These additional checks strengthen the validity of the estimates further. In addition, because business and households provide information in confidence, only those National Statistics staff processing the survey results can see the individual returns. As a result before the information leaves the processing area checks ensure the information cannot be deduced from aggregated results and so remains confidential.

Stage 6: Publication

The final stage involves the publication of the data – which may relate to an individual survey or may bring together a number of different datasets from a number of surveys and sources – via First Release (i.e. the first release of this particular data set) or a Press Release. This release will coincide with the data becoming available electronically but may precede the more detailed paper publication, for example the *UK National Accounts Blue Book*, which takes a little more time to print. This happens because of a commitment to supply data as soon as it is available.

Making administrative data useable

Like survey data, data obtained from an administrative system are also likely to require processing before they are ready to publish. In the main, the process is likely to begin by making any necessary adjustments required to bring the 'concepts' into line. For example, when they become available, data from the Inland Revenue are used to update much of the annual information on incomes in the accounts. However for the Inland Revenue's (taxable) purposes, an individual's income figure will exclude any pension contributions which are not taxable, as well as excluding all of the income earned by someone whose income falls below the tax threshold. For national accounts purposes estimates for the pension contributions and those earning below the tax threshold need to be added in.

The data are then likely to proceed through similar aggregation, checking and publication processes as the survey data above. In fact, within the national accounts, the information is likely to be brought together with the survey data at the aggregation stage.

Seasonal adjustment

Any analysis of time series data will involve an examination of the general pattern of the data, the long-term movements within the series, and whether there were any unusual circumstance – such as strikes or bad weather – that may have affected the data. However this type of analysis is not easy using raw time series data because there may be short-term effects associated with the time of year which will obscure other (possibly interesting) movements in the series. For example retail sales go up in December due to the effect of Christmas. Seasonal adjustment is the process used to identify and remove the seasonal component from a time series allowing a more meaningful comparison of consecutive months or quarters.

In the presentation of many economic series the emphasis is placed on the seasonally adjusted series. This seasonal adjustment is done at component or sub-component level and, in general, the seasonally adjusted aggregates are calculated as the sum of the seasonally adjusted components. For example, the seasonally adjusted households' expenditure total is calculated by summing over one hundred seasonal adjusted components such as fruit, fish and electricity.

Seasonally adjusting in this way is believed to give a clearer interpretation of the changes in the final seasonally adjusted series: GDP is composed of many series which may be influenced by different seasonal effects which are better identified (and therefore removed) at a disaggregated level. In addition, the component series and sub-component series within the integrated economic accounts system, are important to users in their own right.

At the Office for National Statistics, seasonal adjustment is carried out using a package known as X11 ARIMA (which stands for Auto Regressive Integrated Moving

Average, which is essentially a smoothing technique). One of the main aims of the program is the identification and estimation of the *seasonal component* in order to produce a *seasonally adjusted series*. However, seasonally adjusting the components or sub components of the economic accounts is not simply a mechanical process. A good knowledge of the series, as well as an understanding of the X11 ARIMA package, is crucial in the production of the seasonally adjusted series. The compilers of the data series have a very detailed knowledge of their series and are able to look and adjust for any likely problems; for example, the impact of trading day or Easter effects or extreme weather conditions.

Data quality

In general the aim of the Office of National Statistics is to produce timely, consistent and coherent statistics which accurately represent activity in the economy. As a rule all key outputs are subject to regular quality reviews.

As already mentioned above the national accounts system – which provides estimates of GDP – has a number of checks and balances built in. This brings in extra information about the reliability of raw data and the consistency with other sources adds significantly to the reliability of the estimates. To help users monitor the estimates, the revisions to growth rates of GDP are published periodically in the *Economic Trends* publication. In addition, sampling errors – which can be estimated for random samples – are being published for all major business surveys, as they become available.

THE PUBLISHED SERIES AND FURTHER INFORMATION

Data are made available in a wide range of formats to best meet different users' needs. First Releases or Press Releases produced on regular and pre-announced dates provide immediate access to the most up-to-date and important information. A wide range of paper bulletins and publications provide information and analyses on specific topics or social groups. Examples of the key publications include (monthly) *Economic Trends*, the quarterly *UK Economic Accounts*, and the annual *UK National Accounts* and *UK Balance of Payments*.

The National Statistics Information and Library Service (NSILS), see Data appendix, provides a shop, enquiry point and library. NSILS aims to give researchers, academics and the wider public access to all National Statistics as well as data from a range of international organisations.

Information is also available in a number of electronic formats. CD-ROM versions of many of the most popular paper publications are available – in some cases the CD-ROM contains several editions of a publication. A range of data is available on the Internet through the website, **http://www.statistics.gov.uk**. These data are available free of charge via a number of services including 'latest figures' and 'Statbase®'. Researchers can also gain access to some National Statistics datasets through the Economic and Social Research Council's (ESRC) Data Archive run by Essex University at **http://dawww.essex.ac.uk**. The Business Statistics Data Analysis Service (see Data appendix) is a chargeable service that allows users to define their own data needs by selecting series on a 'mix and match' basis.

3 Trends and Fluctuations

Steve Hurd, Director, Statistics for Education

FOCUS QUESTIONS

- What are the main sources of time-series data?
- What do we need to know about units of measurement and the use of indices?

- What is the best way to graph time-series data and when is it good to use logarithms?
- How can we distinguish between seasons, cycles, shocks and trends?
- How do we fit a trend line to a data series?

WHY DO WE NEED TO KNOW ABOUT TRENDS?

How well is our business doing? Is our performance improving? Are we doing better or worse than our sector in general? How do changes in our own, other business sectors, and in the general economy affect our overall sales performance? In order to answer questions such as these firms need to be able to compare data on their own performance with appropriate external statistics. They need to know where suitable data can be obtained, and how it can be interpreted. These are the issues we address in this chapter.

SOURCES OF TIME-SERIES DATA

Observing the changes in important variables over time requires the use of data in the form of a time-series. This is a set of observations of the same variable at different points in time, for example daily, weekly, monthly or yearly. Time-series data may be obtained from various sources.

In-house

During their normal day-to-day operations, firms generate a host of data on such things as the flow of orders, sales, production, sources of revenue and expenditures. For well-managed firms that are in the habit of reflecting on past performance such data provide valuable indicators of how well the business is doing. If firms are to prepare accurate forecasts of their cash flow and borrowing needs, then it is important to understand how the pattern of orders varies over time. If there are regular periods during a typical year when orders and revenue are low, then firms need to make allowance for this in their cash flow and borrowing decisions. Examining mis-matches between sales and production allows firms to manage the volume of finished goods that they stockpile and to adjust their orders for raw materials and other inputs.

Trade associations

Many firms belong to trade associations. These organisations represent the common interests and provide services to firms in a particular industry. One of the most important of these services is the provision of industry-related statistics. It is common for member firms to submit regular returns on their production and sales. Naturally, this is provided on the understanding that commercially sensitive information remains anonymous and is not passed on to competitors. However, the trade association is usually permitted to combine data from different firms in order to produce statistics, which reveal the state of the sector in general. Industry statistics generally include such information as the shares of the market held by different members and product groups, and the total production and sales of various categories of goods within a product class. Trade association data is very valuable to firms for it allows them to see how well they are doing in relation to the market as a whole.

Official statistics

National Statistics collates data from official sources, such as the government and other public bodies, for use by both public and private sector organisations and individuals. As we saw in Chapter 2, much information is gathered during the normal processes of government. For example data gathered by the Inland Revenue and Customs and Excise for the purpose of tax collection provide invaluable information on incomes, output and expenditure, and is used in the preparation of the National Accounts (see chapter 8 for more on the National Accounts). Such time-series data are invaluable to firms for they allow them to monitor the overall movements of output and changing patterns of consumer expenditure, both in the economy as a whole and disaggregated (i.e. broken down) by sector.

UNITS OF MEASUREMENT

When we want to see how a particular variable has changed over time, then it is important to have a clear understanding of the measurement units. There is often a choice of unit, and we need to choose the measure that is most suitable for the purpose in hand.

Totals of physical commodities

In the case of a fairly homogeneous physical commodity, like *tonnes* of pig iron, then the meaning of the term total is unambiguous. With less homogeneous commodities, such as motor cars, however, we will have different elements making up the total. We can ascertain, for example, that the number of new cars registered in the UK in the year 2000 was 2.09 millions[1]. This figure would be useful if we were trying to estimate the pressure on road space, or the demand for lubricating oil. However, for other purposes, we might need to have an idea of the distribution of car sales according to engine size and, possibly, price category. This might be so if we were trying to estimate the likely impact of changing car registrations on the sales of petrol, and motoring related services, such as insurance, both of which depend upon the distribution of cars by size or by value. Whenever totals relate to a composite commodity we may need to be prepared to obtain separate data for each component category.

Nominal expenditure

Many of the totals that we deal with in business are measured in terms of money. A firm selling a wide range of commodities will express its total sales as a money or nominal figure. Money is a convenient unit for totalling amounts of disparate commodities such as sweets and newspapers. We say that money is acting as a common numeraire, or common unit of account. In such cases, nominal expenditure totals are obtained by multiplying the physical quantities of each component by their price, and then summing the various sub-totals.

---

1 Based upon a forecast made by the Society of Motor Manufacturers and Traders Limited in *The Motor Industry Monthly Statistical Review*, July 1999.

Current expenditure

When starting an investigation it is usual to ask simple questions to establish the size or magnitude of the relevant aggregate totals. In a study of the market for vehicles, for example, we are likely to begin by asking: 'What is the current level of expenditure on vehicles?'

This question is less straightforward than it appears at first sight. The word 'current' implies that we want information on expenditure 'now', but it has to be remembered that it takes time for information to be gathered, collated and published. In official statistical publications the most recent data available on many variables are likely to be two quarters old by the time we get it. This leaves us in the strange position of having to begin by estimating the level of sales now, before we can begin to predict what they are likely to be in one or two years time.

As well as meaning 'now', when we are dealing with financial amounts, the word 'current' is also used to mean financial totals measured in prices that prevail at the moment, i.e. current prices. So total current expenditure on vehicles is obtained by multiplying the quantity of each make (and indeed model) of car bought by the current price, and then adding this to the sub-total for every other type of car:

Total current expenditure on vehicles
$$= p_1q_1 + p_2q_2 + p_3q_3 + \ldots \text{etc} = \Sigma\, p_iq_i$$
Where p = the nominal price, q = the quantity purchased, i represents each different make of car, and Σ implies the summation of the expenditures on each type of vehicle.

Nominal versus real expenditure

The *Monthly Digest of Statistics* reveals that household expenditure on vehicles was £4969 million in the fourth quarter of 1999. This figure is in current prices. It is, therefore, the nominal expenditure on vehicles. Nominal expenditure figures are useful when we want to make comparisons of expenditure on different commodity groups at one point in time, or to find out the expenditure on vehicles as a percentage of total current consumers' expenditure.

For many purposes, however, we need to obtain expenditure figures that are expressed in real terms. As explained in Chapter 2, figures for real expenditure have been deflated to remove the effects of price changes. This is done by comparing the price component of expenditure with the price levels that prevailed in a chosen base year. The real expenditure on vehicles in the fourth quarter of 1999 was £4515 million. In this case, the figure has been revalued on the basis of second quarter 1995 prices. The effects of deflating the figures for inflation can be seen in Table 3.1. Whereas nominal expenditure on vehicles increased by 16.18%, the rise in real expenditure was only 5.56%.

The 10.62% discrepancy is assumed to measure the change in the average price of vehicles that has taken place in the

Table 3.1 *Household expenditure on vehicles*

Units: £millions	Nominal expenditure in current prices	Real expenditure in constant 1995 prices
Quarter 2 1995	4277	4277
Quarter 4 1999	4969	4515
Percentage change	**16.18%**	**5.56%**

Source: NS, Monthly Digest of Statistics

intervening period. However, we have to remember two very important points. There may be changes in the composition of cars sold and newer vehicles tend to embody improvements in technology. The price component will, therefore, also capture qualitative improvements. It is, for these reasons, very difficult to separate pure price effects from quantitative and qualitative changes. Nominal totals contain and disguise all of these factors. Constant price figures only provide a partial solution to the separation of price and quantity effects. For most practical purposes, however, we simply have to make do with this.

Measuring relative magnitudes

Figures rarely mean anything in isolation. To appreciate their magnitude it is useful to compare them with related variables. In the case of household expenditure on vehicles suitable aggregates to use for comparison would be: expenditure on other categories of goods, total household expenditure on all goods and services and disposable income, that is household income after tax and other standard deductions have been made. Such a comparison has been made in Table 3.2.

This table sets out the figures for household expenditure on vehicles and for comparable variables: food, total household expenditure and disposable income. It is important to ensure that the variables are all measured in common units. In this case, all the figures are in real terms, expressed in constant 1995 prices. By working out the figures for expenditure on vehicles, as a percentage of the other totals, we can begin to get a feel for the relative magnitudes involved. Households spend about a third as much on buying and running vehicles as they do on food (34.8%). That said, however, vehicle expenditure took up only 3.4% of total household expenditure, and 3.2% of total disposable income, in the fourth quarter of 1999.

Seasonal adjustment: a note

The footnote to the table indicates that the figures are not seasonally adjusted. This is important! The Monthly Digest of Statistics contains figures for most variables in current and constant prices, and in seasonally adjusted and unadjusted forms. When making comparisons, it is important to compare like with like. In the case above, all the figures used are in constant 1995 prices and they are all unadjusted for seasonality (i.e. they have not been smoothed to remove seasonal fluctuations). You will find further information on the processes of seasonal adjustment in chapter 2.

Table 3.2 *Household expenditure and income in real terms, Quarter 4, 1999*

£ millions (1995)	Expenditure on Vehicles	Expenditure on Food	Total household expenditure	Household disposable income
Total	4515	12973	133722	142034
Expenditure on vehicles as a percentage of the above totals	100	34.80	3.38	3.18

All figures are non-seasonally adjusted

Making comparisons over time using a simple base index

When we examine raw data on different variables that change over time, it is often difficult to get a clear impression of rates of change, especially when figures are of quite different orders. Examine, for example, the data contained in Tables 3.3a and 3.3b. We can see from Table 3.3a that there have been substantial real increases in household expenditure on durable goods, food and clothing and footwear, very little change in expenditure on energy products and a real fall in expenditure on alcoholic drink and tobacco. The raw data also allow us to see the rank ordering of expenditures in 1999 from the highest category, food at £51972 million, down to the lowest, energy products at £27561. However, we can get a clearer idea of changes over time using a simple conversion.

Table 3.3b takes the same data and converts it to an index using 1990 as the base year. The 1999 figures are then calculated by reference to the figure in the base year using the formula:

$$\frac{\text{Expenditure in current year} \times 100}{\text{Expenditure in base year}}$$

Applying this in the case of durable goods gives:

$$\frac{54125 \times 100}{38101} = 142.1$$

So a simple index expresses the current figure as a percentage of the corresponding amount in the base year. Although we lose any sense of the order of magnitude of the figures when we convert them to an index, the advantages of doing so are evident from Table 3.3b. We can see, at a glance, the percentage changes in the figures since the base year. From the indices it is readily apparent that clothing and footwear have experience the largest percentage increase in expenditure, a 51.6% increase in real expenditure since 1990. By contrast household energy consumption fell 2.7%, and alcoholic drink and tobacco expenditure was only 88% of 1990 levels, a fall of 12%. We will see later that converting time-series data to simple indices is very useful when we want to illustrate the data graphically. In the various publications of National Statistics many of the statistical series

Table 3.3a *Household consumption expenditure (£ million, 1995 prices)*

	Durable goods	Food	Alcoholic drink and tobacco	Clothing and footwear	Energy products
1990	38101	47055	41654	22105	27389
1999	54125	51620	36657	33504	26648

Table 3.3b *Household consumption expenditure (1998=100)*

	Durable goods	Food	Alcoholic drink and tobacco	Clothing and footwear	Energy products
1990	100	100	100	100	100
1999	142.1	109.7	88.0	151.6	97.3

Source: National Statistics, Economic Trends Annual Supplement, 1999

Table 3.4 *Index of output and relative weights*

Industry	Base weights 1995 (Output =100)	Index of Output 1998	Current weights 1998
Agriculture, hunting, forestry and fishing	18	102.0	17
Total production industries	266	102.5	252
Construction	52	106.4	51
Distribution, hotels and catering, repairs	146	108.3	146
Transport, Storage and distribution	82	121.3	92
Business services and finance	211	117.3	228
Other services	225	105.6	219
Gross domestic product	1000	108.4	1000

are already presented in the form of indices. However, we shall still need access to the raw data in order to get an impression of the relative sizes of the variables we are investigating.

As the Index of Output in table 3.4 is only shown to one place of decimals and the final results are shown as integer values, there are rounding errors. So, instead of the current weights summing to 1000, they come to 1005. However, the component figures still allow us to see that the sectors showing the largest relative growth are transport, storage and distribution, and business services and finance. While, at the same time, the production industries (mining and manufacturing) experienced a relative decline, as did agriculture, construction, and non-financial services.

GRAPHING TIME-SERIES DATA

Having explored some of the important issues concerning units of measurement, let us now examine the ways in which graphs can help to elucidate trends and fluctuations.

Bars or lines?

Graphs of time-series data usually measure the target variable or variables along the vertical axis, and an appropriate unit of time on the horizontal axis. When the number of observations on a single variable is small many people choose to use bar graphs, as they make a strong visual impact. The normal convention for graphing time-series data, however, is to use a line graph. (See Figure 3.1) Line graphs convey the impression of a flow over time, which is usually what we are trying to portray.

The line graph is a particularly effective method of representation when two or more time-series variables need to be illustrated on a single graph. Figure 3.2 for example, illustrates the trend of retail sales for different categories of goods and services.

Calculating changes

Converting raw data to a simple index is one way to transform data in order to extract additional meaning. An index permits ready comparisons to be made to a base year, by showing proportional differences from that base. Simple indices do not, however, help in measuring other changes. Often when we are

Figure 3.1 *Bar chart versus line graph*

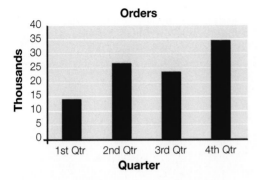 

Figure 3.2 *Line graph representation of UK retail sales*

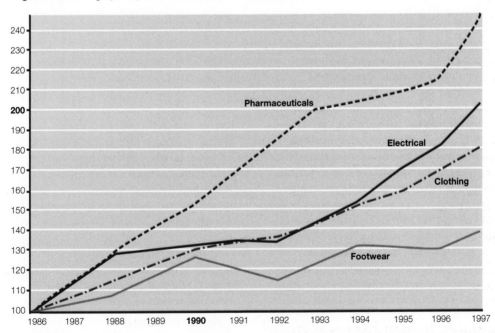

Source: National Statistics, Monthly Digest of Statistics

Table 3.5 *Beer production in the UK: thousands of hectolitres (1 hectolitre = 100 litres)*

	Beer Production Q_t	Absolute difference $Q_t - Q_{t-1}$	Percentage change $(Q_t - Q_{t-1}* 100$
1998 Oct	4745	-	-
1998 Nov	5252	507	10.7
1998 Dec	5437	185	3.5
1999 Jan	2970	-2467	-45.4
1999 Feb	3716	746	25.1
2000 Mar	4646	930	25.0

Source: National Statistics, Monthly Digest of Statistics

describing time-series we will want to say something about changes from one period to another. There are two ways to present these. We can measure either absolute differences or percentage differences. This is illustrated in Table 3.5 with reference to changes in the production of beer in the final quarter of 1998 and first quarter of 1999. The first column of the table contains figures for UK beer production measures in thousands of hectolitres.

The figures in the absolute difference column show the change in beer production from the previous period - they are first differences between the value in the current and previous periods $(Q_t - Q_{t-1})$. The final column shows proportional or percentage differences. These show the percentage change from one period to the next. Note, we are unable to calculate a figure for the first year as the previous year's data is missing. So whenever differences are calculated we lose the first observation. Absolute difference figures are useful to firms for operational decisions related to the planning of production and sales, when the likely absolute variation in orders from period to period is relevant to decisions on the use of inputs. Measuring percentage changes standardises the figures by the division process. It provides a 'unit independent' way of describing changes from period to period. From the figures in Table 3.5

we can see clearly the steady absolute (though not proportionate) rise in beer production in the three months leading up to Christmas and the New Year. A 45% fall in production in January and a progressive restoration of production levels follow this by March 1999 towards the previous October total.

Logarithmic series and growth rates

Although it is possible to see clearly the ups and downs and turning points of a series using a line graph, it is quite difficult to see how the rate of change (i.e. the growth rate) is changing along a line. A technique that allows us to see clearly whether the growth rate is changing involves transforming the data to logarithms before graphing, or plotting the graph on semi-logarithmic graph paper. Table 3.6 and Figures 3.3 and 3.4 illustrate the effects of using logarithmic (i.e. log) series.

In Table 3.6 we start with the number 100 in 1995 and apply a constant 50% per annual growth rate to it up until the year 2000, and a constant growth of 10% thereafter. This creates our column of data units in the form of standard numbers. The final column of the table comprises logs to base 10 of the data units column (Note. Any base will do. Logs to base e, i.e. natural or naperian logs, are also commonly used for this purpose).

Figure 3.3 is a line graph of the last two columns of Table 3.6. The lower line shows

Table 3.6 *Applying logarithms to a constant growth series*

	Annual Growth Rate %	Standard Units	Log Data Base10
1995	-	100.00	2.00
1996	50	150.00	2.17
1997	50	225.00	2.35
1998	50	337.50	2.52
1999	50	506.25	2.70
2000	50	759.37	2.88
2001	10	835.31	2.92
2002	10	918.84	2.96
2003	10	1010.72	3.00
2004	10	1111.80	3.04
2005	10	1222.98	3.09

Figure 3.3 *Line graph of a series in natural numbers and logarithms*

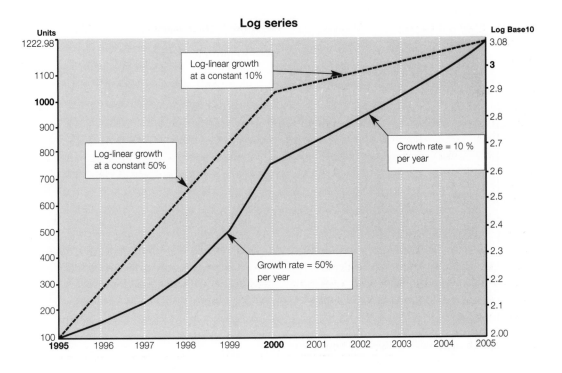

the growth rate of the standard units, which are represented on the left axis. Although there are different 'constant' growth rates on either side of the year 2000, we have graph lines that are getting progressively steeper. This is because the constant percentage of a progressively growing total adds a greater absolute amount to the graph each time. The higher line shows the log values displayed on a linear scale on the right-hand axis. In this case the axis measurements are not so easy to interpret, but the fact that the lines are straight on each side of 2000 tells us that the growth rate was constant in 1995-2000, but changed in 2001-2005 to a lower constant rate.

Before the advent of computers it was common to plot time-series graphs on semi-logarithmic graph paper. The vertical scale uses the standard numbers but the scale is spaced logarithmically. Equal absolute distances become increasingly compressed,

but the degree of compression preserves a constant proportional growth rate. Graphing the standard numbers from Table 3.6 has the same effect as plotting the log series on a natural scale. But, once again, the two periods when the growth rate is constant are evident as is the year in which the growth rate changed.

PATTERNS WITHIN TIME SERIES

The time lapse between each measurement of a variable in a series is called the *frequency or periodicity*. Most official statistics at national, regional or sectoral level are published with either annual or quarterly frequencies. Annual data are useful for making broad-brush comparisons and for looking at trends over longer time periods. Quarterly data are essential for finding out how a variable fluctuates according to the season of the year. However, as quarters tend to be counted from

Figure 3.4 *Plotting a constant growth series on semi-logarithmic graph paper*

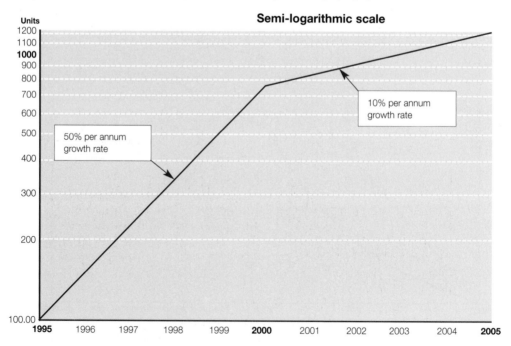

January 1st each year, they do not coincide with the seasonal patterns of orders for every sector. Monthly data series, when they are available, make it possible to identify more complex patterns than can be shown using quarterly figures.

Sometimes we are able to use data with a higher frequency still. For example, firms might keep records of orders on a daily or hourly basis. Supermarkets' computerised check outs keep 'real-time' records at the point of sale. Security prices on the stock market are also recorded on a real-time basis. In a dynamic market firms have to be able to adapt to changes in the pattern of orders from their customers.

When examining time-series graphs it is usually possible to identify four types of feature:

* seasonal variations - fluctuations in demand according to the time of year;
* cycles - variations in business activity as a result of booms and slumps in the economy as a whole;
* shocks - random and unexpected events affecting either the economy in general or the particular market in which a business operates;

* trends - favourable or unfavourable structural changes that cause longer term movements in a particular market.

If firms are to respond appropriately to indicators of change then it is important to be able to distinguish these different features in time-series data. Figure 3.5 identifies the four concepts introduced above.

Seasonal Variations

These are fluctuations according to the time of year. They are seasonal variations in demand, which affect the sales of many products e.g. increased energy consumption in the winter months, or the boom in retail sales in the run up to Christmas each year. Because seasonal changes in demand occur every year, they are largely predictable and firms are able to make provision for them, They can do this, for example, by holding stocks, which act as a buffer between production and sales. With careful stock management firms can cope with normal seasonal fluctuations and maintain a steady flow of production throughout the year. Alternatively, firms can cope with seasonality by adjusting purchasing and production schedules.

Figure 3.5 *Fluctuations and trends*

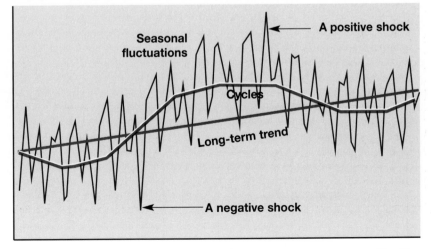

Economic Cycles

Even the best run of economies suffers from economic cycles. There are periods of boom, when incomes and demand levels are rising faster and there is upward pressure on prices, followed by slumps, when the economy slips into recession, and the growth rate of incomes and demand decline and price inflation slows or, even, reverses. Recessions have an adverse effect on firms' sales and cause them to put back, or even put off, their plans for investment in new plant and machinery.

Trends

These describe the long-term path of a market. So long as trends persist they bring some certainty to a market. When they are upward or downwards they require firms to change their production levels, and to modify their employment and investment accordingly. Trends tend to be sector or product dependent. A factor of importance in creating trends in consumer demand is income. Goods, which are regarded as inferior, such as cheap cuts of meat, experience falling sales as incomes rise. Others, with low income elasticities of demand, such as basic foods, experience slow growth in sales as consumers become more affluent. Goods and services with high income elasticities of demand, such as leisure and tourism, take up an increasing share of consumers' incomes over time.

Shocks

Markets are continually affected by unexpected events. Shocks can take many different forms, and we have to distinguish between those which are short-term in duration, and those that persist as a longer-term structural change in a market.

Unusual spells of good or bad weather cause short-term changes in the demand for goods and services as varied as home heating, beer and soft drinks, clothing, pharmaceuticals and attendance at sporting and other outdoor events. Sudden shortages or gluts in the market for a finished product or an essential supply, such as those provoked by health and safety scares, can also cause sudden positive and negative changes.

The entry into the market of new competition, whether from a new product or from the entry of a foreign competitor into the domestic market, may cause a sudden and unexpected shift in demand which persists for some time afterwards. Demand may fall when cost changes, such as the cost of raw materials, wages and taxes, are passed on to consumers in higher prices. Some of the biggest economy-wide shocks have been the result of changes in world commodity markets, such as the major rise in oil prices in the 1970s when the Organisation of Petroleum Exporting Countries (OPEC) formed a cartel and restricted supplies of oil coming on to world markets. This type

Figure 3.6 *Structural changes in a trend*

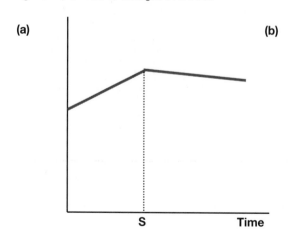

(a)

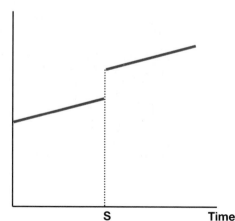

(b)

of external or exogenous shock, affects all parts of the national and international economy, remaining beyond the national control.

Large and persistent shocks lead to re-allocations of demand and structural changes within a market. The evidence for this in time series graphs is re-alignment of trends. Trend lines can alter their slope, shift vertically or do both at the same time. Figure 3.6 shows two different types of structural breaks which you find in time-series. Part (a) is an example of a change in the slope of a trend from strongly upward to steadily declining. Although we should be careful with such loose descriptions, unless we can see the scale on the vertical axis! In part (b) the general upward slope of the trend remains unchanged, but a structural change has caused a sudden and persistent vertical shift.

DISTINGUISHING TRENDS FROM FLUCTUATIONS

Fluctuations in production levels are costly to firms. In periods of low production, expensive capital equipment and labour are under-utilised. When orders and production levels are high there may be a temptation on the part of managers to run machines for more hours than is recommended and to overwork their labour force. Short-term fluctuations in production and sales may also disguise changes in long-term trends, and leave firms unprepared for new market conditions. When fluctuations are larger than normal, firms can find it difficult to regulate production and stocks in line with emerging orders.

To make it easier to identify trends there are a number of techniques which can be used for smoothing the data before graphing.

Figure 3.7 *Identifying a trend using a regression line*

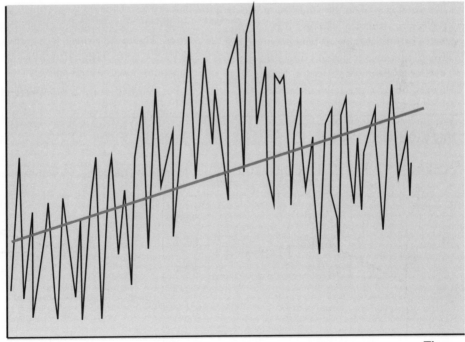

Straight line fitting

This involves fitting a line of best fit through the data points on a graph.

Ordinary least squares is the normal method used to do this. The fitted line, called a regression line is that which minimises the sum of the squared distances between each of the original points and the fitted line[2]. (See Figure 3.7) Many statistical and spreadsheet programs contain a regression or line fit procedure. Once you have mastered the idiosyncrasies of the program you are using, then the method is relatively straightforward, and it provides a trend line with a simple linear equation of the form:

$$y = a + b.t$$

Where 'y' is the variable being analysed, 'a' the intercept on the vertical axis, 'b' the slope of the line and 't' the time period. Most standard packages also generate diagnostic statistics which allow you to judge the strength of linear dependence between the variable you are tracking and time.

The drawback of simple line fitting is that it may disguise structural changes that have occurred within the period being analysed. It is always advisable to observe raw data series by eye for evidence of structural breaks, and to take account of any prior knowledge that would lead you to suspect such breaks. In such cases, the data can be partitioned into two or more periods, and separate regression lines fitted to each period.

Moving Averages

This method is widely used within industry to smooth out data, so as to identify general trends. A three-period moving average consists of finding the average of a particular data point and the data points on either side of it. With a 5 period moving average, two points are taken on either side of each data point, and so on. When an even number is used for moving averages it is not possible to place an equal number of data points on each side of each data point. By convention the odd one left over is placed before the point. So a four-period moving average takes each data point, the two before it, and the one after to work out an average. (See Table 3.8)

The effect of working out a moving average is to smooth out a series of numbers. The larger the number of periods over which you work out the average the smoother the resulting series. Figure 3.8, which shows a four-month moving average from the previous table, illustrates how the data points at the extremes of the graph are lost by the averaging process.

Table 3.8 *Calculating moving 3 and 4 period moving averages*

Quarter	Actual Output	3 Month Average	4 Month Average
1	89	—	—
2	97	96.0	—
3	102	96.3	94.5
4	90	95.0	95.5
5	93	89.0	92.3
6	84	86.3	87.3
7	82	87.0	88.5
8	95	—	—

---

2. The distances are squared to prevent positive (above the line) and negative (below the line) distances cancelling each other out.

Figure 3.8 *Moving average trend lines*

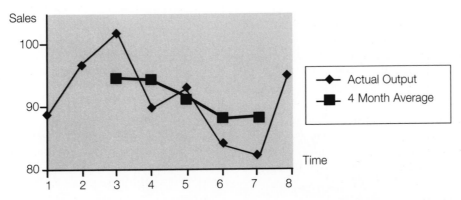

Exponential smoothing

This method uses a weighted average of past time-series values to derive a fitted value. The method used for exponential smoothing can be expressed as follows:

$$F_t = aY_t + (1 - a)F_{t-1}$$

Where, F_t = Fitted value of the time series in period t

Y_t = Actual value of the time series in period t

F_{t-1} = Fitted value of the time series in the previous period t-1

'a' is the smoothing constant and must have a value between 0 and 1. Due to the fact that the current fitted value is influenced be the previous fitted value, which in turn depends upon the one before it, all fitted values are a weighted average of all previous actual values.

However, more weight is given to the most recent values and less weight to the past ones. It should be noted that in time period 1, when there is no previous value, we use the current value 50 as the fitted value. This is illustrated in Table 3.8 and Figure 3.9.

The lower the value of a the greater is the degree of smoothing. In this case the column and line where a = .1 has the greatest smoothing, and a =.9 shows the least smoothing.

The closer a is to zero, the greater is the weight given to past values, and the stronger the degree of smoothing.

Forecasting: a note

It is beyond the scope of this book to discuss the intricacies of forecasting. However, forecasts can be derived using all three of the

Table 3.8 *Actual and exponentially smoothed values*

Time period	Actual value	Fitted values (F_t)		
t	Y_t	a = .1	a = .5	a = .9
1	50	50	50	50
2	80	53.0	65.0	77.0
3	21	49.8	43.0	26.6
4	71	51.9	57.0	66.6
5	48	51.5	52.5	49.9
6	20	48.4	36.3	23.0

Figure 3.9 *Exponential smoothing with different smoothing constants*

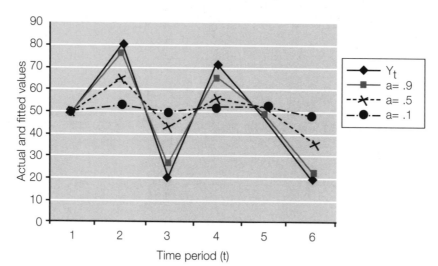

methods for fitting a trend line.

Once we have the equation of the straight-line fit we can forecast any chosen date by entering that date for the value t in the regression equation. We can use the moving average value from the past, say, three months as the prediction of the fourth month and so on forwards. Similarly we can project an exponentially smoothed series forward by using the last smoothed value as the next forecast value, and continue this forward in the same way as a moving average forecast.

All of these methods involve projecting forward an existing trend. They rely, therefore, on the crucial assumption that the past trend will continue into the future. Although they each have a part to play, more sophisticated forecasting methods tend to be model based. They take into account external or exogenous factors, such as prices and incomes, that can cause sales patterns to change. A brief account of model-based forecasting is given in Chapter 6.

4 Market Segments

Barry Harrison, Senior Lecturer, Nottingham Trent University

FOCUS QUESTIONS

- What do we mean by market segmentation?
- What features of market segments can we identify using published statistics?
- How well is our firm performing in each market segment in comparison with the segment as a whole?
- How can firms obtain, use and interpret relevant cross-sectional data?

- What can we learn from official sources of cross sectional data: the Family Expenditure Survey, The General Household Survey, *Social Trends*, *Regional Trends*?
- What factors should be considered in surveys for collecting primary data?
- How can we usefully present cross-sectional data, using graphs and measures of average?

DEFINING MARKET SEGMENTATION

We are all familiar with the terms 'market' and 'market segment'. Nevertheless we need to establish precise definitions of these terms since they are the subject of this chapter and it is important that we interpret them in the same way. **Markets** consist of buyers and sellers of particular products. For example, the car market includes all buyers and sellers of cars; the housing market comprises buyers and sellers of housing, and so on. **Market segmentation**, on the other hand, is the division of a market into distinct groups of buyers who are differentiated in some way from other buyers in the same market.

One point you need to be aware of is that market segments are not always apparent. They do not always have an obvious structure and there are no clearly defined criteria against which you can test the existence of different segments and reach a definitive conclusion about them. It is one of the tasks of management (maybe one of your tasks) to identify broad groups of customers who can be combined together in terms of their particular requirements and therefore targeted more effectively by the company. In fact, firms now design products to target particular segments of the market and so identifying the different segments is particularly important. It is useful to ask yourself which segments of the market your own company, or one you are studying, targets. So, on what bases can markets be segmented? How do you go about identifying a market segment?

BASES OF MARKET SEGMENTATION

In general you would probably begin by identifying some of the more obvious ways in which markets might be segmented. The following discussion is general and for the specific products your own company supplies you might well be able to add other bases for market segmentation.

1. **Geographical segmentation** is the division of a market into geographical regions such as a county, a region or even a set of postcodes. For multi-national organisations, geographical segmentation of the market occurs at the national level. In the UK, soccer kits are manufactured by a small number of firms and soccer clubs, located in different towns and cities who segment the market for different strips.
2. **Demographic segmentation** occurs when it is possible to group consumers by such things as age and gender. This is the most common motive for segmenting a market since consumer requirements most obviously vary with age and gender. It is also very easy to measure the relevant variables in demographic segmentation. Demographic segmentation is often coupled with geographic segmentation so that having defined different regions the market is further segmented according to the age and/or gender structure of the population. It might be further segmented according to occupation or ethnic characteristics and so on.
3. **Psychographic segmentation** is the division of a market into groups based on differences in social class or lifestyle. In terms of lifestyle, a market might be segmented into fitness seekers or family oriented segments.
4. **Behavioural segmentation** involves grouping consumers according to their product knowledge, attitudes, usage (existing users, ex-users, new users) and preferences for different products. There are many examples of this kind of segmentation. For example, the rapid growth of the organic food market is an example of segmentation on the bases of consumer attitudes. The various cereals produced by Kellogg show the way that different products cater for the requirements of consumers in diverse

segments. Sultana bran caters for the health segment, the diet segment is catered for by Special K; Rice Krispies cater for the children's segment, and so on.

CONDITIONS NECESSARY FOR SEGMENTATION

Identifying a market segment is a matter of judgement, but, having identified one, there are other issues you need to consider. Effective market segmentation is only possible if certain conditions are satisfied.

1. It must be possible to estimate the size of the market segment. How else could you estimate production runs, raw material and advertising budgets, and so on?
2. It must be possible for the firm to serve the identified market. Can you produce sufficient quantities of the product at the price consumers wish to pay? Can you deliver to the market? No doubt many opportunities go unexploited because of logistical problems.
3. Any segment identified must be potentially profitable. Again this is why it is important to estimate the size of the segment. In a nutshell you need to be confident that, over some acceptable period of time, revenue is going to exceed costs by the required margin.
4. Sales into any segment depend on the marketing mix and it is a requirement of effective segmentation that you and your colleagues can design marketing mix programmes for each market segment.

Having identified a market segment, what can you do to test the conditions for effective segmentation? In fact, there are a whole host of factors to consider here. Many are beyond the scope of this chapter such as the price the market might bear in different segments, the potential impact of competition, the availability of supply and distribution networks and so on. Here we focus on some data you might very well gather.

CROSS-SECTIONAL DATA

Market segments might be determined by income group, social class or region and gathering data on these will often be your first step in identifying a market segment. Such an approach involves collecting and analysing cross-sectional data. Firms may use this information:

- in establishing which groups of the population or what region to target. Which group is the largest consumer of a particular type of product? If the product is aimed a particular age group, what is the regional breakdown of this group in the UK?
- identifying the stratification of a sample to select to carry out a more detailed study of their own. Are there particular groups in the population that they are more interested in?
- to establish trends in each sector over time and to consider whether cross sectional differences in consumption will reflect changes in different groups over time. For instance, will the buying habits of the top decile become the habits of the 9th decile as incomes increase? Is there any evidence of such a trend?

It is to an analysis of cross-sectional data that we now turn.

What are Cross-Sectional Data?

Whereas time-series data describe the behaviour of some variable over time, cross-sectional data look at variables at some point in time. It is like a still photograph that captures images at a particular point in time. For example, in the car market, time-series data might plot the pattern of sales for some particular model every month over the last five years. You would use this if you needed to identify trends and to project forecasts. Cross-sectional data, on the other hand, might plot the proportion of total sales for all manufacturers of cars within the last quarter. This enables you to make comparisons. In our example of the car market, cross-sectional data

make it possible to compare the size of different market segments. Despite these fundamental differences it is sometimes useful to analyse time-series data and cross-sectional data simultaneously.

Official Sources of Cross-Sectional Data

National Statistics carry out several large cross-sectional studies that are published on an annual basis.

1. The Family Expenditure Survey

This is based on an ongoing multi-stage stratified random sample. In each financial year 11,000 private households in the UK are selected, of whom around 6,500 reply. This provides information on household expenditure and income, broken down, for instance, by income deciles and regions. The original reason for the survey was to provide information on spending patterns for the Retail Price Index but it now serves a much wider role. *National Statistics* will provide a more detailed breakdown of the data and tabulations on request for a fee.

The National Food Survey is a random sample of private households in the UK that provides more detailed information on household expenditure on food. This is to be combined with the Family Expenditure Survey in the future.

2 The General Household Survey

This is a continuous stratified survey of the population resident in private households in Great Britain. For example, in 1998 approximately 16,000 people from 8,500 households were surveyed. The main element is a *continuous survey* that is unchanged over a 5-year period. The continuous survey has a household questionnaire and an individual questionnaire. The former covers demographic information, household accommodation, housing tenure, consumer durables and migration. The latter deals with employment, pensions, education, health and use of health services, smoking, drinking in the last 7 days, family information and income. There are also supplementary surveys, called *trailers*, which do not appear every year and indeed may only appear once. The trailers for 2000/1 include questions on, for example, 'informal carers' and 'alcohol consumption' over the previous 12 months.

Firms may use this information to:

- establish which groups of the population or what regions to target. Which group is the largest consumer of a particular type of product? If the product is aimed a particular age group, what is the regional breakdown of this group in the UK?
- identify the stratification of a sample to select to carry out a more detailed study of their own. Are there particular groups in the population in which they are more interested?
- establish trends in each sector over time and to consider whether cross-sectional differences in consumption reflect changes in different groups over time. For instance, will the buying habits of the top decile become the habits of the 9th decile as

incomes increase? Is there any evidence of such a trend?

An illustration of the type of information that can be obtained from the Family Expenditure Survey is given in the following two examples.

Figure 4.1 shows the large differences in average expenditure on life assurance and pension funds by income deciles. The graph illustrates that the lowest two deciles (20% of households) on average spend a very small amount (approximately 3%) of the amount spent by the highest decile (richest 10%). Even the 9th decile spends only about half the amount spent by the highest decile.

Figure 4.2 compares the expenditure by different income groups on tea and coffee. The average weekly expenditure by households on tea varies little with income, but the expenditure on coffee is considerably greater in the higher income groups.

Given that information from National Statistics is generally much cheaper than from commercial sources, it is always worth

Figure 4.1: *Average weekly household expenditure in £s on life assurance and contributions to pension funds, by income decile, 1998*

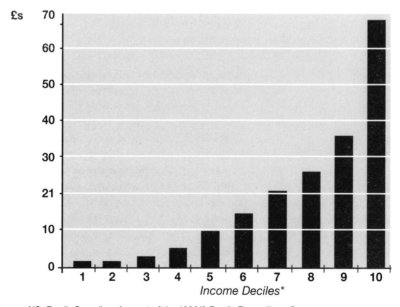

Source: NS, *Family Spending*: A report of the 1998/9 Family Expenditure Survey

* each decile comprises 10% of households

Figure 4.2: *Average weekly household expenditure in £s on tea and coffee, by income decile, 1998*

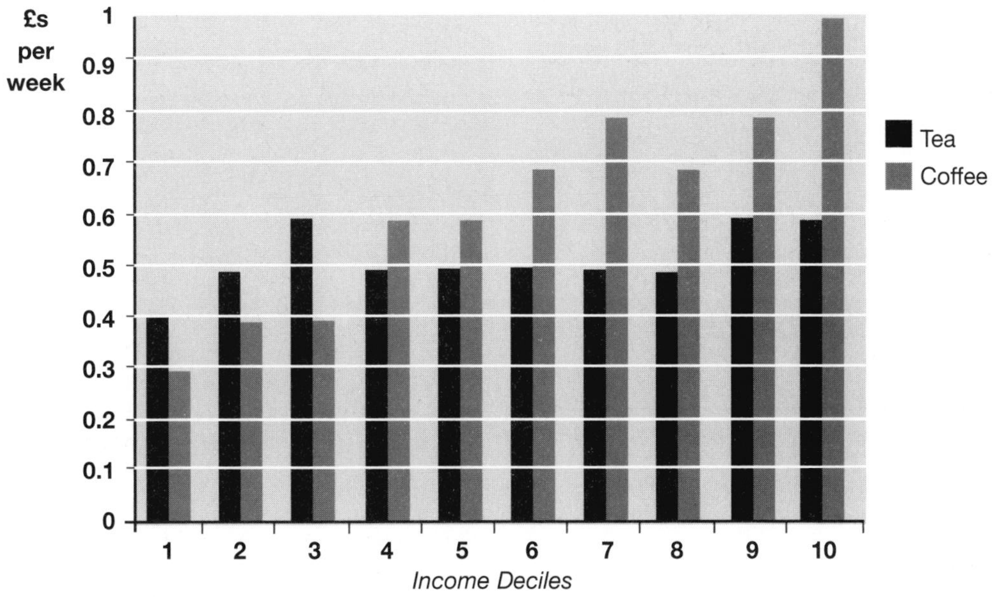

Source: NS, *Family Spending*: A report of the 1998/9 Family Expenditure Survey

checking the availability of suitable official data before resorting to more costly options. Sometimes surprisingly detailed information is available on particular topics. For instance, the General Household Survey includes the results of questions on deafness. The data includes the percentages by sex and age that have hearing difficulty and do, and do not, wear a hearing aid, the reason given for not wearing a hearing aid and the reason for buying a private hearing aid. The latter is reproduced in table 4.1. A short summary of the findings is

also given in the NS publication *Living in Britain*.

USING DATA TO IDENTIFY MARKET SEGMENTS

It might seem that a problem with annual data published by *National Statistics* is that the material is already out of date at the time it is published. This is inevitable. It takes considerable time for information to be

Table 4.1: *Reasons for buying a private hearing aid**

Persons aged 16 or over that have bought a private hearing aid

Better choice	65%
Not available on the NHS	28%
Obtain aid more quickly	15%
Other	37%

*The reasons given total to more than 100% because respondents could give more than one reason.
Source: NS, *Living in Britain*

Table 4.2 *Percentage shares of equivalised post-tax income of households ranked by quintile group*

Quintile Group	1978/79	1998/99
Bottom Fifth	9.5	6
Next Fifth	13	11
Middle Fifth	18	16
Next Fifth	23	22
Top Fifth	37	45

Source: NS, *Social Trends*

collected, compiled, analysed and processed. However, the fact that data are not always strictly current need not be a major problem. Most of the information you are likely to require to identify a market segment is unlikely to alter much from one year to the next. In any case, data from *National Statistics* will often be the most reliable statistical data available to you.

As well as the publications based on particular surveys, National Statistics also publish several useful reference sources that draw together data from various sources on particular themes. Two of the most useful of these are *Social Trends* and *Regional Trends*.

Social Trends

This is an annual publication, widely available in public and college libraries, containing cross-sectional and some time-series data on a variety of subjects. Much of the data spans several years so that trends that are important in analysing changes in the characteristics of different market segments can be identified. *Social Trends* contains useful data on population change and on the distribution of income. Both are very important determinants of demand for most products. Table 4.2 shows the distribution of after-tax income in the UK in 1978/79 and in 1998/99. Notice how, in this case, cross-sectional data is combined with time-series data to show how the different components of aggregate equivalised income have changed over time.

Table 4.3 *Household expenditure: percentages by income grouping, 1997/98*

	Quintile groups by households					
% of expenditure	Bottom fifth	Next fifth	Middle fifth	Next fifth	Top fifth	All households
Food	23	20	19	16	14	17
Leisure goods and services	13	15	16	17	20	17
Motoring and fares	11	15	16	19	18	17
Housing	16	16	15	15	16	16
Household goods and services	13	13	14	13	14	13
Clothing and footwear	6	5	5	6	6	6
Fuel, light and power	6	5	4	3	3	4
Alcohol	4	4	4	5	4	4
Tobacco	3	3	2	2	1	2
Other goods and services	4	4	5	4	4	4
All household expenditure (=100%)(£ per week)	**171**	**218**	**305**	**407**	**556**	**331**

Source: NS, *Social Trends*

Interpreting the information in this table is not a problem once we know the meaning of 'equivalised income'. In fact, equivalised income is used by statisticians to measure the degree of inequality. It is superior to unadjusted measures of income because account is taken on household income of the number of household members ranked by age. The sum of the rankings is then divided into income to give a value for equivalised income. For example, a married couple have a ranking of 1.0, the next additional adult has a ranking of 0.42 and so on. Without this kind of adjustment, simple comparisons of household income would give you a misleading view of how the distribution of income affects different households.

As well as information on the distribution of income at the present time, you will almost certainly require information on the way in which the distribution of income has changed over time. Table 4.2 clearly shows that there was a marked change in the distribution of income over the period and by the end of the period you can see that income was distributed more unevenly across the population than it was at the beginning of the period. The most striking feature of the change in the distribution of income is that, while the share of total income for all groups

except the top quintile group fell, the greatest proportionate changes were at the top end of the scale and at the bottom end of the scale. The clear implication is that the proportionate increase in income at the top end of the scale was at the expense of those at the lower end of the scale. Such information is very important in understanding the changing characteristics of market segments.

It is well known that different groups in society spend their income in different ways and Table 4.3 shows household expenditure associated with different levels of equivalised household income in 1997/98. The data in Table 4.3 reveal that in 1997/98 the households in the bottom fifth of equivalised income distribution allocated around 30 per cent of their total expenditure on the essentials of food, fuel, light and power - almost double the proportion for those households with the top fifth of equivalised income. Conversely, those with the top fifth of equivalised income spent proportionately more on leisure goods and services than those with the bottom fifth of equivalised income. Perhaps more surprising is that for many of the categories of expenditure there is little difference between the different groups. For example, all groups spend between 5 and 6 per cent of equivalised income on clothing and footwear and between 15 and 16

Table 4.4 *Quintile groups of individuals ranked by net equivalised income (%)*

% of income	Bottom Fifth	Next Fifth	Middle Fifth	Next Fifth	Top Fifth
North East	24	25	20	17	14
North West	22	21	21	21	15
Yorkshire & Humber	24	22	20	19	14
East Midlands	20	22	21	21	16
West Midlands	22	20	21	21	16
East	17	18	19	21	25
London	19	19	18	22	30
South East	14	16	18	22	30
South West	19	21	22	20	18

Source: NS, *Regional Trends*

per cent of equivalised income on housing.

Regional Trends

Thus far we have considered the national scene, but the markets for your own company's products might well be segmented regionally. *Regional Trends* is also an annual publication. In order to identify a regional market segment you will again no doubt need to collect data on regional income levels and the distribution within different regions. Table 4.4 presents information on the distribution of income by quintile group in the different regions of Great Britain.

Presenting information in this way often makes differences between different regions strikingly clear. For example, the differences in the distribution of income in the North East compared with the South East are apparent - even from a cursory glance at Table 4.4.

Information on the distribution of income in different regions is clearly important in identifying market segments, but it is by no means the only factor you need to consider. Information on the size and structure of the population is necessary for this, as well as information on patterns of expenditure. Table 4.5 gives information on the regional population levels for the United Kingdom in 1998, decomposed by age.

Table 4.5 gives an idea of the potential size of the market on a national scale but also breaks the market down into potential segments on a regional basis. It is well known that the most densely populated regions are London and the South East and while Table 4.5 confirms this, it also gives an indication of the relative size of other regions that make up the UK. For most products the age structure of the population is an important consideration, and brand image is often tailored to appeal to a particular age group. This gives you an initial indication of the potential size of the market segment in different regions, but the relative size of different groups within the region might also be important.

Raw data of this nature can easily be manipulated to provide other information that might be useful to your particular firm. For example, Table 4.5 reveals that those aged 60 and over form a larger proportion of the total population in the South West than anywhere else in the UK. This might be an important consideration in segmentation, not only if your firm plans to market a product aimed at those either retired or close to retirement, but also because they represent almost 30 per cent of the electorate. They therefore have a relatively large impact on the outcome of local (and national) elections and therefore on the type of amenities local councils provide!

Where suitable data cannot be found in the main published data sources then companies can contact specialist services provided by National Statistics, see the Data Appendix.

MARKET RESEARCH: COLLECTING PRIMARY DATA

Where the data required are not available through *National Statistics*, firms may decide to gather their own information. It is common to contract the job of collecting primary data to specialist firms who attempt to identify a representative, and preferably random, sample of people to complete questionnaires. This approach is not as popular as it once was and a company might prefer to gather its own data direct from its customers.

Sampling

Statistical information is obtained, not by examining the whole population but by obtaining a sample, whose characteristics are representative of those of the population as a whole. So how can you obtain a suitable sample?

Obtaining a random sample.
The basic principle underlying sample selection is that it should ideally be completely *random*. A sample is said to be random (or unbiased) when every member of the population has an equal probability (or chance) of being selected as a member of the sample. However, this implies that before you can select a completely random sample, you

Table 4.5 UK Resident population by age										Thousands and percentages
	0-4	5-15	16-19	20-24	25-44	45-58	60-64	65-79	80 and over	All ages
All person percentages										
United Kingdom	6.2	14.2	5.0	5.9	29.9	18.3	4.8	11.7	3.9	100.0
North East	5.9	14.4	5.2	5.8	29.2	18.4	5.1	12.5	3.6	100.0
North West	6.1	14.8	5.0	5.7	29.4	18.4	4.9	11.8	3.8	100.0
Yorkshire and the Humber	6.2	14.5	5.0	6.0	29.5	18.2	4.9	11.9	4.0	100.0
East Midlands	6.0	14.2	4.9	5.8	29.4	18.9	4.8	12.1	3.9	100.0
West Midlands	6.4	14.6	5.0	5.7	29.2	18.6	4.9	11.9	3.7	100.0
East	6.2	13.9	4.8	5.5	30.0	18.8	4.8	12.0	4.0	100.0
London	7.0	13.7	4.8	7.4	33.9	16.2	4.0	9.4	3.5	100.0
South East	8.1	13.9	4.8	5.5	30.0	18.8	4.7	11.8	4.4	100.0
South West	5.7	13.6	4.7	5.4	28.2	18.9	5.0	13.5	5.1	100.0
England	6.2	14.2	4.9	5.9	30.1	18.3	4.7	11.7	4.0	100.0
Wales	5.9	14.5	5.1	5.6	27.6	18.9	5.1	13.1	4.3	100.0
Scotland	5.9	13.9	5.1	6.2	30.3	18.2	5.0	11.8	3.5	100.0
Northern Ireland	7.2	17.3	6.0	6.9	29.1	16.3	4.2	9.9	3.1	100.0

1 See notes and definitions
Source: NS, Regional Trends

need to first define the total population. This is not always easy. For example, how can you identify all of the consumers of a particular product? The simplest solution to the problem is known as *systematic sampling*. For example if you are sampling consumers of a particular product you might include in your sample the responses from every fourth or fifth person from whom you obtain information.

Stratified sampling
When the sample population is heterogeneous, it is important to ensure that the sample reflects any bias in the population sample. It is unlikely that this result will be achieved by systematic sampling and better results can often be obtained by *stratified sampling*. To use this technique you must first divide the whole population into mutually exclusive sub-groups or strata. Units are then selected randomly from each stratum. The strata are based on some pre-determined criteria such as geographic location, size or demographic characteristic. Sometimes several criteria are used. For example, population strata might be defined in terms of income and then divided

into sub-groups according to age and sex.
Let's take a simple example. Suppose you want to determine the spending patterns of guests at a large, London hotel. The most obvious distinction is between business users and leisure users. Suppose 80 per cent of the guests are tourists and the remainder stay on business. Now those guests visiting London for leisure are likely to have a different spending pattern from those visiting on business, but a purely random sample may well, by chance, include an insufficient number of business travellers.

We might think an adequate sample size would be 100 and so we need at least 100 members for the business segment and four times that number for the leisure segment because the ratio of leisure visitors to business visitors is 4:1, for a total sample of 500. This is referred to as *proportional stratified sampling* and it ensures that the views of all groups are represented in the sample. If, for some reason, an adequate number of respondents cannot be obtained a *disproportionate stratified sample* might have to be used. This technique involves weighting a sample to obtain the correct proportions. For example, if your budget only allows for a population of 300 to be sampled, but you still require 100 responses from the business guests, then you will need to assign a weight of 2 to responses from those staying at the hotel and visiting London for leisure. In other words a total of 200 responses will be obtained from this group and multiplying this by the weight assigned to them gives an effective response rate of 2 x 200 = 400.

Planning a survey

Ensuring that you obtain an entirely random sample is a notoriously difficult problem. However, it is not the only problem you face in sampling. Here we focus on some important issues you need to be aware of in designing a sample.

Survey design

Define your objectives. A great deal of survey work involves analysing responses to a questionnaire and it is therefore important that you ask questions relevant to your needs. Ask yourself constantly how every question is going to help you obtain the information you require.

Decide how you are going to obtain the information. Basically you have a choice between using *personal interviews* or *postal enquiries*. Personal interviews are very time consuming and tend therefore to be relatively expensive. They are useful when more general information is required such as finding out how people spend their leisure time. However, for individual products, specific information is required. For many consumer durables, a great deal of information is gathered from postal returns. Purchasers of durables are targeted because they are inevitably invited to complete a questionnaire that is returned with their guarantee registration card. This is a relatively inexpensive method of gaining information. On the other hand, response rates tend to be fairly low and only purchasers of the product are

sampled, so the sample is not random. This does limit the amount and value of any information you receive in this way. Box 4.1 gives an example of a typical questionnaire.

PRESENTING CROSS-SECTIONAL DATA

Using graphs to illustrate information

Throughout this chapter we have illustrated information using bar charts. One reason for illustrating cross-sectional data in this way is that the visual impact often enables you to identify important characteristics in your data more easily.

Instead of using a bar chart to illustrate the relative size of the different components of an aggregate, you might prefer to use a pie chart. In this case a circle is divided into segments and, since there are 360 degrees in a circle, each component of the aggregate is a proportion of 360. If you choose to illustrate your data using a pie chart you should be careful to include some information on the size of the different segments. If this is missing, pie charts are less useful as a means of illustrating data than bar charts where a scale should always be included.

Figure 4.3 shows the use of pie charts to illustrate differences in the distribution of income between the North East and South East of England. The charts emphasise the relatively high concentration of households in the upper quintiles (fifths) of the income distribution in the South East.

Measures of average

Much statistical data are collected to enable comparisons to be made and, in making comparisons, you will often refer to 'the average'. However, the term 'average' can be interpreted in three different ways and statisticians usually refer to the average as a *measure of central tendency*.

Box 4.1

Postal Questionnaires

When products are sold with a guarantee, consumers are frequently asked to complete a series of questions. These are often given on the same form as the guarantee registration and, if completed, provide the company with considerable information on customer profiles. Typically the type of questions asked takes the following form:

Age
☐ 18-24   ☐ 25-34   ☐ 35-49   ☐ 50-64   ☐ 65 and over

Approximate Income
☐ Less than £10,000   ☐ £10,000-£29,999   ☐ £30,000-£49,999
☐ More than £50,000

Gender
☐ Female   ☐ Male

Occupation
☐ Manual   ☐ Clerical   ☐ Professional   ☐ Retired   ☐ Not employed

How Did You Learn About the Product?
☐ Friend/relation   ☐ Advertising on TV   ☐ Newspaper advertisement
☐ Other (Please give details)

Where Did You Buy the Product?
☐ Retail store/supermarket ☐ Specialist supplier ☐ Mail order ☐ Telesales ☐ Internet

If your own company compiles information in this way, you might be involved in collating the information. In this case you will need to consider some important issues relating to the data you have. How reliable are the data you have received? What is your estimate of the response rate from purchasers? Why might you be interested in the response rate? How do you process the information and once it is processed what is it used for?

Figure 4.3: *Quintile groups of individuals ranked by net equivalised income (%)*

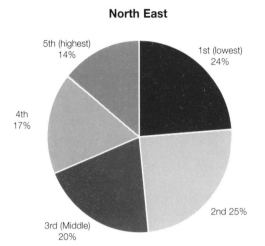

North East

5th (highest)
14%

1st (lowest)
24%

4th
17%

3rd (Middle)
20%

2nd 25%

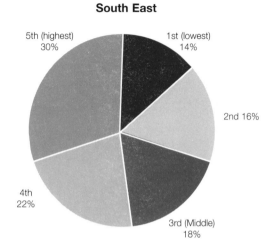

South East

5th (highest)
30%

1st (lowest)
14%

2nd 16%

4th
22%

3rd (Middle)
18%

The mean

The mean is the most widely used measure of central tendency and is the most commonly used interpretation of the term 'average'. If you take a series of numbers such as 1, 8, 3,10, 9 and 11, the mean is calculated as:

(1 + 8 + 3 + 10 + 9 + 11)/6 = 7.

The mean is simply the sum of the series divided by the number of terms in the series. The mean is said to be the representative value of the series. Notice that, although the mean is seven, the number seven does not appear anywhere in the series. The mean is not therefore representative in the sense that it is typical. However, if you subtract the mean from each of the terms in the series you will generate the following series:

-6 + 1 - 4 + 3 + 2 + 4

and the sum of this series is zero. The differences from the mean are called deviations and the sum of the deviations from the mean is always zero. This tells us that the mean is the value around which the terms in the series cluster. The mean by income decile has been used as the average for the data in Figures 4.1 and 4.2

The median

The median is another measure of central tendency. To calculate the median, simply arrange a series of numbers in ascending or descending order. The median is the middle term when the series has an odd number of terms and when there is an even number of terms, the median is the mid-point between the middle terms. Look at the following series:

2, 5, 12, 16, 18, 22, 30

In this case the median is 16. However, if you another term to the series, for example, 36, the median becomes (16 + 18)/2 = 17

The mode

Another measure of central tendency is the mode. This is simply the term that occurs most frequently in a series. Look at the following series.

2, 3, 6, 2, 5, 2, 12, 4, 8, 7, 17, 1, 2, 12, 2

The mode is 2.

We have three different measures of central tendency so, which is the best measure? The very fact that there are three different measures tells you that different measures are preferable in different situations. The most commonly used is the mean. It captures the bulk of the data and is the best measure where data are normally distributed. The median is more suitable when a series is affected by extreme values so that the distribution is skewed. The advantage of the mode is that it is useful when describing behaviour. For example, you might wish to claim that the average family drives a particular type of car implying that a particular type of car is more popular than other types. However, the usefulness of the median and the mode are limited because they both tend to ignore the bulk of the data and are derived from a limited number of observations. The mean is therefore the most useful and most frequently used measure of central tendency.

5 Analysing Costs and Prices

Julian Gough, Principal Lecturer, University of Teesside Business School

FOCUS QUESTIONS

- How can we analyse changes in costs and prices?
- How do we compare the figures for one firm with the industry as a whole?
- What use can be made of official data in analysing a firm's performance?

- What should be the relationship between costs and prices?
- What method should a firm use to set its prices?

INTRODUCTION

The objective of this chapter is to show how data on costs and prices can be analysed to make key decisions within a business. The discussion focuses on two broad types of analysis:

- **Dynamic** – here we are here concerned with the trends in costs and prices **over different time periods**, how they can be interpreted, and how the firm can compare these trends with the industry as a whole. In particular we investigate how the firm can use official data from *National Statistics* to assist in the analysis of its own business performance.

- **Static** – here we are concerned with how the firm's costs are related to prices at a **given moment of time**. We investigate how the firm uses its own data to arrive at the price it charges for its product or service – perhaps the most important decision any firm has to make. This analysis is slightly more theoretical, but it will offer

an insight into two particular approaches to pricing policy.

The concepts relevant to each of these areas are different, but they are introduced by reference to a common illustrative example.

DYNAMIC ANALYSIS

Here we are concerned with how the performance of the firm changes over time. Businesses need to know whether their performance is improving or deteriorating; they also like to compare their own experience with others in the same industrial sector. When they have this knowledge they can plan appropriate action. So how do we go about this task?

Imagine we have set up a firm to manufacture personal computers. We produce a single model which has certain advantages over rivals in terms of its processing speed, memory and reliability of components. We acquired premises for the factory, bought necessary capital equipment, arranged for supplies of components, hired the necessary labour and set up distribution channels for the final product. We sell the product directly to the public without going through a wholesaler or retailer

The firm was set up some time ago and we started trading in 1995. Five years later the firm has expanded but wants to look back at how well it has done comparatively over the period. It does this mainly for its own benefit to get a sense of perspective and as a guide to whether a change in business policy is called for. If costs are rising faster than in the industry as a whole, then this may be a cause for concern and call for remedial action. Such a comparative analysis could be seen as a duty to its shareholders, to provide them with statistical data with which they can judge business performance. Many large companies provide such a statistical summary as an appendix in their Annual Report and Accounts.

Assume that the present is the year 2000, but information for 1999 both within the firm and for other firms in the same industry is incomplete and subject to revision. The firm therefore confines its comparison to the period 1995 to 1998.

Let us start on the cost side with the biggest element, wages and salaries. Information from the company's accounts shows the following expenditure on wages and salaries, in column (1) of Table 5.1. During the period the company took on more workers rising from 8 to 10 as shown in column (2). From this we are able to compute Average Earnings per employee, column (c), by dividing total expenditure in any year by the number of employees.

We can move on to calculate an index of labour costs for the firm. An index shows the trend in the data over time in a more convenient form. A "base year" is chosen for the purpose with a value of 100 given to this year. In this case it would seem sensible to choose 1995 as the base year, as we are interested in the performance of the company since this date. Index numbers are then worked out for the other years relative to this base using the methods outlined in chapter 3. For 1996 we take the ratio of average earnings in 1996 to 1995 and then multiply the answer by 100.

$$13,444/13,125 = 1.024$$

Multiply by 100 = 102.4

Similarly for 1997 we have $13,600/13,125 = 1.036$

Multiply by 100 =   103.6

By the same method the index for 1998 is 106.7. The complete series is shown in the final column of Table 5.1. The great attraction of an index is that it shows the relative change in the series of data over time. For example,

	(1) Total Labour Cost (£)	(2) Employment (No.)	(3) Average Earnings (£)	(4) Index of Earnings (1995 = 100)
1995	105,000	8	13,125	100.0
1996	121,000	9	13,444	102.4
1997	136,000	10	13,600	103.6
1998	140,000	10	14,000	106.7

Table 5.1 *Earnings: wages and salary costs*

Source: Author

Table 5.2 *Comparison of earnings indices*

	Index For firm	Official Index Manufacturing Industries
1995	100.0	100.0
1996	102.4	104.2
1997	103.6	108.8
1998	106.7	113.7

Source: Author and *Economic Trends*

the index of 106.7 in 1998 relative to the base of 100 in 1995 shows that average earnings grew by 6.7% over the period.

The firm may wonder if this change in earnings was typical of the industry as a whole. Here it would need to consult official publications such as *Economic Trends*, *Labour Market Trends* or the *Monthly Digest of Statistics*, which are all published by *National Statistics* (NS). We could look at the **Average Earnings Index** for all manufacturing industries as shown in the publication *Economic Trends (Table 3.7)*. This is shown in the second column of Table 5.2. It can be compared with the index we have just derived for the firm.

Fortunately, the Average Earnings Index is also based on 1995 = 100 so it is easy to make a comparison. It is evident that earnings in the firm have grown significantly slower than in manufacturing industries as a whole – by only

6.7% over the period as against 13.7% overall in manufacturing.

However, the index for manufacturing covers a wide range of industries and it would be more useful to look at a sector closer to that of our firm. The most appropriate sector is Electrical and Optical Equipment, data for which are published in the *Monthly Digest of Statistics (Table 18.7)*. However, there is a problem here in that the base of this index has changed over time and is not based on 1995 = 100. Data for 1998 and 1997 are based on March 1996 = 100 whereas data for 1996 and 1995 are based on 1990 = 100. We will therefore have to make some adjustments to the official indices to bring them to a comparable base. This is adjustment is known as **chain linking** and is shown in Table 5.3.

We note that official data are only available for 1997 and 1998 for the index with base of March 1996 = 100. However, it is possible to derive values for 1996 and 1995 using the previous base of 1995=100, because we have data for 1997 on both bases. To derive the value for 1996, on the March 1996=100 base, we take the ratio of 1996 to 1997 on the 1990 base and apply this to the index for 1997 on the March 1996 base.

$$140.2/147.9 \times 105.7 = 100.2$$

By a similar procedure for 1995 we have 132.9/147.9 x 105.7 = 95.0

Hence we now have a complete series on the March 1996 = 100. We now need to re-base

Table 5.3 *Average earnings in electrical and optical equipment*

	Index (1990=100)	Index (March 1996 = 100)	Index (1995=100)
1995	132.	(95.0)	(100)
1996	140.2	(100.2)	(105.5)
1997	147.9	105.7	(111.3)
1998		110.1	(115.9)

Source: NS, *Monthly Digest of Statistics*

this series on 1995 = 100, which is simply done by dividing the index in column two by the value in the base year (95.0) and multiplying the answer by 100. Hence for 1996 we have:

100.2/95.0 x 100 = 105.5

Similarly we get 111.3 for 1997 and 115.9 for 1998. It therefore appears that average earnings in this sector rose slightly faster than for manufacturing industry as a whole over the period (15.9% as against 13.7%). The comparison for our individual firm is therefore even more marked with its earnings rising only 6.7% over the same period. The point to be noted here is that the firm should use the index that is nearest to its own sector. *National Statistics* produces a wide range of indices, broken down by industrial sector, so it is a matter of finding the category which most nearly fits that of the firm. The more refined the index, the more accurate the comparison will be.

It should be noted that the process of chain linking is useful, but only an approximation of what actually happened. Official data are systematically re-based, and the sample of firms on which the data are based, are changed in line with movements in the pattern of industry.

A particularly important re-appraisal took place in 1998 where it was suspected that the official data were not accurately measuring national trends, and possibly sending misleading information to the Monetary Policy Committee of the Bank of England. This Committee sets base interest rates in the United Kingdom, which is a benchmark interest rate which then affects interest rates on personal loans, overdrafts and mortgages. Base rate is set each month by the Committee with the objective of keeping inflation close to a target of 2.5% per year.

However, the index in early 1998 seemed to be failing to pick up the growing importance of smaller firms in the economy whose earnings were growing more slowly than in larger firms. This led to an overestimation of earnings growth and possibly an unnecessary rise in interest rates in June 1998 to counteract the apparent, but false, rise in average earnings. The Average Earnings Index had to be temporarily suspended, pending an investigation of the series. It was subsequently revised and the new series published in March 1999. Hence any comparison against national trends should carry the proviso that official data itself is subject to estimation error and possible revision.

Returning to our example, we have found the results encouraging for our firm. But there are further matters to be considered. Over the period the productivity of the workforce may have improved, so what we get for our expenditure on labour may have increased. Let us assume that the following information on output is available for each year from the firm's records, so that we can get a measure of labour productivity. This is shown in Table 5.4.

As can be seen in column 2, the number of

Table 5.4 *Labour Productivity*

	(1) Employment (No.)	(2) Output (No.)	(3) Productivity (per worker)	(4) Productivity (Index) Firm	(5) Productivity (Index) Manufacturing
1995	8	500	62.5	100.0	100.0
1996	9	570	63.3	101.3	99.3
1997	10	640	64.0	102.4	100.0
1998	10	650	65.0	104.0	100.5

Source: Author and NS, *Economic Trends*

Table 5.5 *Unit wage costs*

	(1) **Earnings Index For firm**	(2) **Productivity Index for firm**	(3) **Unit Wage Cost Index (Firm)**	(4) **Unit Wage Cost Index (Manufacturing sector)**
1995	100.0	100.0	100.0	100.0
1996	102.4	101.3	101.1	105.0
1997	103.6	102.4	101.2	108.7
1998	106.7	104.0	102.6	113.1

Source: Author and NS, *Economic Trends*

computers produced rose from 500 in 1995 to 650 in 1998. Dividing output by employment in each year gives productivity, in terms of output per employee, as shown in column 3. We can then turn this into an index, using the method described earlier, and this is shown in column 4. Finally, we can compare this with an official **index of productivity** in manufacturing industries, taken from *Economic Trends (Table 3.8)*, which is shown in the final column. It will be seen that productivity in our firm grew by 4.0% over the four-year period, significantly faster than the 0.5% experienced in manufacturing industries over the same time.

We can then use the index of productivity for the firm to adjust our index for earnings. This will give us a measure of what is known as unit wage costs, or the cost per unit of output. Unit wage costs are calculated by dividing the earnings index by the productivity index in

each year, and then multiplying the answer by 100. Hence for 1996 we have

$$102.4/101.3 \text{ x } 100 = 101.1$$

Similarly we get 101.2 for 1997 and 102.6 for 1998. (Table 5.5 column 3)

This can be compared with the official index of **Unit Wage Costs** in manufacturing industries (*Economic Trends, Table 3.8*). It is clear that unit wage costs have increased far slower in our firm than in manufacturing industries as a whole as shown in column 3 and 4 – only 2.6% as against 13.1% over the four year period.

We have so far only considered the labour element of the costs of production. While this is the largest single item, it is quickly followed by purchase of materials and components used in the assembly of the computers. We could undertake a similar analysis of these costs.

Data for costs of bought-in components and

Table 5.6 *Unit component costs*

	Total Component Cost (£)	**Output (No.)**	**Unit Component Cost (£)**	**Cost Index (Firm)**	**PPI Index Manufacturing sector**
1995	75,000	500	150.0	100.0	100.0
1996	84,000	570	147.4	98.3	98.8
1997	93,800	640	146.6	97.7	90.6
1998	94,900	650	146.0	97.3	82.3

PPI = Producer Price Index
Source: Author and NS, *Economic Trends*

materials could be obtained from the company's records and accounts. Dividing these by the output of computers in each year gives the cost per unit. We can derive an index of unit component costs in a similar fashion to that for labour costs. This is shown in Table 5.6.

This index can be compared with an official index – the **Producer Price Index (PPI)** for inputs of materials and fuel purchased by manufacturing industries. This is conveniently based on 1995 = 100 and is published in *Economic Trends (Table 2.1)*. The decline in the official index mainly reflected the fall in oil prices over the period coupled with the strength of the pound sterling, which reduced the prices of imported materials. It will be seen that the fall in component prices for our firm of 2.7% was far less that the 17.7% fall in input prices for manufacturing industries as a whole.

We could repeat the analysis for all the cost components, but for simplicity, we will group all the remaining items under the heading of "Other Costs". Deriving data from the company accounts and going through the same procedure as before we get the information in Table 5.7.

Most of these costs are unrelated to output and there will be enough spare capacity to cope with the higher output levels over time. For example, the premises, administrative support, accounting and legal inputs could

manage the increase in output from 500 to 650 units per year. It will be seen that costs only rise gently reflecting the impact of inflation over time. Hence, unit "other costs" fell sharply (by 20.2%) as they coped with the large increase in output over the period.

The different patterns of the cost components over time are shown in Figure 5.1 below, which are obtained from the indices in Tables 5.5, 5.6 and 5.7 above. The contrast between the modest rise in labour costs, slight fall in component costs and rapid decline in other costs is clearly evident.

Figure 5.1 *Cost components*

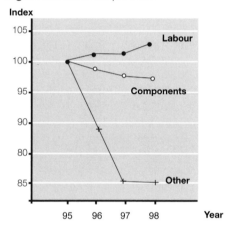

Having derived indices for wages, components and other costs, we can now put them together

Table 5.7 *Unit "Other Costs"*

	(1) Total Other Cost (£)	(2) Output (No.)	(3) Unit Other Cost (£)	(4) Other Cost Index (firm)
1995	70,000	500	140.0	100.0
1996	70,800	570	124.2	88.7
1997	71,800	640	112.2	80.1
1998	72,600	650	111.7	79.8

Source: Author

Table 5.8 *Weights for combined cost index*		
	£	Weight (% total)
Wages	105,000	42
Components	75,000	30
Other	70,000	28
Total	250,000	100

Source: Author

to derive an overall index of unit costs for the firm. We need to weight the three elements by their relative importance to the firm. The most common method is to use the weights that apply in the initial base year (of 1995), and then use these for subsequent years. The weights in 1995 are derived Table 5.8.

We then take each index and multiply it by its respective weight from the above table and add the elements together.

Hence for 1996 we have:

$$(101.1 \times 42\%) + (98.3 \times 30\%) + (88.7 \times 28\%)$$

$$= 42.5 + 29.5 + 24.8$$

$$= 96.8$$

We repeat the process for 1997 and 1998 and derive the following index for overall costs (Table 5.9).

It is evident that the firm has succeeded in reducing its overall unit costs by 5.4% over the period. This was composed of a slight rise in labour costs, a slight fall in component costs and a substantial fall in other costs.

We have so far assumed that the value of money is stable over this period of time. In reality, however, the prices of most goods and services rise over time – i.e. there is an increase in the price level, which we call inflation. As a result we should really adjust all of the above data for inflation to bring them back into what economists call "real" terms.

To convert the data to constant prices we need a measure of inflation. The most widely used official measure of inflation is the **Retail Prices Index (or RPI)**. This measures the retail prices of a wide range of goods and services bought by the typical household. The weights attached to each item are carefully calculated from a survey of the buying habits of a large sample of households. This pattern of weights is kept stable for several years, but is occasionally updated to reflect the changing patterns of household purchases. Sometimes new items, such as mobile phones, computer games and chilled foods have to be added. Similarly old items which are now bought in low quantities, such as net curtains, tinned meat and laundry services, are deleted. The RPI has been published for over 50 years and over this period the spending patterns of households have changed due to rising incomes, new technology and new lifestyles and social customs.

The "All Items" RPI is the best understood

Table 5.9 *Overall cost index*				
	(1) Labour Index	(2) Component Index	(3) Other Index	(4) Overall Index
1995	100.0	100.0	100.0	100.0
1996	101.1	98.3	88.7	96.8
1997	101.2	97.7	80.1	94.2
1998	102.6	97.3	79.8	94.6

Source: Author

Table 5.10 *Real index of overall unit costs*

	(1) Overall Cost Index	(2) RPI All Items (Jan 1987 = 100)	(3) RPI All Items (1995=100)	(4) Real Overall Cost Index
1995	100.0	149.1	100.0	100.0
1996	96.8	152.7	102.4	94.5
1997	94.2	157.5	105.6	89.2
1998	94.6	162.9	109.3	86.6

Source: Author and NS, *Economic Trends*

measure of inflation in the UK and is used for the up-rating of old age pensions, state welfare benefits and tax allowances. It does, however, have two important variants.

RPIX All items excluding mortgage interest payments. This is the measure of "underlying inflation" in the economy as used by the Bank of England in its task of controlling inflation.

RPIY All items excluding mortgage interest payments and indirect taxes.

In addition, the RPI is broken down into about a dozen broad categories of goods and services, and in detail to almost one hundred individual goods or services. Hence *National Statistics* provides a wide range of official price indices that may be of use to the firm. Consumer prices are also measured by a separate index for comparison across countries in the European Union. This is called the **Harmonised Index of Consumer Prices (HICPs)** and is published in *Economic Trends* and the *Monthly Digest of Statistics*.

For the purpose in hand we simply want to take out the effect of general inflation from our data on costs. The All Items RPI is probably the most widely used deflator – partly because it has a wide coverage of goods and services and also because it is well recognised by the public as being an official measure of inflation. Indeed, there is bias in business towards using the All Items RPI

simply because it is the most widely known index. However, it is important to choose a deflator that best matches the basket of goods of concern. The RPIX, for example, is better at measuring the underlying rate of inflation, but other deflators should be used as appropriate. For the purposes of our current example we will confine ourselves to the RPI.

We can then deflate our overall index of unit costs to constant prices as in Table 5.10.

The first column shows the overall index as calculated in Table 5.9. The second column shows the official RPI Index as published in *Economic Trends*, Table 3.1. This is based on Jan 1987 = 100, so we convert this series to a base of 1995=100 in column three. Finally we use the index in column three to deflate the index in column one. For example for 1996 we take the index of 96.8 and divide it by the index of 102.4 and then multiply the answer by 100

$$96.8/102.4 \times 100 = 94.5$$

Similarly we derive the "real" overall cost indices for 1997 and 1998. From the final column we see that in real (constant price) terms the firm reduced its costs by 13.4% over the four-year period.

It is interesting to compare the total cost index in its original form as in Table 5.9 with the deflated "real" index in Table 5.10. This is shown in Figure 5.2, which illustrates the impact of allowing for a change in the general level of prices. Real costs have therefore fallen much more sharply when we allow for inflation.

Figure 5.2 *Monetary and real indices of the firm's costs*

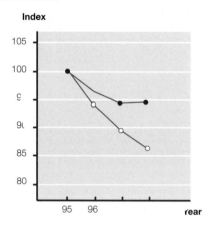

We have so far been concerned solely about the performance of the firm on costs. We finally, turn to a brief consideration of pricing. Here we would have to know what pricing policy the firm adopted in the period. Let us assume that the firm used an **average cost pricing** policy in 1995, adding a profit margin of 50% on average costs to arrive at the retail price of £750. This policy will be discussed in detail in the second part of this chapter. If the firm continued with this procedure we could

work out the price charged in each year as shown in Table 5.11.

Columns 1 to 3 show the totals for labour, components and other costs, which are summed in column 4. Output in each year is shown in column 5, which when divided into total cost gives Average Cost in column 6. We then apply a 50% profit margin to derive the price of the computer (to the nearest £) in column 7. In the final column is the price index for computers using the data in column seven and based on 1995 equal to 100. It will be noticed that this index is exactly the same as the overall cost index derived in Table 5.9, since prices are the same ratio above average cost for each year.

We could then compare this index with price indices for the sector to which the firm belongs. This is shown in Table 5.12

Column 2 shows the **Producer Price Index (PPI)** for the output of all manufacturing industries, while the column 3 shows the PPI output index for the electrical and optical equipment sector. It is evident that the index for our firm has shown a decline in price of 5.4% over the period, in marked contrast to the 4.2% growth in all manufacturing industries. However, the decline has not been as steep as in the electrical and optical equipment sector as a whole, which showed a fall of 11.4% over the same period.

Table 5.11 *Determination of price (based on average cost)*

	(1) Labour Cost £	(2) Component Cost £	(3) Other Cost £	(4) Total Cost £	(5) Output No.	(6) Average Cost £	(7) Price £	(8) Price Index
1995	105	75	70	250	500	500	750	100
1996	121	84	70.8	275.8	570	483.9	726	96.8
1997	136	93.8	71.8	301.6	640	471.3	707	94.2
1998	140	94.9	72.6	307.5	650	473.1	710	94.6

Source: Author

Table 5.12 *Price index comparison*

	(1) Price Index Of firm	(2) PPI (Output) Manufacturing Industries	(3) PPI (Output) Electrical and Optical equipment
1995	100.0	100.0	100.0
1996	96.8	102.6	97.8
1997	94.2	103.6	93.6
1998	94.6	104.2	88.6

PPI = Producer Price Index

Source: Author and *Monthly Digest of Statistics*

It conclusion, we have shown that the firm can use indices for a variety of purposes. Including to:

- construct an index of an element of its costs;
- construct a composite index of costs;
- adapt costs to unit costs using a productivity index;
- compare a firm's costs with an official index for its industrial sector;
- deflate cost figures to constant prices;
- analyse price indices for the firm over time;
- compare a firm's price index with an official index for its industrial sector.

STATIC ANALYSIS

We now turn to our second area of analysis to investigate how the firm uses its cost data to determine prices. Here we are essentially using statistics internally recorded in the firm and applying them to a business use. In this process we here use some elementary economic theory to help us measure the costs and apply them to pricing. The reader may find the analysis a little more theoretical than in the previous section, but emphasis is put on how the theory can actually be used by the firm. The reward for our extra effort in this section will be an understanding of two possible pricing policies which are available, with this added bonus of knowing that one of these will actually deliver the maximum profits from our computing business.

Perhaps the most vital decision for any firm is the price it charges for its product or service in the market place. It is this decision that will determine whether the firm will survive and, if so, how much profit it will make. Nearly all firms in the economy have such a decision to make, whether they are small retailers on the high street or giant manufacturers competing with just a few other firms. Firms nearly always have *some* discretion over price, and therefore a decision to make, because of the differentiation in their product or service from those of rivals. This may reflect many factors such as the product quality, design, technical features, location, brand image, after sales service etc. This discretion over price varies with the degree of competition they face. It is greatest for a firm with a near monopoly (perhaps through a patented product) and least for a small retailer facing intense competition from many rival shops nearby.

Prices must be related in some ways to cost, but what is the link between the two?

What information does the firm seek and how does it use the data to arrive at a price to charge the consumer?

Let us set up a simple example to illustrate the problems and examine two possible solutions.

We return to our previous example of the computer manufacturer which was set up in 1995. Imagine we go back to this year and investigate how the firm might first set a price for the computer? We investigate two possible approaches, one using average costs and the second based on marginal costs.

(1) Average Cost Approach

The first approach is to use information on our costs and then add on a profit margin so that the venture brings us a return on our investment in manufacturing capacity. This is known in economics as the average cost method of pricing.

The approach is very simple in that price is determined by the following rule:

Price = Average Cost + Profit Margin

The relevant concept of cost therefore is average cost, defined as total cost divided by the number of units of output (computers) made per time period. The firm will therefore have to identify the various elements of costs that will be incurred within a given time period, say a year. The firm has a manufacturing capacity that could produce a maximum of 600 computers a year, but is planning to produce only 500, to give it a margin of leeway of reserve capacity and ability to take out some equipment occasionally for repair or servicing.

Assuming that the planned output is 500 per year, the manager in consultation with his accountant and production engineer, makes the list of all the costs that will be incurred for this output (see Table 6.13).

Hence the average cost of production is estimated at £500 on the planned level of output. To this will be added a profit margin to make the venture worthwhile. But what margin should be added? There is no simple answer to this and the decision will be a matter of judgement for the manager. He or she will be influenced in this by the prices and profit margins that are being earned by

Table 6.13 *Costs at an output of 500 per year*

	Total Cost (£ per year)
Wages and salaries	105,000
Rent of premises	7,000
Heat, lighting & power	15,000
Components bought in	75,000
Telephone, postage	5,000
Business rates	6,000
Insurance and security	7,000
Accounting and legal	10,000
Depreciation of equipment	5,000
Management	15,000
Total	**250,000**
Average Cost	**250,000** = **£500** **500**

Source: Author

other firms in the industry producing similar products. With a little research in terms of looking at cost data in the Annual Reports and Accounts of these firms, the sort of profit mark up may be estimated. In addition the manager will subjectively take a view of the premium in the market that this computer, with its superior specification, can command in relation to its rivals. Let us say that the manager decides on the basis of these factors that a margin of 50% can be added on. Hence the price becomes:

$$
\begin{aligned}
\text{Price} &= 500 + 50\% \text{ of } 500 \\
&= 500 + 250 \\
&= £750
\end{aligned}
$$

(Note we are neglecting here the complications of Value Added Tax, which is normally added to the price of most products)

All this would seem very straightforward. The data are available, the concepts are simple and the computation is easy. Indeed, there is evidence that many firms price in such a fashion. But, unfortunately there are several drawbacks to what we have done:

1. the initial planned output of 500 may have been convenient, but that decision was purely arbitrary in a business sense;
2. the 50% profit margin was subjective, with only the "conventional" profit margin of other firms being used as a guide;
3. there is no guarantee that the firm will be able to sell the 500 computers at this price;
4. the firm is extremely unlikely to achieve maximum profits from such a pricing procedure.

These four points are of some considerable weight, but the third warrants particular attention. The procedure we have outlined concentrates almost wholly on the costs of the firm. The demand for the product and the relationship between demand and price have played no part in this process.

In economics there is the "law of demand" which states that for almost all products the higher the price the lower the quantity demanded by consumers. Let us imagine we knew the demand curve for the particular model of computer being manufactured and plotted on a diagram as in Figure 5.3 below.

Figure 5.3 *Demand and excess supply*

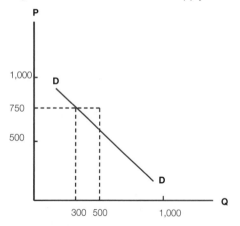

Now let us look at our planned output of 500 computers and the price of £750 we have decided upon. It is evident from the diagram that the demand for computers at that price is not 500 but substantially less – say 300. So the firm will be producing 500 and only selling

300 and stocks will accumulate. What will it then do? Perhaps it will cut output back to 300 to match demand? Or should it reduce price to clear the unsold output?

Another possibility is that demand is much stronger as shown in Figure 5.4.

Figure 5.4 *An increase in demand for computers*

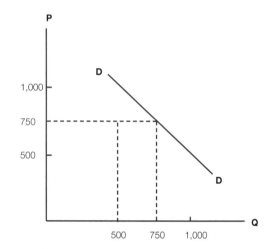

Here the demand at the price of £750 is 750, way above the normal output 500 and even above the maximum capacity of the factory of 600. What will the firm do? Will it start a rationing procedure with customers having to wait in a queue for their machine? Or will it increase the price of the computer to cut back demand to the 500, which it originally planned?

We do not answer these questions here, but simply pose the problems that are inherent in the Average Cost pricing method. What is missing in the above procedure is any planned business objective for the firm, and a set of cost and pricing rules to achieve this.

(2) Marginalist Approach

We now turn to our second approach to the pricing problem. This assumes that the manager and shareholders want the firm to generate the maximum amount of profit possible. This may secure maximum income for the manager if he is paid according to the profit made by the firm. It will also achieve maximum dividends for the shareholders. Indeed, this motivation is the one that is assumed in the conventional economic theory of the firm that has been developed over the last century or so.

To achieve this objective the manager has to use a different concept of cost. Instead of thinking in terms of averages the decision taker has to consider **marginal costs** – defined as the cost of producing one extra unit of output (in this case one extra computer). The decision taker will compare the extra revenue from the sale of the computer (called **marginal revenue**) with the marginal cost. If marginal revenue is greater than marginal cost then profits will rise, so the extra computer will be produced. If, however, the marginal revenue from the extra computer is less than the marginal cost of producing it, then the computer will not be made. Hence the rule for the optimum output of computers in the year is to find the sales and output level where:

Marginal Cost = Marginal Revenue

Note that we will determine the optimum quantity that will be produced by the firm, not just arbitrarily assumed it would be a convenient figure of 500, as in our previous average cost pricing approach. Having determined the optimum output we will then use the demand curve for computers to decide upon the price to be charged. It will be seen that this approach involves the interaction of both the costs of the firm and the demand for the product in determining the optimal level of output and optimum price in which to maximise profits.

This may all be very well, but how do we actually perform this task with the cost data previously specified? We need a measure of marginal cost, a concept which is intrinsically more difficult to grasp than average cost. To do this we need to look back at our cost data and divide the cost elements into fixed and variable elements. Fixed costs are those that would be incurred by the firm even if it were to temporarily shut down production completely for the year. Variable costs are those other

Table 6.14 *Fixed and variable costs*

The fixed costs are likely to be:

	Fixed Cost (£ per year)
Rent of premises	7,000
Business rates	6,000
Insurance and security	7,000
Accounting and legal	10,000
Depreciation of equipment	5,000
Management	15,000
Total fixed cost	**50,000**

While the variable costs are likely to be:

	Variable Cost (£ per year)
Wages and salaries	105,000
Heat, lighting & power	15,000
Components bought in	75,000
Telephone, postage	5,000
Total variable cost	**200,000**

Source: Author

costs, which vary in some way with output. These costs are shown in Table 6.14.

Now the variable costs are those expected if the planned output were 500 computers per year, whereas the fixed costs are those that would be incurred if output were zero. We can plot this data of total cost (TC) against output on a graph as shown in Figure 5.5

The fixed costs (FC) of £50,000 are shown as the intercept on the vertical axis when output is zero. The second point shows total costs of £250,000 when output is 500 units. Hence the variable costs of £200,000 can be attributed to the rise in output from zero to 500. If we had no other information about costs we could make the simple assumption that marginal costs were the same throughout this range. Hence we join the two points on the graph by a straight line and the marginal cost (MC) is simply the slope of this line. This is equal to the change in total cost divided by the change in output. In this case it is

Figure 5.5 *Total costs of computer production*

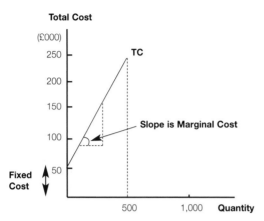

Figure 5.6 *The estimated demand for computers*

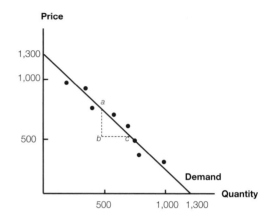

£200,000/500 or £400 per computer. Hence with this simplifying assumption we can easily get an estimate of marginal cost.

It should be noted that we would not expect this linear relationship to hold as we reached the maximum capacity of the machinery (600 computers per year). Under such conditions costs are likely to rise sharply as labour has to work overtime, machines are operated near capacity and reliability and quality starts to fall. However up to the normal output of 500 a linear relationship may not be too unrealistic.

We now have to measure marginal revenue. For this we need to have an estimate of the demand curve for the new computer – i.e. the relationship between demand for the computer and the price charged, with other factors such as household incomes, price of rival computers and advertising held constant. This is not an easy task and we can only briefly sketch the process in this chapter. However, it is vital to making the optimal decision on price.

Let us imagine the firm has hired a market research consultancy to undertake a survey of annual demand for the product at different prices. It has interviewed several thousand potential customers and derived their response as to whether to buy the computer at say eight hypothetical prices. The market research agency has then aggregated the responses and plotted demand against these prices as shown in Figure 5.6, as shown by the dots.

The firm would then need to fit a line through these points to derive the demand curve. An inspection of the data reveals that the points lie approximately on a downward sloping line. There is a statistical technique, known as regression analysis, which will fit the "best" line through these points (see Chapter 6). Instead we could proceed by simply drawing a line "by eye" through the points so that that the line goes through "the middle" of the data points. This is a very approximate process but it will do for our purpose.

It will be seen that the line cuts the vertical price axis at the value of £1,300 – this indicating that demand will fall to zero if the firm sets its price this high. The slope of the line can be measured by drawing a small triangle anywhere on the line. The slope is then the vertical distance **ab** divided by the horizontal distance **bc**. In this particular example the distance **ab** is exactly equal to **bc**, so the ratio of ab/bc is exactly 1, but negative because as P goes down 1 unit Q goes up one unit.

Now the general equation of any straight line is

$$Y = a + bX$$

Where **a** is the intercept on the vertical axis
        b is the slope of the line

In this case our variables are P and Q, rather than Y and X

Hence we have

P = a + bQ

However the relationship between P and Q is inverse so the value of b is negative.
   We have estimated that a = 1,300 and b = -1
   Hence our equation is:

P = 1,300 + (-1) Q

or

P = 1,300 − Q

This is the average revenue equation.
   Now the marginal revenue curve can be derived from the average revenue curve. Marginal revenue is always less than average revenue for a downward sloping demand curve. This is because the lowering of price has two effects:

• It *decreases* revenue for the firm to the extent that each unit is now sold at a lower price than it was previously;
• It *increases* revenue for the firm to the extent that more units are sold than before, because the price has fallen.

Marginal revenue reflects the outcome of these two opposing effects. For a straight line average revenue curve, the marginal revenue curve is also a straight line starting from the same point on the vertical (price) axis but having double the slope of the average revenue curve.
   Hence in our case if the average revenue curve is:

P =   1,300 − Q

Then the associated marginal revenue curve is:

MR   =   1,300 − 2Q

The slope of −1 on the average revenue curve doubles to −2 on the marginal revenue curve and the intercept of 1300 stays the same.
   We are now in a position to determine the optimum output of the computer firm.

We need MR = MC

We know that MC = 400 and that

MR = 1,300 − 2Q

Hence

1,300 − 2Q = 400

2Q = 1,300 − 400

2Q = 900

Q = 450

Hence the optimal output to be produced is 450 computers per year. If we put this value into the average revenue equation we will find the optimal price to be charged.

P = 1,300 − 1 x 450

P = £850

Hence the firm should charge a price of £850 per computer and produce 450 per year. This can also be shown diagrammatically as in Figure 5.7. Marginal cost is the horizontal line at £400 per computer. It is however, likely to rise as capacity of 600 computers per year is reached. The average revenue (demand) curve and marginal revenue curves for the product are shown by downward sloping functions. Optimum output is where MC = MR at output level of 450. Taking output up to the demand curve shows the optimum price to be charged of £850 per computer. This is the maximum price that can be charged, while still securing sales of 450 computers.

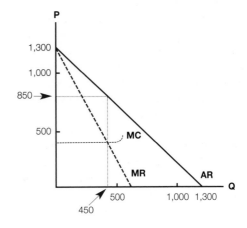

Figure 5.7 *Profit maximising price and output*

The absolute profit can easily be worked out.

Total Revenue

= Price x Output

= 850 x 450 = £382,500

Total Cost

= Total Fixed Costs + Total Variable Costs

= Total Fixed Costs + Output x Marginal Cost

= 50,000 + 450 x 400

= 50,000 + 180,000

= £230,000

Hence the maximum profit is:

= 382,500 - 230,000

= £152,500

It may be useful to compare this with the average cost pricing method.

Under the average cost pricing method the firm decided to produce a "normal" level of output of 500 and sell it at a price of £750. Using the average revenue curve of:

P = 1,300 – Q

Substitute in the value of 500 for output.

P = 1,300 – 500

P = £800

Hence the firm should be charging a price of £800 per computer to make demand match available output, but only charges £750. Demand will exceed the firm's output at this price and some customers will have to wait for their computers. Some may not be willing to wait in a queue and defect to competitors in the computer industry.

We can work out total profits under the average cost pricing rule.

Total Revenue

= Price x Output

= 750 x 500 = £375,000

Total Cost

= £250,000

Profit

= 375,000 – 250,000

= £125,000

Hence the average cost price method results in substantial profits of £125,000, but a problem of excess demand for its product. But it could have made even more profit (£152,500 per year) by reducing output to 450 and increasing the price to £850 per computer. The latter is the maximum profit available under these conditions and would also bring output exactly in line with demand at this price.

Summarising this section, we note there are two main approaches to using costs to determine prices and output. The average cost method is simple and widely used but suffers in that it pays little attention to demand. The result is that the firm produces too much or too little output, and forgoes the maximum profit which is available. In contrast, the marginal route pays equal attention to cost and demand, but requires that we think in marginal rather than average terms. The estimation process is more difficult and the informational requirements much higher. However, the prize is greater profit and a match between optimal output and demand at the chosen price.

We have confined our analysis to a firm producing only one product. Many firms, however, produce a variety of products and this causes additional complications for both methods. In particular, the fixed costs of the firm would have to be somehow "shared" between the various products being manufactured, while the variable costs would have to be exactly allocated to each product. This adds in additional informational requirements for the pricing decision, and the employment of allocation rules for sharing out the fixed (overhead) costs of the firm.

CONCLUSION

In this chapter we have illustrated how the firm can use statistics to assist decision-making in the field of cost and pricing. This has involved the use of both the firm's own data from its accounting records and nationally available statistics (mainly from *National Statistics*). The techniques and concepts appropriate for dynamic and static analyses have been outlined and a range of possible applications investigated. Appropriately used, the use of business statistics can brief decision-makers on the comparative performance of the firm and contribute to an improved pricing policy.

6 Demand Forecasting

Shabbar Jaffry, Principal Lecturer, University of Portsmouth Business School
Frank Asche, Lecturer, University of Bergen, Norway

FOCUS QUESTIONS

- Why is it useful to use a model to forecast demand?
- How can official data be prepared for analysis using a spreadsheet?
- How can line and scatter graphs be used to investigate factors influencing demand?

- How can a demand function and a forecasting equation be constructed?
- What is multiple regression analysis and how can we interpret its findings?
- How do we prepare and interpret a model-based demand forecast?

INTRODUCTION

Why is demand so important? The study of demand is vital to all businesses, whether to make a business plan to raise money to expand or for routine annual planning. Businesses need to know how much to produce, where and to whom to sell their products. They also have to assess the effect on the demand for their products of changes in their price, the budgets of final consumers, advertising expenditure levels and the prices charged by their competitors.

The techniques introduced in this chapter apply equally whether one is estimating demand at the level of the firm or of the industry. It should be noted, however, that the demand for the product of an individual firm would often be more responsive to price changes than the product group as a whole. When suitable in-house data are not available, an industry level demand function can be very useful. It provides a valuable benchmark for business planning against which a firm can measure its own performance. The example

developed in this chapter shows how *National Statistics* data can be used to estimate demand at the industry level. It uses throughout the example of the clothing industry, but the methods are equally applicable to other market sectors.

Firms can use information from *National Statistics'* sources to estimate aggregate industry demand for a product category or categories similar to their own. For example, if the firm's product were their summer collection of clothing for men, then they might use industry data to estimate the demand for either clothing as a whole or men's shirts in particular. An advantage of constructing and estimating an equation to represent demand is that it can be used to forecast future industry demand. This is achieved by using independent forecasts of National Income and the Retail Price Index in forthcoming quarters and years. We show how this can be done by means of a spreadsheet model, which is quite easy to use and can be readily updated as new information becomes available. Such an in-house spreadsheet demand model can provide the firm with early warnings of a slow down or pick up in the demand for its product group.

One of the crudest methods of deriving a forecasting involves using **extrapolation**. This is where a target series is projected forwards into the future on the assumption that the past trend will continue unchanged (see chapter 3). Extrapolation has the advantage of being relatively easy to use, although some methods used for fitting a time-series trend are very sophisticated. The disadvantage is that simple line fitting does not pick up the turning points in series very well.

An alternative is to investigate the underlying causes of demand changes. This involves analysing the relationship between the demand for a good and relevant causal variables, such as the incomes of consumers and product prices. This is known as **demand analysis** and allows us to answer quantitative questions like *"what happens to the demand for our good if the price is raised by 3%"*.

The techniques of extrapolation and demand analysis can also be amalgamated. We can begin by extrapolating the explanatory variables in our demand equation to obtain estimated future values. These values can then be inserted into our demand equation to derive a forecast of future demand.

DATA REQUIREMENTS

Industry level data can be obtained from *National Statistics* in both printed and electronic formats. For example, if one wants to estimate the industry demand for clothing, then information on consumer expenditure for clothing, total consumer expenditure and disposable income is found in the *Monthly Digest of Statistics*, and, if longer series are required, in *Economic Trends*. More detailed consumer expenditure series, down to four-digit Standard Industrial Classification (SIC) product codes are available from the publication *PRODCOM (*formerly called *Business Monitor)*.

Table 6.1 shows relevant industry quarterly data on consumer's expenditure on clothing excluding footwear. The data, obtained from *National Statistics'* electronic data bank (see www.statistics.gov.uk and the Data Appendix), are used to estimate the demand for clothing by all consumers. The first row contains the codes that are used to identify the series precisely. The second and third columns have the consumer expenditure on clothing at current prices, CCEAQU, and constant 1995 prices, CCBQQU, respectively. The fourth and fifth columns have the total household consumption expenditure at current, ABPBQU, and constant 1995 prices, ABPFQU, respectively. The last column has the household disposable income at 1995 prices, NRJRQU. All the series are in £ million. QU indicates that the data are quarterly.

These data are used later in the chapter to estimate a demand function for clothing. However, before estimating a demand function at the industry level, it is necessary to manipulate some of the data to generate the variables required, in the correct units of measurement. For example, at the industry level, price data are usually not available. Therefore, a suitable real price series needs to be generated. This is normally achieved by following these simple steps:

1. **Calculate the price of clothing.**

   Divide each figure in the column of data for consumer expenditure on clothing at *current prices* by the corresponding figure in the column of data in *constant prices*. We can think of the constant price figure as a measure of quantity, whereas the current price figure includes the effects of price changes. The latter is therefore revenue and is made up of quantities times prices. When we divide one by the other, the quantities effectively cancel each other out and leave us with a measure of the change in the price of clothing. This is often referred to as the implicit price of clothing (see chapter 3)

Table 6.1 *Spreadsheet of consumer expenditure on clothing and income (£ million)*

	A	B	C	D	E	F	G	H	I	J	K	L	M
		CCEAQU	CCBQQU	ABPBQU	ABPFQU	NRJRQU							
1													
2	yearqtr	CLOTHN	CLOTHR	TOTALN	TOTALR	RPDIR							
3	1963Q1	307	1400	4456	47435	51740							
4	1963Q2	372	1688	4936	51959	52259							
5	1963Q3	371	1685	4984	52888	54154							
6	1963Q4	496	2245	5189	54022	54409							
7	1964Q1	330	1489	4791	49921	54831							
8	1964Q2	394	1769	5212	53301	55065							
9	1964Q3	383	1748	5303	53952	55692							
10	1964Q4	523	2314	5562	55470	56081							
11	1965Q1	358	1574	5131	50754	55908							
12	1965Q2	420	1839	5516	53615	55982							
13	1965Q3	417	1818	5646	54706	57007							
14	1965Q4	545	2374	5858	55927	57290							
15	1966Q1	377	1627	5456	51957	59637							
16	1966Q2	434	1856	5914	55485	57229							
17	1966Q3	422	1800	5912	55141	57053							
18	1966Q4	553	2340	6109	56124	57467							
19	1967Q1	385	1624	5661	51969	57195							
20	1967Q2	437	1839	6082	55550	58351							
21	1967Q3	439	1853	6262	57103	59854							
22	1967Q4	581	2442	6574	59229	59201							
23	1968Q1	411	1725	6256	55813	60130							
24	1968Q2	475	1983	6418	56187	60344							
25	1968Q3	473	1961	6689	57924	59204							
26	1968Q4	621	2559	7088	60211	59215							
27	1969Q1	429	1753	6498	54410	59945							
28	1969Q2	514	2062	6909	57270	60523							
29	1969Q3	498	1979	7081	58366	60289							
30	1969Q4	651	2559	7566	61155	60278							
31	1970Q1	464	1804	6929	55342	60575							
32	1970Q2	552	2116	7468	58731	63209							
33	1970Q3	546	2062	7807	60694	63353							
34	1970Q4	737	2733	8343	62972	62881							

2. Calculate the general consumer price level.

Divide the total consumer expenditure at *current prices* column of data by the total consumer expenditure at the *constant prices* column. This will generate the implicit price of total consumer expenditure, or the movement of prices in general.

3. Calculate the relative price of clothing.

Dividing the implicit price for clothing by the implicit price for total consumer expenditure gives the relative price of clothing. This series is the real, that is inflation adjusted, industry implicit price of clothing. The process is known as deflation. It tells us the extent to which clothing prices have risen or fallen relative to prices in general.

Now we have the real price level for clothing, we can use it with data on real household income levels (i.e. personal disposable income at constant prices) to estimate an industry demand function for clothing. Of course, some of the above manipulations would not be needed if we were estimating a demand function for the firm's products using in-house data. However, official national income data would still be needed along with a general price index as a deflator.

GRAPHICAL ANALYSIS

Before conducting any formal statistical analysis of data it is always advisable to explore the data characteristics using graphs. We can plot simple line graphs of each series to examine the general movements of each variable over time. Chapter 3 explains how to

Figure 6.1 *Consumer expenditure on clothing at 1995 prices*

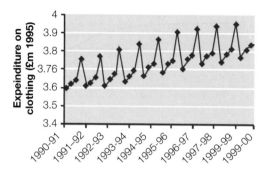

(negative and positive respectively). This suggest that a different, and possibly better, way to obtain information about what determines consumer expenditure on clothing would be to estimate a demand function (or equation) using price and income data.

CONSTRUCTING A DEMAND FUNCTION

When constructing a forecasting model it is necessary to take considerable care to identify the key factors that affect the demand for the commodity in question. Here we draw upon the conclusions of well-established economic theories of demand.

Key factors that affect the demand for most goods are the incomes of consumers, the price of the good itself and of competing goods. Taking information about these factors into account, it is often possible to increase the precision of the forecasts. Moreover, "what…if?" questions such as: "What happens to consumption if the price increases?", "What happens to consumption if the general income level increases?" can be answered.

Consumption and income

A consumer's problem is how to derive the most benefit from a given budget (or income level). In any period, t, suppose that the consumers demand for a good Q_t, can be expressed as a function of the consumers

do this. Figure 6.1 clearly shows that the consumption expenditure on clothing has a seasonal pattern. Seasonally adjusting this series may allow us to identify a general trend, which could then be extended into the future using the trend forecasting techniques discussed in chapter 3. It would not, however, allow us to take advantage of any knowledge we have, from published forecasts, of the effects of expected changes in important variables, such as incomes and prices.

We can begin to investigate causal relationships between different variables by plotting scatter graphs to look at the general correspondence between the different series. Figures 6.2 and 6.3 show that the real consumption expenditure on clothing has a clear association with price and income

Figure 6.2 *Relative price and household consumption expenditure on clothing at 1995*

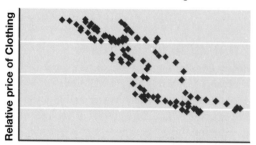

Consumption Expenditure (£m 1995)

Figure 6.3 *Household income and consumption expenditure on clothing at 1995 prices*

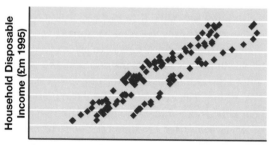

Consumption Expenditure on Clothing (£m 1995)

income in period, *It*. This can be expressed as the linear relationship:

(1) $Q_t = a + bI_t$

Here, *a* and *b* describe the relationship between demand and income and differ in value for different goods. The *a* is a constant term that describes the part of consumption that is not influenced by changes in income. The value of *b* is of central interest. The sign and magnitude of *b* indicates how a change in income affects the demanded quantity of the good in question. If *b* is positive, demand for the good will increase when income increases and more so the higher the magnitude. If *b* is negative the demand for the good will decrease when income increases. It might seem counterintuitive that the demand for a good can decrease when income increases. However, it is perfectly reasonable when one thinks about it. There are a number of goods that one buys mainly because they are cheap when your income is low, but which one would not even consider when one has reached a higher income level. One example of such a good may be a tin of baked beans. Goods with a positive income effect are said to be *normal*, while goods with a negative income effect are said to be *inferior*.

A problem with linear relationships such as (1) is that *b* is dependent on the units of measurement of both quantity and income. Economists therefore often prefer what is called an elasticity to measure the relationships between variables. An elasticity gives the percentage change in the left-hand side variable given a one percent change in the right-hand side variable, in our case the percentage change in quantity demanded due to a one percent change in income.

If we transform the data into logarithms, the estimated value for *B* will be the *income elasticity*, that is the responsiveness of the quantity demanded with respect to income.

(2) $\ln Q_t = A + B \ln I_t$

In this case ln denotes the natural logarithm of

Q_t and I_t respectively. We distinguish between negative and positive elasticities, a negative elasticity denoting an inferior good and a positive elasticity a normal good. In addition, we need to consider whether the elasticity is larger or less than one. The reason for this is that with an income elasticity of one, a one percent increase in income will increase consumption of the good by one percent. Hence, in this case the budget share of the good is constant. If the income elasticity is less then one, we say that demand is income inelastic, and the budget share of the good will be reduced when income increases. If the elasticity is larger than one, the budget share of the good will increase with increased income. In this case we say that demand is income elastic (very responsive), or that the good in question is a luxury good.

Introducing the effect of price

While the relationship between income and consumption is important, it is also desirable to include the price of the good in an equation to explain demand. Adding an additional term to the relationship in equation (1) does this, so our new demand equation becomes:

(3) $Q_t = a + bI_t + cP_t$

Here P_t is the price of the good and *c* gives the effect of a change in the price on the quantity demanded, if everything else remains constant. We expect *c* to be negative, as a price increase will generally lead to a reduction in the quantity demanded. This is known as the **Law of Demand**, and is

Figure 6.4   *Demand and price*

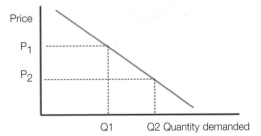

represented graphically as in Figure 6.4. When the price is P1 the quantity Q1 will be demanded, and when the price is P2 the quantity Q2 will be demanded.

As mentioned above, elasticities are a convenient way to represent the strength of the relationship. The demand equation is therefore often expressed in terms of natural logarithms, Box 6.1 Equation (4).

C is known as the **price elasticity of demand**. We expect the elasticity to be negative. Furthermore, it can be important to distinguish between elasticities larger or less then -1. If the elasticity is less then -1 (for instance, -2.7) then demand is elastic. If the elasticity is larger then -1 (for instance, -0.8) then demand is inelastic. This benchmark is important since with a demand elasticity of -1, a one percent increase in the price will lead to a one percent decrease in the quantity demanded, if other things remain constant. Hence, at this point changes in the price will not change the total revenue obtained from the market. The revenue lost by the decrease in the quantity demanded exactly offsets the revenue gained due to the increased price. If demand were elastic, so that a one percent change in the price leads to more than a percentage change in the quantity demanded, the revenue from the market would increase if the price were reduced. If demand were inelastic, so that a one percent change in the price leads to less than a percentage change in the quantity demanded, the revenue from the market would decrease if the price were reduced. Hence, depending on the price sensitivity of demand for a good, it may or may not pay to reduce the price.

Introducing competing goods

It is not only the price of the good in question that influences the quantity demanded. The prices of competing goods may be important, for example different brands of clothes. These can be introduced into our demand equation by including the price of competing goods or substitutes. If we assume that there are two potential substitutes, and that their prices are S1 and S2, this is represented in Box 6.1 Equation (5).

E_1 and E_2 give the effect of changes in the prices of these competing goods on the quantity demanded. Since the equation is in logarithms, the estimated effects will be elasticities. These elasticities are known as **cross-price elasticities**. If they are positive, an increase in the price of a competing good will increase the demand for our good. The goods are then competing, as the price increase of the competing good increases the demand for our good. It is also possible for these effects to be negative. In this case, the goods

---

Box 6.1

Extended demand models

Standard model with demand dependent upon household incomes and relative price:
(4) $lnQ_t = A + BlnI_t + ClnP_t$

Adding the influence of the sales of two substitute goods on demand:
(5) $lnQ_t = A + BlnI_t + ClnP_t + E_1lnS1_t + E_2lnS2_t$

Adding 3 dummy variables to pick up quarterly seasonal effects:
(6) $lnQ_t = A + BlnI_t + ClnP_t + E_1lnS1_t + E_2lnS2_t + L_2D2_t + L_3D3_t + L_4D4_t$

Adding the effect of a trend towards or away from the good in question:
(7) $lnQ_t = A + BlnI_t + ClnP_t + E_1lnS1_t + E_2lnS2_t + L_2D2_t + L_3D3_t + L_4D4_t + GlnT_t$

are said to be complements as the price increase of the complement good decreases the demand for our good (e.g. cars and petrol). If any of the cross-price elasticities are zero, changes in the associated price do not affect the demand for our good. If this is the case, the two goods are not competing. Hence, the cross-price elasticities can also be used to test whether two goods are competing, by testing statistically whether the cross-price elasticity is different from zero.

Nominal versus real prices

When there is inflation, one cannot really compare the price of a good with the price of the good at another time. However, we can make the two prices comparable by adjusting for inflation. This is done by dividing the money values of prices and income used in the demand equations by a price index, in order to deflate their values. Some data published by *National Statistics* is already deflated and is referred to as **constant price data**, or data in real terms. This was considered earlier in this chapter in the data section.

Seasonality and trends

Some goods are more popular in certain seasons of the year. To capture the effect of seasonality on a good's demand we can include special variables, called **seasonal dummies**, into the equation. Such variables take on the values zero or one, according to the season or quarter to which the data applies. To capture the effect of quarterly seasonality the demand equation becomes Box 6.1 Equation (6).

In the equation $D2$, $D3$ and $D4$ represent the last three quarters of each year. Notice the above equation does not contain a dummy variable for the first quarter. The intercept term, A, works as a base quarter and the other three quarters' demand is compared to this base quarter's demand.

Another factor that could potentially affect the demand for a good is an underlying trend operating in a market. For instance, in the case of food products, demand for some of the products may change over time due to taste

changes, which may not be fully explained by price, income or seasons. Another good example is the demand for computers, which has been rising in recent times as their popularity has increased. To capture the trend factor in the demand for a good the demand equation can be extended as in Box 6.1 Equation (7).

In this equation, the variable T takes the ascending values 1, 2, 3 and so on, representing successive time periods. G represents the change in demand for a good due purely to changes in time.

ESTIMATING AND INTERPRETING A DEMAND EQUATION

We are now in the position to start estimating demand equations. The first thing to do is to decide which explanatory variables to include. While prices, income and a price index are almost mandatory, some thought must be given to which substitute prices are to be included and whether trend and seasonal factors need to be included. We shall use a modification of the general form of relationship found in equation (7), using only one substitute.

The procedure is to use **multiple regression analysis**. This is a standard feature of many spreadsheet and statistical packages. It provides estimates of the effects of the explanatory variables on demand, and a number of statistics to indicate how well our equation explains variations in the quantity demanded.

An example of the results of a multiple regression using quarterly data is the following estimated demand equation for cotton shirts: Shown in Box 6.2 Equation (8).

The income elasticity, B, is +0.8, indicating a normal good. The price elasticity of demand, C, is −1.31, indicating a price elastic demand. There is just one competing good in this example. The cross-price elasticity, E_1, of +0.5 indicates that the good in question is a substitute for cotton shirts, as a 1% increase in this price will lead to a 0.5% increase in the demand for cotton shirts. The trend term has a parameter of 0.02, this indicates that there is a 2% growth per quarter in the demand for cotton shirts independently of other factors. The three quarterly dummies indicate that, compared to the first quarter, demand is slightly higher in the second quarter, lower in the third quarter and much higher in the fourth quarter.

ESTIMATING AND FORECASTING DEMAND USING MULTIPLE REGRESSION ANALYSIS

Table 6.2 presents the data from Table 6.1 in the form of logarithms. The log of the industry price of clothing is LRPRICE, $\ln P$. LCLOTH, $\ln Q$, is the log of consumer expenditure at constant prices and LRPDI, ln I, is the log of personal disposable income at constant (1995) prices. $D2$, $D3$ and $D4$ are the dummy variables which take on the values 0 or 1 to capture the seasonal pattern of consumer expenditure for clothing. For this estimation we include the variables identified as possibly important from our graphical analysis. However we exclude substitute good prices and trends.

Table 6.3 presents the regression results generated using the Microsoft Excel spreadsheet. The regression analysis in Excel comes under *Tool Data Analysis Regression*

commands. In the table XVariable 1 is the log of price and XVariable 2 is the log of income. The estimation includes 3 dummy variables representing Quarter 2 (XVariable 3), Quarter 3 (XVariable 4) and Quarter 4 (XVariable 5). The intercept represents the first quarter.

The effects of the explanatory variables are given in the highlighted cells B17:B22. Rounding to two places of decimals, the estimated equation is that shown in Box 6.2 Equation (9)

The price elasticity is negative (-0.35), implying that for every one percent rise in the price of clothing, the real consumer expenditure on clothing goes down by 0.35 percent. The demand is price inelastic. The income elasticity is greater then one and it means that clothing is a luxury good. The seasonal dummies imply that in quarter 2, 3 and 4 expenditure on clothing is higher than the first quarter, more so in the final quarter of the year. In relative terms increase in expenditure in the fourth quarter is over 4 times the quarter 2 and almost 3 times to the quarter 3.

These results can be used to both:

1 Carry out 'what if' analysis. For example, if the company wants to increase the price by 5%, what will be the likely effect on the quantity demand?
2 Forecast consumer expenditure (quantity demanded) of clothing in the future.

Box 6.2

Extended demand models

An estimated demand equation for shirts based upon model (7), with a single substitute:

(8) $\ln Q_t = 0.5 + 0.8 \ln I_t - 1.3 \ln P_t + 0.5 \ln S1_t + 0.03 D2_t - 0.05 D3_t + 0.1 D4_t + 0.02 \ln T_t$

An estimated demand equation using the clothing data based upon model (7) with substitute commodities and the trend removed:

(9) $\ln Q_t = -1.82 + 1.08 \ln I_t - 1.35 \ln P_t + 0.04 D2_t + 0.05 D3_t + 0.17 D4_t$

Table 6.2 *Clothing expenditure, prices and personal disposable income in real terms*

	A	B	C	D	E	F	G
1	Log values and dummy variables						
2		LCLOTH	LRPRICE	LRPDI	D2	D3	D4
3	1963Q1	3.146128	0.3681641	4.713826	0	0	0
4	1963Q2	3.227372	0.3854561	4.718161	1	0	0
5	1963Q3	3.2266	0.3685531	4.733631	0	1	0
6	1963Q4	3.351216	0.3617523	4.735671	0	0	1
7	1964Q1	3.172895	0.3634763	4.739026	0	0	0
8	1964Q2	3.247728	0.3574993	4.740876	1	0	0
9	1964Q3	3.242541	0.3481433	4.745793	0	1	0
10	1964Q4	3.364363	0.3529655	4.748816	0	0	1
11	1965Q1	3.197005	0.3521466	4.747474	0	0	0
12	1965Q2	3.264582	0.3463296	4.748048	1	0	0
13	1965Q3	3.259594	0.3468363	4.755928	0	1	0
14	1965Q4	3.375481	0.3407879	4.758079	0	0	1
15	1966Q1	3.211388	0.3437235	4.775516	0	0	0
16	1966Q2	3.268578	0.341206	4.757616	1	0	0
17	1966Q3	3.255273	0.3397802	4.756278	0	1	0
18	1966Q4	3.389216	0.3366878	4.759419	0	0	1
19	1967Q1	3.210586	0.3377259	4.757368	0	0	0
20	1967Q2	3.264582	0.3365374	4.766048	1	0	0
21	1967Q3	3.267875	0.334535	4.777093	0	1	0
22	1967Q4	3.387746	0.3311352	4.772329	0	0	1
23	1968Q1	3.236789	0.3274913	4.779091	0	0	0
24	1968Q2	3.297323	0.321607	4.780634	1	0	0
25	1968Q3	3.292478	0.3198809	4.772351	0	1	0
26	1968Q4	3.40807	0.3141734	4.772432	0	0	1
27	1969Q1	3.243782	0.3115744	4.777753	0	0	0
28	1969Q2	3.314289	0.3151864	4.78192	1	0	0
29	1969Q3	3.296446	0.3168489	4.780238	0	1	0
30	1969Q4	3.40807	0.3130763	4.780159	0	0	1
31	1970Q1	3.256237	0.3126657	4.782293	0	0	0
32	1970Q2	3.325516	0.3120865	4.800779	1	0	0
33	1970Q3	3.314289	0.3135656	4.801767	0	1	0
34	1970Q4	3.43664	0.3086531	4.798519	0	0	1

Table 6.3 *Estimated regression results for equation (9)*

SUMMARY OUTPUT

Regression Statistics	
Multiple R	0.993155361
R Square	0.986357571
Adjusted R Square	0.985848525
Standard Error	0.021824099
Observations	140

ANOVA

	df	SS	MS	F	Significance F
Regression	5	4.614452059	0.92289	1937.66	4.53E-123
Residual	134	0.063823036	0.000476		
Total	139	4.678275095			

	Coefficients	Standard Error	t Stat	P-value	Lower 95%	Upper 95%	Lower 95.0%	Upper 95.0%
Intercept	-1.824385523	0.364675054	-5.00277	1.74E-06	-2.545648	-1.1031122	-2.54564814	-1.1031223
X Variable 1	-0.35192223	0.067013479	-5.25151	5.77E-07	-0.484463	-0.219381	-0.48446307	-0.2193814
X Variable 2	1.081563741	0.071749103	15.07425	1.2E-30	0.9396567	1.2234708	0.93965668	1.22347081
X Variable 3	0.042467926	0.005220619	8.134342	2.46E-13	0.0321421	0.0527936	0.03214207	0.05279379
X Variable 4	0.047671904	0.005221183	9.130479	9.22E-16	0.0373453	0.0579985	0.03734532	0.05799848
X Variable 5	0.172549032	0.005247195	32.88405	5.05E-86	0.162171	0.1829271	0.16217101	0.18292706

FORECASTING FROM A REGRESSION EQUATION

Equation (9) was estimated using quarterly data starting from Quarter 1 1963 to Quarter 4 1997. Now let us assume that the pundits are forecasting that in the next quarter the average household income is likely to rise by 5%. This may tempt the company to increase its prices by 5 percent to cash in on the good times. What will be the net effect on the level of quantity demanded of clothing in the first quarter of 1998? Using the estimated equation gives the change in the quantity demanded $(\Delta Q_t\%)$ as:

10) $\Delta Q_t\% = -0.35\ lnP + 1.08\ lnI$
$= -0.35(5\%) + 1.08(5\%) = +3.62$

If the company increases its price by 5 percent, and household income is likely to go up by 5 percent, then the increase in the quantity demanded in first quarter will be equal to +3.62. This implies that household income has a greater effect than price on the demand for clothing. So, how much price can rise before consumers reduce their current level of expenditure on clothing, when their average household income is likely to rise as fast as 5% per quarter? According to the above equation the clothing businesses have to

raise their prices by over 15% before the consumers reduce their clothing expenditure in the first quarter.

11) $\Delta Q_t\% = -0.35(15.36) + 1.08(5) = 0$
In this way it is possible to carry out a spreadsheet-based simulation exercise and observe the effects of changes in prices and income on the quantity of clothing demanded.

Now let us assume that we want to forecast consumer expenditure for clothing for 1998. The price and household disposable income values for the 4 quarters of 1998 are asshown in Table 6.4.

We need to take logs of these values and replace logP and logI with the values derived from the above for each quarter. We also need to use the estimated effect of the dummy variables, as in equation (9), to reflect seasonality in the consumer expenditure on clothing to derive the forecasts in Table 6.5.

Although underestimating the demand, the regression model has produced reasonably accurate forecasts of consumer expenditure on clothing 1998. The differences between actual and forecast values are quite small. The plot of the actual and forecast values in Figure 6.5 shows the forecasts following the trend as well as the turning points in the actual expenditure.

Figure 6.5 *Actual and estimated real clothing expenditure for 1998*

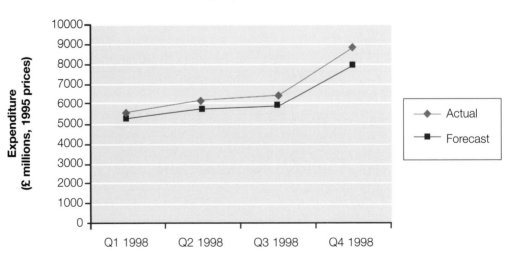

Table 6.4 *The real price of* clothing and real income in 1988

	Real Price	Real Income
Quarter 1	0.9242969	131078
Quarter 2	0.9439255	130174
Quarter 3	0.9111404	130874
Quarter 4	0.9341011	132783

Source: Derived from the data in the Monthly Digest of Statistics

Table 6.5 *Forecast and actual values of consumer expenditure on clothing for 1998*

	log(Actual)	log(Forecast)*	Actual	Forecast	Difference
Quarter 1	3.7454652	3.72258115	5565	5279	-286
Quarter 2	3.7866805	3.75858666	6119	5736	-383
Quarter 3	3.8121778	3.77172694	6489	5912	-577
Quarter 4	3.9466487	3.89958799	8844	7936	-908

* Forecasts are based upon equation (9)

For any business, following the underlying trend and being able to predict the turning points is very important. These results imply that it would be reasonable to carry out forecasts based on this model if estimated values for the independent variables (prices and income, in this example) were available. It should be remembered, however, that even when a forecasting model proves to be reasonably reliable the equation should be continually re-estimated using the latest values.

7 The Economy and Business

Professor Nigel Healey, Dean of the Business School,
Manchester Metropolitan University

FOCUS QUESTIONS

- How do changing macroeconomic conditions affect business sales and profitability?
- In what ways do macroeconomic developments differentially impact individual companies, depending on the characteristics of the demand for a company's products and its organisational and financial structure?
- What do we need to know about the major macroeconomic variables such as economic growth, unemployment, inflation and the balance of payments?
- How can macroeconomic data help a firm to identify trends and guide business planning?

INTRODUCTION

Well-managed businesses plan for the future. They may plan to expand capacity when an upturn in demand is anticipated. They may plan to reduce bank borrowing when a rise in interest rates is imminent. They may plan to switch sales from overseas markets to their home markets when the exchange rate is expected to rise. This chapter is about the impact of macroeconomic changes on businesses and, more specifically, about how businesses can use macroeconomic data to inform planning and decision-making.

Identifying and assessing the implications of macroeconomic developments can clearly improve business planning. The adoption of the euro by eleven of the EU's fifteen member states, for example, represents a major economic shock, with far-reaching implications for British business. The introduction of a minimum wage, the onset of a deep recession and a rise in interest rates are also examples of macroeconomic developments that may impact British companies.

Business planning, however, involves more than simply identifying significant developments. Companies must also absorb the implications of such changes for their market or industry – and for themselves – and craft a suitable response. The same macroeconomic changes can have very different effects on different companies.

For example, suppose that there is an increase in British interest rates. This increase will tend to lead to an appreciation in the exchange rate (e.g. from DM2.90/£ to DM3.10/£), as international capital flows into British banks, increasing the demand for sterling. Exporters will be damaged by the appreciation of the exchange rate, which will make their products more expensive in overseas markets.

Higher interest rates will also increase the cost of company borrowing (e.g. to finance investment or holdings of stocks) and reduce the demand for goods typically purchased with borrowed funds (e.g. capital equipment like plant and machinery, housing, expensive consumer durables like cars).

Heavy engineering companies which have large capital investment programmes and high stock:output ratios will be adversely affected by the rise in the cost of borrowing. Housebuilders (e.g. Barratt, Wimpey) will also suffer from the rise in interest rates, which will increase the cost of financing work-in-progress (i.e. partly-built houses) while reducing consumer demand for finished houses. Heavy engineering companies which export a high proportion of their output (e.g. GKN, Marconi, British Aerospace) will be doubly affected by the combination of a higher exchange rate and higher interest rates.

Conversely, importers of consumer durables (e.g. Hyundai, Toshiba, Yamaha) will benefit from the appreciation in the exchange rate, which will reduce the sterling selling price of their products, but suffer reduced demand due to the rise in interest rates. Holiday tour companies (e.g. Lunn Poly, Thomas Cook) will similarly benefit from the increased strength of the pound and are likely to be less affected by the higher interest rates.

This example illustrates the importance of being able to work back from the effects of a change in the macroeconomic environment to the impact on a specific company. Figure 7.1 shows the different levels involved. The 'macroeconomic environment' is the broad economic framework within which all companies operate. The 'operating environment' is the specific market/industry within which the company operates (e.g. the market for executive cars, the market for new

Figure 7.1: *The general to specific approach*

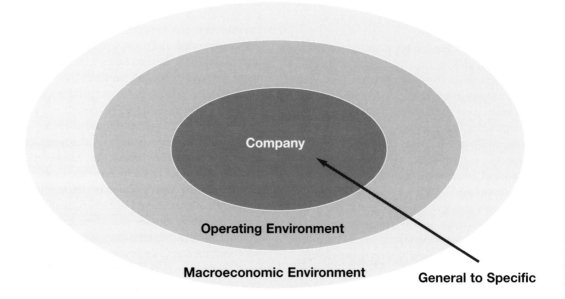

residential homes). The company is the organisation itself, with its particular mix of business operations, financial structure, human resources and product portfolio.

Effective business analysis involves being able to go from the 'general-to-the-specific'; in other words, being able to identify a significant development like a rise in interest rates and work out first the implications for businesses in general, then for the company's operating environment and only then, after taking into account the special characteristics of the company vis-à-vis its competitors, the impact on the company itself.

INTERPRETING MACROECONOMIC DATA

While macroeconomic developments are mediated by a company's operating environment and its organisational and financial shape, they ultimately impact on its 'bottom line' (i.e. its profits) by changing its revenues or costs. An increase in consumer spending may, after taking into account the relevant elasticity of demand, lead to higher revenues, but also inflate costs by causing a tightening of labour markets and upward pressure on wages. Higher consumer spending may encourage the central bank to raise interest rates to counter inflationary pressures, boosting the cost of servicing bank debt or increasing the revenues from accumulated bank deposits. Whatever the characteristics of a company, there is a handful of key macroeconomic variables to watch:

* Economic growth (which is identically equal to the growth of aggregate demand);
* The composition of aggregate demand;
* Unemployment and wage inflation;
* Inflation and interest rates;
* The current account and the exchange rate.

Each of these variables provides a guide to the way that macroeconomic trends are likely to affect a company's costs or revenues. Consider each in turn.

Economic Growth

Economic growth refers to the rate at which gross domestic product (GDP or total output) – and, by definition, aggregate demand – is growing (see chapter 2). Table 7.1 sets out the rate of growth of GDP and per capita GDP (i.e. average income per person) for the EU member states. It shows the variation in the growth records of different countries over the period 1991-2000, with Ireland posting extraordinary average annual growth of 6.5% pa, while Italy could only manage 1.3% pa. Britain's performance, at an average growth rate of 2.1% pa, was slightly above the EU average of 1.9%.

By and large, poorer countries, as measured by per capita GDP, tend to grow more quickly, as the same investment in capital and equipment will have a bigger impact on a poor, less-developed country than an advanced developed neighbour. To some extent, this is reflected in Table 7.1. Those EU countries with growth rates above the EU average of 1.9% over the period 1991-2000 tended to have below average standards of living, as measured by per capita GDP, in 1990 and have generally improved their position relative to the EU average by 2000; and *vice versa*. Ireland, for example, outperformed the rest of the EU in growth terms and lifted its per capita GDP from 70% of the EU average in 1990 to 11.8% above the average by 2000.

Changes in the rankings can be misleading, however, because economic growth is the rate of change of GDP measured in the national currency, at constant prices. Comparisons of per capita GDP for the different EU states, on the other hand, are calculated by converting per capita GDP measured in the national currency into a common currency, in this case the euro. Britain's apparently spectacular improvement in the per capita GDP rankings, up from 89.2% of the EU average in 1990 to 113.0% in 2000, does not chime with its only marginally faster than average rate of economic growth over the same period. Most of the apparent 'catch up' stems from the recent

Table 7.1: *Economic growth in the EU*

	Per Capita GDP[1] (EU = 100)		Annual Change in Real GDP, 1991-2000
	2000	**1990**	**(% pa)**
Austria	112.2	109.6	2.0
Belgium	104.9	103.0	1.9
Britain	113.0	89.2	2.1
Denmark	143.0	135.0	2.5
Finland	110.7	142.7	2.0
France	106.1	111.5	1.7
Germany	112.0	123.5	1.8
Greece	52.1	43.3	2.3
Ireland	111.8	70.0	6.5
Italy	88.0	101.1	1.3
Luxembourg	191.5	148.9	5.3
Netherlands	110.4	102.8	2.7
Portugal	49.8	37.1	2.6
Spain	66.9	68.8	2.4
Sweden	121.1	144.0	1.6
EU 15	**100.0**	**100.0**	**1.9**

Source: European Economy

Note: [1]. at current market prices

appreciation in sterling vis-à-vis the euro, which has increased the euro value of Britain's per capita GDP by approximately 15% between 1998 and 2000.

Economic growth is, in the minds of most business planners, the key macroeconomic variable. When the economy is growing, consumer and business confidence is strengthened. Households have more secure jobs and rising disposable income: they accordingly tend to spend more, taking more frequent or more expensive holidays, and borrowing to purchase larger houses and newer cars. Companies enjoy buoyant profits and invest in new plant and equipment to meet the growing demand for their goods and services.

The relationship between economic growth and business profitability is not, however, a direct one. Some sectors are more strongly pro-cyclical than others. The link is via the income elasticity of demand (see also Chapter 6). Companies producing 'superior' goods (with an income elasticity greater than unity) will find demand increases at a faster rate than the economy as a whole: for example, an income elasticity of demand for a product of 1.5 implies that, all other things equal, if GDP increases by 3%, then demand for the product will increase by 4.5% (i.e. 3% x 1.5). Conversely, the demand for 'inferior' goods (which have an income elasticity of demand less than unity) will grow more slowly than the rate of economic growth.

Financial analysts use a concept broadly related to income elasticity to measure the relative profitability of a company over the economic cycle. The 'Capital Asset Pricing Model' essentially measures the variability of a company's profitability relative to all the companies quoted on the stock market. Beta values greater than unity imply that profits

Table 7.2: *Beta values (1999)*	
British Airways	1.35
Lloyds TSB Group	1.32
P & O	1.28
National Westminster Bank	1.20
EMI Group	1.06
Vodafone Group	1.06
Allied Domecq	0.98
Scottish Power	0.98
Cadbury-Schweppes	0.93
Marks and Spencer	0.73
British Telecom	0.67
Boots Co	0.65

Source: London Business School

vary by more than the market average; and *vice versa* for values less than unity. A company's market value (i.e. the total value of all its equity shares) simply reflects the market's view of the company's profits over time: higher expected profits in the future mean a higher market price today. If a company has a beta value of, say, 1.5, this implies that, in a growing economy in which the market prices of all shares rise by 10%, the market price of the company's shares will rise by 15% (i.e. 1.5 x 15%). As Table 7.2 shows, Boots, British Telecom and Marks and Spencer have beta values of significantly less than unity, implying that their profits are less than proportionately affected by changes in economic growth; British Airways, unsurprisingly, has the highest beta value, reflecting the disproportionate impact of faster economic growth on greater business and leisure travel.

The composition of aggregate demand

Discussing business prospects in terms of the outlook for economic growth implicitly assumes that all the components of GDP – household consumption, business investment, government expenditure and 'net exports' (i.e. exports less imports) – grow at the same rate, so that the composition of demand does not change. Table 7.3 illustrates the shares of the main components of GDP in 1999. The first four components – consumption, investment government final expenditure and exports – are often known as 'total final expenditure', from which must be deducted that part of consumption, investment and government spending devoted to imported, rather than domestically produced, goods and services. In the short run, the balance between these four components can vary significantly and, to the extent that different businesses are more or less dependent upon a single component of spending, this can have a major influence on different companies (See Table 7.4).

Changes in the composition of aggregate demand stem from the fact that the different components are driven by different factors. The growth in consumption broadly tends to mirror the behaviour of GDP as a whole, since households consume a reasonably stable proportion of extra income (i.e. the so-called 'marginal propensity to consume). As Table 7.4 indicates, the rate of growth of consumption has broadly mirrored changes in GDP since 1990. However, changes in retail finance and home ownership mean that, for short periods, consumption and GDP can diverge: for example, with house prices soaring and equity withdrawal widespread, consumption raced ahead by 3.9% in 1999, despite the slowdown in GDP growth to 2.1%.

Table 7.3: *The composition of UK aggregate demand, 1999 (% GDP)*	
Household[1] Consumption	66.5
Business Investment	19.3
Government Final Expenditure	18.8
Exports of Goods and Services	31.6
less Imports of Goods and Services	-36.3
Statistical Discrepancy	0.2
equals GDP[1]	100

Source: NS, *Economic Trends*.
Note: [1]. including voluntary sector

Table 7.4: *The changing composition of UK GDP (1995 prices, % annual change)*

	Consumption	Investment	Government Spending	Exports	Imports	GDP
1990	0.7	-6.5	2.5	4.9	0.5	0.6
1991	-1.7	-11.6	2.9	-0.2	-5.0	-1.5
1992	0.4	2.7	0.5	4.1	6.8	0.1
1993	2.9	3.0	-0.8	3.9	3.2	2.3
1994	2.9	7.8	1.4	9.2	5.4	4.4
1995	1.7	2.3	1.6	9.5	5.5	2.8
1996	3.6	2.4	1.7	7.5	9.1	2.6
1997	3.9	9.2	-1.4	8.6	9.2	3.5
1998	3.2	10.9	0.7	2.3	8.8	2.2
1999	3.9	1.5	4.4	3.1	7.6	2.1

Source: NS, *Economic Trends*

The rate of growth of investment, which is driven by business confidence and the need to expand or contract production, tends to be more volatile than GDP. This phenomenon is widely known as the 'accelerator effect'. Because investment in new plant and equipment typically increases *annual* output by less than the amount of the investment itself, forecast changes in demand give rise to magnified changes in investment. Table 7.4 shows the deep slump in investment by 11.6% in 1991, compared with a contraction in GDP of only 1.5%, and the spectacular growth in investment of 10.9% in 1998, despite a much more modest rate of GDP growth.

While government final expenditure has historically been strongly counter-cyclical, as past governments increased spending to counter recession and cut spending to take the heat out of economic expansions, in the last 20 years fiscal policy has been used in a much less activist fashion. Exports and imports, in contrast, are relatively volatile, driven by changes in exchange rates and differences in economic growth rates at home and abroad (see Chapter 9 for a more detailed explanation).

Table 7.4 illustrates the very strong recovery in exports between 1993 and 1997,

following sterling's withdrawal from the European exchange rate mechanism in late 1992. Free to float, sterling depreciated by approximately 20% against the US dollar and the German deutschmark. British exports became much cheaper in foreign markets (and foreign goods became more expensive to British consumers) and the economy began to grow, primarily led by the increase in net exports, with consumer spending and investment initially fairly stagnant. Between 1997 and 2000, in contrast, when sterling appreciated significantly in value against the main continental currencies, buoyed by high interest rates in Britain, sluggish growth in Germany and France and the financial markets' concerns over the future strength of the euro, economic growth became underpinned by consumer and investment spending, while export growth slowed and import growth accelerated – leading to a growing current account deficit. Export-oriented manufacturers and those competing with imported goods suffered a slump in demand, while the service sector boomed.

As noted above, the significance of changes in the composition of aggregate demand is that different businesses have different customer bases. Retailers rely on household consumption for their sales; manufacturers of heavy engineering plant and office equipment are dependent upon the rate of corporate investment; for defence contractors and construction companies specialising in road building, their main customer is the government; and most manufacturers and many service sector companies compete with overseas producers. Depending upon the balance of the growth in aggregate demand, some businesses can suffer in a general economic expansion and others boom.

Unemployment and wage inflation

There is an increasing tendency amongst leading businesses to take account of the broader constituency of their 'stakeholders' (i.e. those affected by their activities, which includes their workforce, their consumers and society in general, as well as their

shareholders) when taking commercial decisions. BMW's decision to sell its troubled Rover subsidiary to the Phoenix Group, rather than its preferred buyer Alchemy, in May 2000, appears to be have been, at least in part, influenced by the company's concern for the adverse impact on its public image that the predicted job losses may have entailed. More generally, however, companies are concerned primarily with their 'bottom line' (i.e. their profitability) and the significance of trends in national unemployment figures rests in the message they carry for future costs and revenues.

Table 7.5 shows very considerable variations in the rate of unemployment, from 14.2% in Spain to 2.6% in Luxembourg in 2000 and even greater variation over the period 1991-2000. Unemployment is an elusive concept. These figures are a composite of three main sources of unemployment:

Table 7.5 *Unemployment in the European Union*

	Unemployment[1], 2000 (% labour force)	Average unemployment, 1991-2000 (% labour force)	Unemployment in 2000 relative to 1991-2000 average
Austria	4.1	4.0	+0.1
Belgium	8.6	8.9	-0.3
Britain	5.7	8.1	-2.4
Denmark	4.8	7.0	-2.2
Finland	9.2	12.5	-3.3
France	10.3	11.3	-1.0
Germany	8.7	8.3	+0.4
Greece	9.9	9.2	+0.7
Ireland	5.7	11.4	-5.7
Italy	10.9	10.4	+0.5
Luxembourg	2.6	2.7	-0.1
Netherlands	2.7	5.3	-2.6
Portugal	4.6	5.7	-1.1
Spain	14.2	19.7	-5.5
Sweden	6.2	7.7	-1.5
EU15	**8.6**	**9.9**	**-1.3**

Source: European Economy

Note: [1]. Eurostat definition

1 Frictional unemployment
2 Structural unemployment
3 Cyclical unemployment

Frictional and structural unemployment both stem from 'natural' change in economies. Frictional unemployment arises because workers tend to move between jobs over their lifetimes and often experience a period of transitory unemployment between jobs. Structural unemployment also results from workers changing jobs, but as a consequence of wider, structural changes in the economy. For example, in Britain over the last 15 years there has been a significant expansion in the number of jobs in the service sector and a major contraction of employment in the manufacturing sector, with many traditional 'blue-collar' jobs being lost to new hi-tech production techniques or producers in developing countries. Structural unemployment normally entails longer periods of unemployment for those affected, since there is, almost inevitably, a mismatch between the qualifications, skills and experience of workers displaced by declining sectors and the capabilities demanded by employers in the 'sunrise' sectors.

Taken together, frictional and structural unemployment is sometimes known as the 'natural rate of unemployment'. The natural rate of unemployment is not natural in the sense that it is immutable, nor is it necessarily constant over time. Its main characteristic is that it represents an underlying pool of unemployment, which changes little as the economic prosperity of the country changes, in contrast to the third category of unemployment – cyclical unemployment. Cyclical unemployment is, as the name suggests, unemployment that primarily arises from the business cycle. In a recession, cyclical unemployment will increase. In a boom, cyclical unemployment will fall.

For businesses, it is cyclical unemployment which is the key macroeconomic variable, since it is variations in cyclical unemployment which primarily influence the pressure on

average wage costs. While the natural rate is far from straightforward to estimate, some guide to labour market pressures can obtained from Table 7.5 by comparing unemployment in 2000 with the average rate from 1991-2000. It shows, for example, that in Britain, unemployment is 2.4% less than the 1991-2000 average, while unemployment in Germany is 0.4% above the 1991-2000 average, suggesting that cyclical unemployment is lower in Britain than in Germany.

The significance of changes in cyclical unemployment for businesses stems from their impact on labour shortages and wage inflation. As already noted, unemployment is not evenly spread across the country or across different occupations and labour shortages inevitably bite more quickly in sunrise sectors like information technology than in sunset sectors like steel and textile manufacturing. Nevertheless, monitoring national unemployment rates provides a useful guide to pressures in the wider labour market. Table 7.6 illustrates the relationship between unemployment and wage inflation in Britain over the period 1990-1999.

In order to make some allowance for the underlying natural rate of unemployment, the third column again sets out the rate of unemployment relative to the 1990-99 average: all other things equal, positive variations suggest a rise in cyclical unemployment and negative figures a fall. 'Wage inflation' is shorthand for the increase in (nominal) average earnings, with the latter term including overtime and bonus payments. Table 7.6 illustrates the slowdown in the growth of nominal average earnings *per annum* as unemployment rose in the period 1990-94 and average earnings growth has picked up as unemployment declined throughout the rest of the 1990s. The last column shows the behaviour of real average earnings (i.e. nominal average earnings adjusted for inflation), which is the measure most important to businesses. In the long run, real average earnings should grow in line with the growth of real GDP, which averaged 1.9% *per*

Table 7.6: *Unemployment and wage inflation in the UK*

	Unemployment, ILO definition (spring Labour Force Survey)	Unemployment relative to 1990-99 average	Nominal average earnings (% change per annum)	Real average earnings (% change per annum)
1990	1.4	10.1	0.7	-
1991	8.4	0.2	6.4	0.5
1992	9.8	1.6	7.2	3.3
1993	10.4	2.2	4.9	3.4
1994	9.7	1.5	2.6	0.1
1995	8.7	0.5	4.6	1.2
1996	8.3	0.1	4.5	2.1
1997	7.2	-1.0	3.8	0.6
1998	6.3	-1.9	5.8	2.4
1999	6.0	-2.2	2.8	1.2

Source: NS, *Economic Trends*

annum over the period 1990-99. Table 7.6 shows that real earnings actually increased in 1992-93, as a result of a much sharper fall in inflation than wage settlements and this led to further downward pressure on nominal average earnings in 1994. In the period 1996-99, real earnings increased at an annual average rate of 1.6%, suggesting that wage settlements were not excessive relative to the performance of the real economy.

Inflation and interest rates

Like all macroeconomic variables, inflation matters to businesses only to the extent that it impacts either costs or revenues. Table 7.7 shows inflation rates across the EU. It shows that, for all countries, there was a surge in inflation during the 1970s, which were characterised by two sharp rises in international oil prices, and a general convergence of inflation rates during the 1990s as countries have prepared for monetary union. Interestingly, the inflation performance of the eleven member states which joined the euro zone (EU11) is hardly different from that of the wider EU15, both over the period 1961-1990 as well as in the 1990s, suggesting that to date the disciplining effect of accession to

monetary union may not have been as great as generally believed.

For businesses, the impact of inflation depends on its relative impact on costs and revenues. Because the inflation rate represents the increase in the cost of living to the average household, it is often used as the basis for negotiating wage increases for employees. Wage and salary costs, for the typical company, amount to 70% of total operating costs, implying that a 2% rate of inflation, all other things equal, will lead to an increase in the total operating costs of 1.4% (2% x 0.7). As noted above, however, the bargaining ability of employees to extract inflation-linked adjustments to their wages depends also upon unemployment: when cyclical unemployment is high, the ability of employers to resist wage claims is greater and incomplete indexation may lead to a fall in real (i.e. inflation-adjusted) wages; and *vice versa*.

Inflation also impacts business costs through its effect on interest rates. The Bank of England controls inflation by raising or lowering interest rates. Since 1997, the Bank of England has been constitutionally independent of the elected Government and it has a statutory obligation, by exercising its control over interest rates, to ensure that forecast inflation remains at a target rate of 2.5% pa. An increase in the forecast rate of inflation implies that the independent 'Monetary Policy Committee' of the Bank of England should, in keeping with its statutory duties, increase the rate of interest in order to bring the forecast rate of inflation back down to the target rate. As a rough rule of thumb, a 1% increase in interest rates equates to an increase of £1.5bn in the annual interest costs of British businesses, although, of course, this falls disproportionately on those companies which are dependent upon borrowing from banks at variable interest rates.

Table 7.8 shows British inflation and interest rates over the period 1990-1999. Generally, it confirms that higher rates of inflation are associated with higher *nominal* interest rates. From a business perspective, the *real* interest rate is as important as the nominal interest rate: the nominal rate determines the amount of cash needed each year to service a given loan; the real, or inflation-adjusted,

interest rate provides a more meaningful guide to the true burden that servicing loans places on a company. The famous 'Fisher equation' captures the relationship between nominal and real interest rates:

nominal interest rate = real interest rate + expected inflation

Table 7.8 shows the spike in nominal interest rates in 1990, following the Bank of England's attempt to slow an overheating economy. Using actual inflation as a 'proxy' for (i.e. estimate of) expected inflation, Table 7.8 also shows that real interest rates have moved within a much narrower band, reaching a high of 5.1% in 1991, but generally remaining in a range of 3.0-4.5%. Historically, these represent high real interest rates. For example, real interest rates in the period 1945-75 were closer to 1.5-2.0%. These higher real interest rates in the 1990s reflect the greater use of nominal interest rates to head off looming inflationary pressures and maintain inflation within its target band.

Table 7.7: *Average inflation rates in the European Union*

	1961-70	**1971-80**	**1981-90**	**1991-2000**
Austria	3.5	6.3	3.6	2.1
Belgium	3.1	7.2	4.6	1.8
Britain	3.9	13.3	6.0	3.2
Denmark	5.8	10.4	5.8	1.8
Finland	4.7	11.5	6.4	2.3
France	4.3	9.8	6.2	1.9
Germany	2.8	5.2	2.6	2.3
Greece	2.5	13.2	18.3	9.1
Ireland	5.1	14.0	7.1	2.8
Italy	3.8	14.6	10.0	4.2
Luxembourg	2.5	6.5	5.0	2.2
Netherlands	4.1	7.6	2.3	2.3
Portugal	2.8	17.3	17.3	5.1
Spain	5.8	15.0	9.3	4.0
Sweden	4.1	9.6	8.2	3.0
EU 11	3.8	10.1	6.4	2.9
EU 15	3.9	10.6	6.5	3.1

Source: European Economy

Table 7.8: *Inflation and interest rates in the UK*

	Inflation	Nominal short-term Interest rates[1]	Real short-term Interest rates
1990	9.4	14.0	4.6
1991	5.9	10.9	5.1
1992	3.9	7.1	3.2
1993	1.4	5.3	3.9
1994	2.5	6.5	4.0
1995	3.4	6.5	3.1
1996	2.4	6.4	4.0
1997	3.2	7.6	4.4
1998	3.4	6.3	2.9
1999	1.5	5.9	4.4

Source: NS, *Economic Trends*; NS, *Financial Statistics*

Notes: [1]. Three-month interbank bid rate

The impact of an increase in interest rates depends upon its impact on a company's costs and revenues. In turn, this depends upon the company's financial structure. While inflation has been successfully maintained within a range of 1.5-3.5% since 1993, Table 7.8 suggests that this has been achieved by manipulating the behaviour of firms and their customers via interest rate changes. Take the example of a construction firm. The purchase of development sites and the cost of the construction work (materials, labour, etc) are typically financed by bank borrowing. At the same time, homes are financed by borrowing the necessary capital over periods of 25-30 years. A rise in interest rates simultaneously increases the costs of financing work-in-progress and chokes off demand for the finished product, eroding revenues – and profitability. Construction is, therefore, highly sensitive to changes in interest rates.

In contrast, a large hairdressing salon carries relatively little stock and customers pay immediately, often in cash, as soon as the service is completed. A successful hairdressing company with significant cash reserves can enjoy a higher interest return on its bank deposit and faces no obvious increase in its costs, probably benefiting, on balance, from an increase in interest rates. The impact of an increase in interest rates clearly depends on the nature of the business.

The current account and the exchange rate

While most business people are aware of the rate of economic growth and inflation, and probably have a good idea of the scale of unemployment (at least in their region), their understanding of the balance of payments is likely to be limited. At first sight, the balance of payments, a system of double-entry bookkeeping of the nation's trade and capital transactions which balance by definition, is an arcane and incomprehensible jumble of figures. Nevertheless, the balance on the current account (i.e. the balance on transactions relating to imports and exports of goods and services, including transfer payments) can provide a useful guide to longer-term developments in the economy. The current account is defined as:

Current Account Surplus (+)/Deficit (-)
= Exports − Imports

When a country's economy is growing quickly, its demand for imports will tend to increase causing a current account deficit; conversely, during recession, imports will be lower and the current account is more likely to be in surplus. The current account is, however, also influenced by other factors, notably the exchange rate, and may be in surplus or deficit for an extended period. If a country has a current account deficit, this implies that it must be 'borrowing' from abroad. For example, when foreign companies build new factories (e.g. Toyota in Derby, Nissan in Washington, County Durham), they acquire assets in Britain, which is a form of lending to this country. In the same way, foreign banks buying shares in British companies on the London stock market are also lending to Britain. Both transactions allow Britain to finance a current account deficit with inflows of foreign capital.

Large and sustained current account deficits translate into large and growing foreign ownership of domestic currency assets (bank deposits and shares) and expose the country to the risk that, if rattled by some unwelcome development, wholesale capital flight may lead to a collapse in the exchange rate. Salutary examples of this danger abound in recent history. Russia, for example, had, until mid-1998, been financing its large current account deficits by borrowing from abroad. The

financial crisis in Asia in August 1997 led to a slump of international investor confidence in all so-called 'emerging economies'. For those countries dependent on capital inflows like Russia, the result was a sharp fall in the value of the rouble twelve months later. British companies which had invested in the Russian market suddenly found the local currency cost of their imported inputs soaring and the sterling value of their past profits slashed by the rouble's abrupt slide.

While the state of the current account carries important messages for the future course of exchange rates in developing and transition economies, the same has not been true of advanced economies like Britain's in recent decades. As Table 7.9 shows, the UK's current deficit in the period 1990-99 has averaged 2.1% of GDP, a figure which has been easily financed by overseas borrowing. In a world where $1trillion of short-term capital is moved between major financial markets daily, the exchange rates of leading currencies are primarily driven by interest rate differentials. Expectations of a modest increase in British interest rates will cause an inflow of millions, or even billions, of dollars into the UK, driving up the value of the currency. The current account responds increasingly to, rather than causes, exchange rate movements.

Table 7.9: *The UK current account and effective exchange rates*

	Current Account Balance (% of GDP)	Sterling Exchange Rate Index (1990=100)	Annual Appreciation/ Depreciation (%)
1990	-3.0	100.0	-2.2
1991	-1.7	100.7	0.7
1992	-2.5	96.9	-3.8
1993	-2.3	88.9	-8.3
1994	-1.4	89.2	0.3
1995	-0.4	84.8	-4.9
1996	-0.9	86.3	1.8
1997	-1.1	100.6	16.6
1998	-3.2	103.9	3.3
1999	-4.7	103.8	-0.1

Source: NS, *Economic Trends*

Table 7.9 illustrates movements in the effective exchange rate index. Such indices are produced in a similar way to consumer price indices, by weighting the movements in various bilateral exchange rates (e.g. $/£, euro/£, yen/£) according to the respective currencies' importance for Britain's trade. Table 7.9 shows the depreciation in the effective exchange rate between 1992 (following sterling's exit from the exchange rate mechanism) and 1995. With a one to two year lag, the current account began to improve, moving from a deficit of 2.5% of GDP in 1992 to a low of 0.4% by 1995. As the effective exchange rate began to appreciate after 1995, its rise contributed to a widening current account deficit, which reached 4.7% of GDP by 1999.

Exchange rate changes affect the so-called 'tradable sector'; i.e. that part of the economy which either exports to overseas markets or, although serving only the domestic market, competes with overseas producers. For example, even if a British car firm never exported a single vehicle, it would still be part of the tradable sector, since it competes directly with imported Volkswagen, Peugeot and Fiat cars. Because almost every company in Britain uses some imported inputs and has some overseas customers, even businesses which may not think of themselves as part of the tradable sector are affected by exchange rate developments. Restaurants in London, for example, will almost certainly use a significant proportion of imported basic foodstuffs, employ foreign cooks and waiters and serve overseas visitors: the appreciation of sterling thus has profound, but mixed, effects on their costs and revenues (see Chapter 10 for further discussion of this).

In simple terms, an appreciation in the exchange rate increases the foreign currency price of British exports and reduces the sterling price of foreign imports. Because most businesses use some imported components, or compete with overseas producers, and may have foreign customers, assessing the overall impact of a rise in the exchange rate is not straightforward. In order to fathom out the implications of a change in the exchange rate, a company needs to look at the imported inputs at the various stages in its supply chain and at the characteristics of its customers.

CONCLUSIONS

Understanding the meaning and behaviour over time of the key macroeconomic indicators can provide useful information about likely developments in the economy. Figures for economic growth, the major components of aggregate demand, unemployment, inflation and the current account can all be a useful aid to informed business planning. At the same time, it is important to understand that the implications of any given macroeconomic development vary from company to company, depending upon its finance structure, production processes and costs and its international linkages. Every company is at least slightly different from 'average' and will be differentially impacted by, say, a rise in interest rates or a depreciation in the exchange rate.

This chapter has illustrated the way in which the key macroeconomic variables affect the profitability – and sometimes the viability – of British business. Understanding the significance of the main macroeconomic data, and being able to spot emerging trends, undoubtedly improves business decision-making, which must attempt to take into account future developments in economic conditions. Given the importance of basing decisions upon informed guesses about the future, there is unsurprisingly a significant industry dedicated to using economic models to forecast the major macroeconomic variables in a systematic way. The way economic forecasts are made is the subject of Chapter 8.

8 National Accounts and Economic Forecasts

Martin Weale, Director, National Institute of Economic and Social Research

FOCUS QUESTIONS

- What is the Gross Domestic Product and how is it measured?
- What do you need to understand to be able to use the accounts of sectors of the economy?
- What is the importance of prices and quantities in the national accounts?

- Which are the crucial macroeconomic variables, both within and outside the framework of national accounts, for businesses to understand and to track?
- What are the aims of economic forecasts and what is their use to businesses?

INTRODUCTION

The uses of macroeconomic statistics for business fall broadly into three categories:

1 providing an indication of what is happening to the volume of transactions and activity in the economy.
2 indicating how prices and costs are changing.
3 providing an opportunity for businesses to see how their performance compares with that of the economy as a whole.

The basic framework for macroeconomic data and recording is provided by the National Accounts. These were set up in 1940 as a tool for wartime planning, allowing the government to calculate where it might find the resources needed to be diverted to the war effort. Since 1945 they have, however, become the basic framework for macroeconomic analysis.

An important aspect of national income accounting is that it should be possible to make reasonably good comparisons between different countries. This in turn means that international standards are needed to ensure this. These change from time to time reflecting the changing structure of the economies the national accounts are intended to describe. The most recent international standards were set out by the United Nations in 1993, with a European System of Accounts derived from this in 1995. The European Standard was adopted by the United Kingdom and Denmark in 1998 with the rest of the European Union following suit in 1999. (See chapter 2 for details of the National Accounts Framework and practice in the UK.)

GROSS DOMESTIC PRODUCT

The single most widely-used indicator of the state of the economy is Gross Domestic Product (GDP). It measures income generated in the economy and also the value of output, and is perhaps the most important single aggregate in the national accounts. We begin our discussion, showing how GDP can be built up in three ways, from expenditures, incomes or the output of the economy. The data for the three approaches for 1998 is given in Table 8.1.

The Expenditure approach

The reference point for the measurement of economic activity in terms of expenditures is the total value of goods and services supplied to final domestic or foreign purchasers or procured by the government, less any goods and services bought from abroad. This provides the definition of Gross Domestic Product as:

GDP = Household Consumption
+ Investment (gross of depreciation)
+ Government Consumption
+ Exports
− Imports

It measures the total value of productive activity in the economy in a particular time period (e.g. a year). On this basis GDP can be thought of as the value of goods supplied to final users, rather than as inputs into further stages of the productive process, but less any goods and services that have been bought from abroad.

The Income approach

Alternatively GDP can be calculated from information on incomes. There are four types of income generated from this productive activity.

1. **Labour costs.**
   These are the first, and largest component. They include payments made directly to workers, such as wages and bonuses, and also expenses such as employees' national insurance contributions, essentially a tax associated with employment.

2. **Operating surplus.**
   This is a catch-all term which includes the operating profits of corporate enterprises.

3. **Mixed incomes.**
   These are, in principle, the incomes of the self-employed. They include an employment compensation (i.e. pay) component and a profit component. But neither the statistician nor, in all probability, the self-employed person can distinguish between the two; hence the name.

4. **Indirect taxes net of subsidies.**
   These are the fourth component of GDP at market prices. They can be as large as operating surplus and, for a few industries such as tobacco products, may be many times larger than the value of compensation of employees and operating surplus.

The Output approach

Finally one may assess GDP in terms of the output of the various industries which comprise the economy. For each enterprise or industry we can set up an account showing the value of sales and the cost composition of sales in terms of the four types of income – compensation of employees, operating surplus, mixed incomes and indirect taxes, but with a fourth item representing the cost of any goods and services which have been bought in as part of the productive process. Adding up incomes not by type of income but by the industry in which each is generated provides the output measure of GDP. Secondly, one can arrive at the output measure by thinking in terms of expenditures rather than incomes. If we take the total value of sales, but deduct the total value of purchases of inputs by enterprises the outcome is a figure for the value of those goods which are sold not to other enterprises but to final buyers (consumption, government consumption, investment and exports - all sales by one enterprise with no corresponding purchase by another) less the value of those goods and

Table 8.1 *UK National Accounts 1998: Output, Income and Expenditure*

OUTPUT APPROACH		INCOME APPROACH		EXPENDITURE APPROACH	
Agriculture	9656	Compensation of employees	463398	Final Consumption expenditure:	
Mining & Quarrying	12748	Taxes less	17619	a) by Households and	
Manufacturing	147306	subsidies on		non-profit institutions	
Electricity, Gas and		production other		serving households	545124
Water	16737	than those on		(NPISH)	
Construction	39262	products		b) by Government	153564
Distribution, hotels and catering	113070	Operating surplus	223212		
Transport, storage and communication	63340	Mixed income	43379	Gross Capital Formation	151823
Business service				Exports	224202
and finance	176977			Less Imports	232714
Public administration		Discrepancy	-64	Discrepancy	1726
and defence	40495				
Education, health and social work	89041				
Other services	38912				
Gross Value Added at Basic Prices	747544		747544		
Taxes less subsidies on products	96181		96181		
Gross Domestic Product	**843725**		**843725**		**843725**

Net Compensation of Employees from the Rest of the World	76
Net taxes less subsidies received from the Rest of the World	-3437
Net Property Income from the Rest of the World	15098
Gross National Income	855462
Net Current Transfers from Rest of the World	-3090
Gross National Disposable Income	852372
Less Depreciation	88771
Net National Disposable Income	763601

Source: NS, *United Kingdom National Accounts*

services which are imported from abroad. Thus the output measure represents a different perspective on the income and expenditure measures rather than a fundamentally distinct concept. There are inevitably minor accounting discrepancies between these three totals, although in the UK these are allocated across the known variables for all except the most recent data. The discrepancies are shown explicitly in Table 8.1. (Refer back to Chapter 2 for an introduction to GDP measurement.)

Market versus basic prices

All of these estimates can be calculated from a number of price bases. The most obvious way is to evaluate **GDP at market prices**, the prices that people actually pay for goods and services. However, as we have seen above, this has the implication that a proportion of income accrues as indirect taxes, in addition to the incomes which accrue to capital and labour as factors of production. While measurement at market prices gives a satisfactory means of assessing the size of the economy as a whole, it may give a very misleading picture when comparing individual industries, for the reason explained above. The tobacco industry appears very large because tobacco is taxed; if some other products were taxed instead, the value of the output of tobacco processing at market prices would be much smaller. For this reason, it is sometimes also found useful to produce estimates of **value added at basic prices**. These include taxes which fall on industries such as motor vehicle licences, but omit those which are levied on goods and services. Whether users should pay more attention to data at basic or at market prices depends, as always, on their particular needs. Someone who wanted to know how big the cigarette market was in terms of outlays by consumers would need to look at market price data. But someone who wanted an indicator of the resources devoted to cigarette manufacture would be given a better impression from data at basic prices.

Transfer payments

In the calculation of income and expenditure the national accountant finds it essential to distinguish those transactions which are transfer payments from those which are payments for goods and services or made for factors of production (wages and profit) in order to assess the scale of the productive activity taking place in the country. The idea behind this is that an increase in the flow of transfer payments does not increase the flow of resources available to satisfy the wants of each country's residents. For any sort of comparative purpose we need to distinguish the two. Thus one would not want to show a country as having a higher level of productive activity because households pay taxes to the government, which then buys in health services from enterprises in order to supply them to households as compared to the alternative where households buy their health services directly from enterprises. The expenditure on services is the same in both cases but the total value of transactions generated is higher in the second case than in the first. The link between GDP and transfer payments is discussed in more detail when we come to sectoral accounts.

Data Sources

The national accounts are compiled from a wide range of sources, including both administrative sources and special surveys. Income tax data are the most important source of information on incomes, but they are not very timely and have to be supplemented by special surveys in order to provide a prompt picture of the state of the economy. Sample surveys of firms and households provide much of the expenditure and output data, while information on some types of consumption is provided by tax data. In collecting data of this sort it is always necessary to balance the demand for reliable data with the desirability of limiting the burden on those who have to supply the data and keeping control over the costs of data collection. (See Chapter 2 for further information on sources of national accounts data.)

Gross Domestic Product and Gross National Income

GDP is probably the most widely used single indicator of economic activity, but we should draw attention to the link with GNI, the Gross National Income of a country and also with Gross National Disposable Income (GNDI). (See lower part of Table 8.1). GDP measures the productive activity in a country independently of the ownership of factors of production. GNI on the other hand is calculated after deducting from GDP the operating surplus accruing to foreign-owned companies and crediting the surpluses of UK companies earned abroad. The labour income accruing to foreign short-term workers in the United Kingdom is also deducted and the income credited to British workers employed abroad is added. Finally taxes paid abroad (such as the UK's VAT contribution to the EU are deducted and any receipts are added). For most large countries these adjustments are typically rather small, but in some cases they can be substantial. Thus in the Irish Republic GDP is some 10% above GNI because there are very high levels of foreign investment in the country which lead to large profits earned in the country and accruing to the rest of the world. Net transfers received are added to Gross National Income to deliver Gross National Disposable Income.

Gross and Net Measurements

These three measures are all gross rather than net of depreciation. Depreciation is the part of the capital stock that is assumed to have been worn out in the process of producing goods and services. The reason why attention focuses on the gross rather than the net measure is because it relates to flows of goods and services. Net Domestic Product and National Income are calculated by deducting depreciation from the corresponding gross figures. Since depreciation flows rely on an essentially arbitrary calculation it is felt that the gross rather than the net figures may be a better indication of economic activity. It is also the case that the depreciation charges are

unaffected by short-term fluctuations in economic activity; monitoring these fluctuations was one of the aims of national income accounting. Thus, while both the net concepts exist in the European System of Accounts, they are not given any great prominence.

SECTORAL ACCOUNTS

The economy is, of course, comprised of a large number of economic agents, and the estimate of GDP is a summary outcome of the activities of all these people and businesses. The system of national accounts shows the interrelationship between, in principle, the activities of any economic agent or group of agents and the rest of the economy.

For practical purposes it is useful to group together economic agents of various types. The convention in the UK is to identify:

* Non-financial corporations
* Financial corporations
* General Government
* Households and Non-profit institutions serving households

A finer disaggregation is obviously possible and more detail is provided in some parts of the national accounts.

If, however, we are to build up a complete picture of economic activity, we must include the rest of the world as an extra sector. We can show the receipts and payments of each sector, with receipts and payments categorized in various ways. Table 8.2 shows these accounts for 1998 on a consolidated cash-flow basis in the most compact form possible: the official sources present the same data but in a number of subsidiary accounts.

Looking at the first four columns of data, we see the receipts of each sector followed by the payments that it makes. The terminology used is that of the European System of Accounts. There are a number of items whose meaning is not self-evident. FISIM (Financial Intermediation Services Indirectly Measured) is an adjustment which reflects the fact that the operating profits of financial institutions are usually calculated inclusive of the profit made on the margin between the interest rates at which they borrow and at which they lend. Since, in the national accounts, interest payments are treated as a transfer payment, it follows that the income which the financial institutions earn in this way has to be deducted from their reported profits when adding up the operating surplus in the country as a whole as shown in Table 8.1. Acquisitions less disposals of valuables are treated as a form of investment. 'Other transfers' includes large amounts of insurance premia, while social contributions include pension contributions whether they are paid to the government as national insurance contributions or into private sector pension funds. Similarly social benefits include payments of pensions by private sector funds. The net increase in the value of pension funds arising from net inflows is shown as the net equity in pension funds.

It also has to be remembered that the accounts shown for the four domestic sectors represent current income rather than production. They show how the sectors use the income generated from their productive activities or given to them by other sectors but they do not show the productive process in full as represented by sales less cost of production. Nevertheless, in each sector the cash flow is fully accounted for with net lending balancing receipts and payments. The account for the rest of the world is shown on exactly the same basis but only those transactions which affect the UK are indicated.

In order to show the link between this structure and the accounts of Table 8.1, we introduce a sixth account which summarises the productive activity of the economy. It receives incomes from sales to final demand and buys in inputs, either as factors of production or as imports. Taxes on production are shown as a payment by this account, because receipts from sales to final demand are valued at market prices.

With this accounting structure we observe that every payment has a counterpart as a receipt, in that the total for each row is the same whether one looks at receipts or payments. Thus the row for social contributions in the receipts table shows the receipts of social contributions by each sector. The row in the payments table shows the payments by each sector and, not surprisingly payments equal receipts. The only exception to this is with the residual; at the same time there is no counterpart in the receipts table to net lending. If, however the residual and net lending on the payments side are added together, they equal the residual on the receipts side, apart from a rounding error. The equality arises because the figures for net lending by each sector are calculated as a balancing item, and therefore include any accounting discrepancies. True net lending must sum to zero across all sectors; the observed total of £1790m is therefore the sum of the unidentified residuals in the sectoral accounts. This plus the residual on the payments side of the production account must equal the residual on the receipts side of the production account.

Transfer payments are both received and paid by the various sectors of the economy. Goods and services are, however, bought by sectors from productive activity while payments for factors of production are made by the production sector to the other sectors. The table shows how GDP at market prices can be calculated on either an income or an expenditure basis. The income calculation is done by adding up the elements shaded in dark blue, while the expenditure measure is calculated by combining the elements shaded light blue, but remembering that imports need to be deducted, not added.

The importance of the sectoral data is that they make it easier for business users to keep track of variables which are pertinent to their own businesses. For example, a non-financial business may wish to monitor how the growth of its operating profit (the value of output less the costs of production) compares with that of

Table 8.2. *Sectoral National Accounts for the United Kingdom 1998* £m

	Non-financial Corporations	Financial Corporations	General Government	Households and NPISH	Rest of World	Production	Total
RECEIPTS							
Consumption						698688	698688
Gross Fixed Capital Formation						147629	147629
Changes in Inventories						3621	3621
Acquisitions less Disposals						573	573
Imports					232714		
Exports						224202	224202
Operating Surplus	175674	18788	12518	45602			252582
Mixed Income				43379			43379
FISIM		-29370					-29370
Compensation of employees				463474	701		464175
Taxes on Production			110363		3437		113800
Property Income	53329	259262	10882	121376	95490		540339
Current Taxes			138650		3481		142131
Social Contributions	3298	66491	64649	342			134780
Social Benefits				170191	1234		171425
Other Transfers	10545	25207	62389	31873	11049		141063
Net equity in Pension Funds				16567	-1		16566
Capital Taxes, Grants and Transfers	1925		4852	4653	744		12174
Discrepancy						1725	1725
Total	**244771**	**340378**	**404303**	**897457**	**348849**	**1076438**	**3312196**
PAYMENTS							
Operating Surplus						252582	252582
Mixed Income						43379	43379
FISIM						-29370	-29370
Compensation of employees					777	463398	464175
Taxes on Production						113800	113800
Imports						232714	232714
Exports					224202		224202
Property Income	119950	223627	34592	51582	110588		540339
Current Taxes	25997	7637		103443	5054		142131
Social Contributions				134680	100		134780
Social Benefits	3298	49925	116605	814	783		171425
Other Transfers	10313	25281	78949	19783	6737		141063
Net Equity in Pension Funds		16566					16566
Capital Taxes, Grants and Transfers	216		8448	2327	1183		12174
Consumption			153564	545124			698688
Gross Fixed Capital Formation	94840	6977	10631	35181			147629
Changes in Inventories	3150	489	107	-125			3621
Acquisitions less Disposals of Valuables	40	70		463			573
Acqusitions less Disposal of Non-produced Non-financial assets	200	-46	-382	246	-18		0
Discrepancy						-64	-64
Net Lending	-13233	9852	1789	3939	-557		1790
Total	**244771**	**340378**	**404303**	**897457**	**348849**	**1076439**	**3312196**

NPISH = Non-profit institutions serving households;.
Source: NS, *UK National Accounts*.
Note: Rounding Errors may lead to totals differing from component sums.

non-financial businesses in the economy as a whole. Or a firm selling to households may wish to see how the value of its sales has grown compared to movements in the disposable income of households, defined as consumption plus capital formation, acquisitions of valuables and non-produced assets and net lending excluding net increase in pension fund equity. Equally, if a business has found a historic link between its performance and the movement of one or other of these variables, it may wish to use a forecast such as that discussed below.

PRICES AND QUANTITIES

As the discussion above makes clear, the accounting structure measures money flows and is set out in money terms. For many purposes, however, it is important to be able to break down money flows into quantity effects and price effects. For some purposes the nature of the decomposition is very clear. For example purchases of wheat can be measured in kilogrammes of wheat. Multiplying this by a price per kilogramme gives the total value of expenditure on wheat. In other cases the distinction between a quantity effect and a price effect may be less distinct. For example motor cars now cost much more than they did forty years ago. Much of this increase is a genuine increase in price. But there is an element that is difficult to quantify, which amounts to an improvement in quality and should more probably be seen as a quantity effect than a price effect. Certainly quality improvements are nothing to do with any general inflation (see Chapter 3).

Finally, for most categories of transaction shown in the national accounts, there is no corresponding flow of goods and therefore no clear means of making the split between quantities and prices. While the money used to pay an income tax bill could always be used to buy goods, it does not correspond to any particular flow of goods, and it is therefore difficult make any definitive split between quantity increases and price increases when discussing either transfer or income payments.

Thus for flows of goods and services, the components of final demand, it is possible to construct price indices. Even with these, as the example above makes clear, there may be some doubt as to quite what constitutes a price change. But to understand the way in which national accounts can be used to indicate movements in the volume of economic activity, these concerns need to be put to one side.

The basic idea is that flows of goods and services can be measured either in current prices, the amounts actually paid for them, or in the prices of some base year (see Chapter 2). Thus it is possible to work out what the total consumption by UK households would have cost in the prices ruling in 1995 even though today's prices are rather different. The ratio of consumption expenditure in 2000 measured in 1995 prices to the value of consumption expenditure in 1995 gives an indication of how much the volume of expenditure has increased since 1995. Obviously, it is also possible to calculate the ratio of expenditure in 2000 to that in 1996 with both measured in 1995 prices in order to obtain an indication of how the volume of consumption expenditure has changed between 1996 and 2000. Table 8.3 shows the expenditure figures from the 1998 accounts both in current prices (as in Table 8.1) and in 1995 prices. It also presents price indices, measured with 1995=100, and allowing the user to deduce immediately the percentage change to prices since 1995.

A moment's thought will indicate that there is nothing special about the use of 1995 prices as a reference point. The calculations could equally well be done in the prices of 2000 or indeed of any other year; this would be bound to deliver a different answer. It is quite incorrect to say that the answer calculated to one price base is right and another is wrong; the fundamental difficulty is that, in any exercise of this type, the aim is to convert a large number of figures - the increases or decreases in expenditures on individual goods and services - into a single summary statistic. There should be no surprise that this can be done in more than one way.

Table 8.3 *Current and constant price expenditure in 1998 £million*

	Current Prices	1995 Prices	Deflator (1995=100)	Volume (1995=100)
Final Consumption expenditure				
By Households and NPISH	545124	505367	107.9	111.3
By Government	153564	142210	108.0	101.3
Gross Capital Formation	151823	148360	102.3	123.9
Exports	224202	241123	93.0	119.1
Less Imports	232714	265261	87.7	129.3
Discrepancy	1726	1581		
GDP at Market Prices	843725	773380	109.1	108.5
Compensation of Employees			110.8	
Gross operating surplus and mixed income			105.2	

Source: NS, *UK National Accounts*

The Table also shows, again as index numbers, the volume of each expenditure as compared with its 1995 figure. These are calculated by dividing each type of expenditure in 1995 prices by its value in 1995 and multiplying the resulting ratio by 100. These figures provide a simple indication of how much each type of expenditure has changed since 1995 after the effects of price changes are removed. The series are calculated so that when the volume index is multiplied by the price index, the result indicates the increase in the value of expenditure in 1998 compared with that in 1995.

Finally, we can also measure the increase in the volume of the output of each industry. These figures are presented, again with 1995=100, in Table 8.4. This table allows us to see immediately that the volume of manufacturing output has risen only slightly since 1995, while transport, storage and communication, and real estate, renting and business services have been extremely buoyant. The Table allows firms to assess their performance relative to the key industries in which they are involved.

Detailed national accounts are available only on an annual basis. Summary data, including

those shown in Tables 8.1 to 8.4 are, however, available quarterly. These data are important for firms concerned with the short-term evolution of the economy, but it is a mistake to think that they are better than annual data at indicating long-term trends. With quarterly data the question of seasonal and working day adjustment becomes important. Consumption

Table 8.4 *Constant price output in 1998 (1995=100)*

Agriculture	102.6
Mining & Quarrying	104.4
Manufacturing	102.1
Electricity, Gas and Water	107.5
Construction	106.0
Distribution, hotels and catering	106.4
Transport, storage and communication	120.8
Finance	103.5
Real estate, renting and business activities	119.1
Public administration and defence	96.0
Education, health and social work	108.2
Other services	112.2
Gross Value Added at Basic Prices	108.6

Source: NS, *UK National Accounts*

always rises in the fourth quarter of the year because of spending associated with Christmas. Seasonal adjustments are made to remove the impact of this and similar effects allowing a direct comparison between data for different quarters. Working day adjustments are needed because, for example, the balance of economic activity between the first and second quarter depends on whether Easter falls in March or April.

KEY MACROECONOMIC VARIABLES OUTSIDE THE NATIONAL ACCOUNTS

While the national accounts provide a coherent framework for most of the macroeconomic variables, showing how they interrelate, there are a number of important variables that do not feature directly in the national accounts. Perhaps the most important of these is the **Retail Price Index**. This measures the prices of a range of goods narrower than total consumption by households on a monthly basis. Its importance is largely historic - in that retail price indices were calculated much earlier than the first national accounts were available. But the fact that, in the United Kingdom, inflation targeting is defined in terms of the Retail Price Index (excluding the effects of interest rate changes on mortgage costs) gives it as much importance as it has ever had.

Perhaps the other variables of great macroeconomic importance but which also lie outside the national accounting framework are **employment and unemployment** data. Classifications of employment on the industrial basis used in the national accounts make it possible to monitor how output per person employed in each industry is changing. This measure of labour productivity should, ideally, be adjusted for changes in hours worked. On many occasions this is possible, but even when it is not, it offers a crude indication of productivity movements industry by industry.

ECONOMIC FORECASTING

National accounts provide a coherent framework for measured data, but they also give a basis for economic forecasting. It would not be quite true to say that the sole aim of economic forecasting is to project forward elements of the national accounts; forecasters are typically interested in a number of other variables, such as the Retail Price Index and employment data as discussed above. They are also concerned about interest rates and exchange rates, again lying outside the national accounting framework.

Nevertheless, the framework offered by the national accounts is the core of any economic forecast. Typically employment and price indices are derived from the national accounting aggregates *via* statistical relationships between employment, capital formation and output and in the light of past interrelationships between the price measures in the national accounts and the auxiliary price indices.

Endogenous and Exogenous Variables

As the accounting framework makes clear, the variables representing the evolution of the economy are interdependent. The level of GDP depends on the level of consumption; the definition of GDP as the sum of public and household consumption, investment and exports less imports provides an identity linking consumption to GDP. But consumption is likely to depend on income, or at least on the household component of income in a manner which is behavioural rather than an identity. In this respect consumption is said to be **endogenous** to the system. Households do not consume all their income and economic modellers have to estimate how consumption depends on current and past income, and perhaps also on expectations of future income.

There are other variables which are simply taken as given, and have no equation to explain them. In models of the UK economy world activity is often treated as **exogenous**. It influences the UK but the UK is small enough not to influence it significantly. This mixture of different types of interdependent variables means that a typical forecasting model is a set of simultaneous equations, comprised of a mixture of identities, behavioural relationships and exogenous variables. All of these variables have to be forecast, and variables which are determined exogenously using the forecaster's judgement in some models may be established by behavioural relationships in other models. Or variables may be exogenous for some parts of a simulation and endogenous for other parts.

Identities are simple linkages which are always true, such as the fact that the income and expenditure measures of GDP are the same. **Behavioural relationships**, on the other hand, are estimated using regression methods. For example, if consumption is believed to depend on income, then a statistical relationship is estimated, showing the influence of income on consumption. It is often found, in such relationships, that there are lags involved, so that consumption may depend on both current and past income. It may also depend on the past value of consumption, for example if people's spending habits are influenced by what they are used to as well as what they can afford[1].

In a typical model there are two types of variable which are usually regarded as exogenous. One, as already noted, includes variables relating to the external environment. The demand for UK exports depends on the state of activity in the rest of the world. It is possible to endogenize this, using a model of the world economy, but most UK models run independently of world models. Similarly world commodity prices and the oil price are not really influenced by activity in the United Kingdom, although they could be derived from a world model. Without such a model the

forecaster typically uses judgement to project paths for these variables.

The other group of exogenous variables are policy variables. The government makes statements about its spending plans over a three-year period; these provide a basis for forecasting some of the components of government expenditure. Less information is given about future tax rates, but again, for the most part the forecaster has to make assumptions about these and treat them as inputs into the forecast process.

Not all policy variables need be exogenous. For example, the interest rate is set with reference to inflation prospects. The interest rate projected by a model should, therefore, logically, be related to its inflation forecast. The degree to which it is possible to do this depends on the extent to which the policy authority (in the UK the Monetary Policy Committee of the Bank of England) explains how it arrives at its decisions. In practice the interest rate is likely to be treated as exogenous in the near future but determined by a behavioural relationship in the longer term. The modeller will choose a relationship which ensures that the inflation target is delivered in the long run.

A particular difficulty arises with short-term interest rate forecasts. These are guesses about the future behaviour of the Bank of England's Monetary Policy Committee. Past experience, combined with their public pronouncements may make it possible to judge how they are likely to react to the economic environment, but it is difficult to make a scientific analysis of this. Users of forecasts need to recognize that the decisions made by the Bank of England do not always turn out for the best. There is some evidence that the Monetary Policy Committee moves interest rates more frequently and further than is desirable.[2] Certainly UK interest

---

1 More complicatedly, consumption may additionally depend on expectations of future income; this creates an additional level of complexity in the solution of any economic model and raises the question whether the expectations of year 2 income which influence the project in year 1 should be the same as the actual forecast of income for year 2. If the forecast has this property, the solution can be described as model-consistent; it is more usually described as being solved with rational expectations.

2 At least until February 2000. Since then they have been more stable.

rates are more volatile than those in the United States or in the Euro Area. Forecasters have to predict what the Monetary Policy Committee is likely to do even if their own past experience suggests it may not be a good idea.

There may be other cases where exogenous adjustments are necessary to behavioural equations. For example, if an equation is underpredicting the variable of concern, the forecaster is likely to assume that this underprediction will continue into the near future, but over the longer run the variable will revert to the value predicted by the forecasting equation. Alternatively, there may be some policy change about which the forecaster has to form some judgement. For example, the replacement of Unemployment Benefit with the Jobseeker's Allowance increased the pressure on unemployed people to find jobs and reduced the rate of inflation associated with any particular level of unemployment. Any forecaster has to come to some judgement as to how important this is likely to be.

Forecasting output in the economy

An economic forecast then is a set of projections of interrelated economic variables linked together by accounting identities and behavioural relationships. Table 8.5 presents the main outputs of the National Institute forecast for January 2000 on an annual basis. Attention in this table focuses on volume data (in 1995 prices) or on output and price indices. The underlying value data can of course be derived from these. The full forecast, published in the *National Institute Economic Review* presents quarterly estimates as well as the annual numbers shown here, and covers a wider range of variables including accounts for the public sector and details of UK transactions relative to the rest of the world. However, forecasters typically do not publish all the forecast variables generated by their models. There are two reasons for this. The first is simply for reasons of brevity. The second concerns reliability which we discuss below.

What does the forecast in Table 8.5 tell us? We should first note that only the figures for 1998 will already have been revealed at the time the forecast was made in January 2000. The figures for 1999, although now past, will not have been collated by *National Statistics* and are therefore part of the forecast. Thus all of the growth rates shown are forecasts. The forecast of household consumption growth in 2001/2 is 2.4%, which is below the 3.6% in 1998/9. A further squeezing of the growth rate in government consumption was expected. Meanwhile, the growth rate of gross capital formation was forecast to increase from the year 2000 onwards, while the economy as a whole, as measured by the GDP forecast, was expected to remain buoyant with growth at well over 2% per annum. The fastest growing sector was expected to be distribution. The various price indices forecast suggest that inflation will remain under control, after a jump in the RPI to 4% in the year 1999 to 2000.

Forecast Uncertainty

In the nature of things forecasts are uncertain. The exogenous variables may evolve differently from what has been assumed. All behavioural relationships incorporate random error terms. And, much to the irritation of the forecaster, relationships break down from time to time. Forecasts, like data, are typically published as point estimates, but it is possible to give an indication of their reliability. In the UK the National Institute and the Treasury provide estimates of mean absolute errors in past forecasts. The National Institute also has, since 1995, used the standard errors of its past forecasts to estimate probability ranges for its forecasts of output growth and RPI inflation, making the assumption that these forecast errors are normally distributed about the published forecast. In much the same way, the Bank of England publishes its 'fan charts' showing the probability that inflation and output growth will lie in particular ranges. The National Institute's work shows, not surprisingly, that the reliability with which

Table 8.5: *A Summary of the National Institute forecast, January 2000*

Components of Expenditure   1995 prices

	Final Consumption Expenditure		Gross Capital Formation							
	House-holds & NPISH	General Govern-ment	Gross Fixed Investment	Change to Inventories	Exports	LESS Imports	Residual	GDP Market Prices	Adjustment to Basic Prices	GDP Basic Prices
1998	504.8	141.8	145.9	3.5	242	266.2	1.0	772.8	84.7	688.1
1999	522.8	147.1	151.9	0.2	249.9	284.9	0.7	787.7	86.1	701.6
2000	541.3	153.8	156.9	1.2	266.2	307.4	0.7	812.7	89.3	723.4
2001	555.7	157.5	162.4	1.1	278.7	324.9	0.7	831.2	91.9	739.3
2002	568.8	161.3	168.6	1.0	292.3	341.4	0.7	851.3	94.4	756.9

Growth Rates

1999/98	3.6	3.7	4.1		3.3	7.0		1.9	1.7	2.0
2000/99	3.5	4.6	3.3		6.5	7.9		3.2	3.7	3.1
2001/00	2.7	2.4	3.5		4.7	5.7		2.3	2.9	2.2
2002/01	2.4	2.4	3.8		4.9	5.1		2.4	2.7	2.4

GDP by Sector

	Manufacturing	Public	Distribution	Construction	Oil	Rest	Total
1998	102.0	105.6	108.7	106.0	107.5	109.6	108.5
1999	101.8	107.5	110.4	106.3	112.5	113.7	110.6
2000	104.2	111.6	114.0	109.4	116.1	116.7	114.0
2001	106.4	113.9	117.9	111.9	118.5	117.5	116.6
2002	108.9	116.2	122.4	114.2	120.9	118.6	119.4

Growth Rates

1999/98	-0.2	1.8	1.6	0.3	4.7	3.7	1.9
2000/99	2.4	3.8	3.3	2.9	3.2	2.6	3.1
2001/00	2.1	2.1	3.4	2.3	2.1	0.7	2.3
2002/01	2.3	2.0	3.8	2.1	2.0	0.9	2.4

Price Indices

	Unit Labour Costs	Import Deflator	Wholesale Price Index	Consumer Price Index	HICP	Retail Price Index All Items	Excl Mortgage Interest GDP	Deflator Basic Prices	GDP Deflator Market Prices
1998	111.0	87.7	102.1	108.4	106.0	109.3	108.6	109.1	109.7
1999	116.1	85.6	101.7	111.1	107.4	110.9	111.1	111.8	112.8
2000	120.3	85.2	103.2	113.5	109.3	115.3	113.7	114.7	116.2
2001	124.2	86.9	105.2	116.3	111.5	119.0	116.5	117.7	119.2
2002	127.3	89.0	107.0	119.0	113.5	121.4	119.1	120.4	121.8

Growth Rates

1999/98	4.6	-2.4	-0.4	2.5	1.3	1.5	2.3	2.5	2.8
2000/99	3.6	-0.5	1.5	2.2	1.8	4.0	2.3	2.6	3.0
2001/00	3.2	2.0	1.9	2.5	2.0	3.2	2.5	2.6	2.6
2002/01	2.5	2.4	1.7	2.3	1.8	2.0	2.2	2.3	2.2

Source: National Institute Economic Review, January 2000

growth and inflation can be forecast depends on how far ahead the forecast is being made. The standard error of the forecast of the growth rate in the current year is just over 1.3% points for the forecast made in February, but only about 1% points for the forecast made in May. The forecast made in the October before the year in question has a standard error of about 1.8% points. The reliability of inflation forecasts is harder to judge because the inflation rate has been extremely stable over the last four or five years.

While the importance of presenting indicators of reliability along with economic forecasts cannot be doubted, it is to be regretted that the practice is not more widespread. In the public debate too much attention is focused on the point estimates produced by forecasters and too little on their inherent reliability. Instead time is devoted to the relatively fruitless exercise of assessing who has been right and who wrong *ex post*.

The value of forecasts to forward-looking businesses is immense. Having some idea of the likely movements in the economy as a whole provides an essential backcloth for firms making marketing, production and investment decisions.

9 Using Economic Data: a multinational perspective

Donald Hepburn, Corporate Economist, Unilever PLC

FOCUS QUESTIONS

- What are the strategic policy issues facing a multinational business?
- How can economic data from international and national sources help businesses to make better decisions?
- Why is it necessary for firms to understand the economic and political environment in which they operate?
- What role does judgement play in using data for business analysis?

INTRODUCTION

Will the USA continue to be the world's economic powerhouse, growing like an Asian "tiger" (over 7% per annum at the end of 1999)? Will it manage a soft landing or nosedive into recession? Will the £ depreciate? Will Europe experience an economic renaissance to match the USA's "new economy"? Will Japan finally pull itself out of its decade-long stagnation? How will the Internet affect business? Can we now forget the Asian crisis? Can we bank on a continuing trend towards market liberalisation across the world, in trade, investment and economic policies? Or will there be a backlash against this consensus, driven perhaps by growing inequalities? How do people spend their money now? How will this change with income, age, price, family size?

This is just a sample of the many macro and micro economic questions that concern an

economist in a multinational company. For any economist they are interesting questions in their own right. For example, it is easy to become wrapped up in the technicalities of forecasting GDP and the econometric models that produce them, but usually it does not matter if growth is 2.5% or 2.75%. What matters much more is how the broad questions posed above can be answered in terms of their impact on business strategy and decisions.

Risk is another important area a business economist has to consider. Often forecasts will cluster around a fairly narrow range. Table 9.1 shows Consensus forecasts for US, Germany, Japan and China for 2000 and 2001.

This shows that most forecasters were expecting a very favourable outlook, with the USA achieving a soft landing, Europe taking over the baton of growth, Japan finally extricating itself from stagnation and China managing the difficult transition to a more efficient economy with no serious impact on

Table 9.1 *Forecasts of GDP growth*

(%)	2000		2001	
	Average	**Range**	**Average**	**Range**
USA	4.3	3.5 - 4.9	3.1	2.6 - 3.9
Germany	2.8	2.5 - 3.5	2.8	2.0 - 3.7
Japan	0.9	0.2 - 1.8	1.6	0.6 - 2.4
China	7.3	6.5 - 7.9	7.5	6.5 - 8.6

Source: Consensus Forecasts, March 2000

its growth performance. At the time of writing this was one scenario, possibly the most likely, certainly the most desirable. At the same time, other scenarios were possible. Surprises like the Asian crisis do happen, even if they are hard to predict. Understanding these alternative scenarios and working out a response can give a company a huge advantage in the market place.

This chapter picks a small sample of these issues to show how a business economist might approach them and their relevance to a multinational business. It will show how, in thinking about the issues, economic data from international and national sources can help businesses to make better decisions. Note here that "data" have been interpreted widely to include economic policies. These, and the political forces that drive them, can be as significant for a business as hard numbers. This clearly poses a problem for an economist who will usually have no expertise as a political scientist. There is no easy way round this problem except to look for the best advice and then make a judgement.

A MACRO ECONOMIC EXAMPLE

One of the most important strategic issues for a multinational company is whether to invest in a new country or region; or, if already present in all regions of the world, where to focus extra resources. Should they be concentrated to take advantage of opportunities in Europe and North America or

should they be channelled towards the big developing markets such as China, India, Russia and Brazil? At the most basic level, this question translates into "where will extra resources provide greatest value for shareholders"?

Size

The first and most basic issue in assessing market attractiveness is 'size'. A large market will be more attractive than a small one because it may offer economies of scale in many areas such as manufacturing, marketing, distribution, advertising and government relations. At first sight, size seems easy to measure. It is the amount of private consumption, which itself is a combination of the number of people and their average spending. Population is a straightforward number. We know that there are roughly 200 million people in Indonesia. Their spending is harder to measure, as the following example, spanning the economic crisis in Indonesia, will show.

Table 9.2 *Private consumption in Indonesia*

	1997	1998	1999
Rupiahs (billion)	387,171	663,460	800,000
Rupiah/£	4,753	16,583	12,709
£ (billion)	81	40	63

Source: IMF, International Financial Statistics and author's estimates.

Table 9.3 *Taking inflation out*

	1997	**1998**	**1999**
Private consumption (Rupiah bn, current prices)	387,171	663,460	800,000
Inflation Index (1999 = 100)	47.5	84.2	100
Private consumption (Rupiah bn, 1999 prices)	815,075	788,177	800,000
Change in Real Private Consumption (%)		-3.3	1.5

Source: IMF, *International Financial Statistics, Consensus Forecasts*, and author's estimates

In Rupiah terms, private consumption increased by 71% in 1998 and 21% in 1999. In £ terms, however, private consumption fell by about 50% in 1998 as the Rupiah collapsed but then rose to reach about three-quarters of its 1997 level in 1999 as the exchange rate recovered from its overshoot. The "right" size of the market then depends on an estimate of the sustainable exchange rate. The 1997 rate was clearly too high, the 1998 rate too low. Relative stability in the rate since then suggests that the 1999 rate may be in the right ball park, subject to the need in the longer term to avoid a return to overvaluation.

These figures are all shown in current prices, i.e. including inflation. So here is another source of distortion. If we are interested not just in the current size of the market but also how it has grown we need to strip out inflation to get to the 'real' situation. Although the rate of inflation (as measured by the private consumption deflator) is hard to calculate in such a complex country, particularly as it is passing through economic crisis, the best estimate is that it rose to 77 % in 1998 and fell back to 19 % in 1999. Table 9.3 shows what happens if we take inflation out and express private consumption in constant (1999) prices. The real changes give a much better idea of the

quantity of goods and services that people actually consumed over this turbulent period.

A final complication comes if we want to compare market sizes of different countries. Is the Japanese purchasing power greater than the Chinese purchasing power? The answer to this question depends on how purchasing power is measured. So far we have used the market exchange rate to convert foreign currencies. This makes most developing countries look very small. If Purchasing Power Parity (PPP) exchange rates are used we see a radically different picture of market size. In terms of purchasing power, China is ahead of Japan. India overtakes UK and Brazil approaches the UK. (See Box 9.1 and Chapter 10 for further details of the impact of exchange rate changes).

As so often in economics, the right answer depends on the question being asked. The market exchange rate gives a good indication of the scope for making current profits. Dividends are, after all, paid with profits from abroad translated at market exchange rates. The PPP exchange rate measure of the market gives more weight to the market in terms of volume and the longer term potential. For example, in China market sizes in terms of tonnes are huge though prices are currently low. As China develops, the exchange rate will tend to rise. This will make China a more

---

Box 9.1

Purchasing Power Parity (PPP)

In developing countries the price of goods and services is much lower than in developed countries when converted at market exchange rates. For example, the 1998 income per head in China is $775, using the then current exchange rate of Rmb8.28/$. This level of income would not seem able to support the standard of living observed in China where many people own colour televisions, washing machines and fridges. The reason for this apparent anomaly is the difference in prices in China and USA. Chinese prices are lower because Chinese wages are lower. The Purchasing Power Parity (PPP) exchange rate takes this into account by comparing consumption of goods and services across countries.

The effect of using PPP exchange rates instead of market exchange rates is dramatic. The table shows how the size of some larger developing countries changes according to whether it is measured at market or PPP exchange rates.

GDP in 1998 ($ billion)		
	Market exchange rates	PPP exchange rates
Japan	3,783	2,887
UK	1,357	1,220
China	961	4,068
Brazil	778	1,085
India	383	1,511

Source: World Bank World Development Indicators, see the World Bank website at
http://www.worldbank.org/data/databytopic/keyrefs.html

---

attractive market. Looking only at the market in current exchange rates would underestimate China's potential.

Segmentation

So far we have talked about the size of the total market, in terms of the private consumption of a country. This, of course, is only a starting point. It is then necessary to drill down to understand how this consumption is split, for example by:

- products and services;
- demographic factors such as age, family structure, income group;
- region within a country;
- distribution channel.

Some of these factors will be covered later in the chapter.

Table 9.4 *GDP growth: actual and forecast rates*

(% pa)	1970-80	1980-90	1990-2000	2000-2008
USA	3.1	3.2	3.2	2.9
UK	1.9	2.7	2.1	2.4
Japan	4.6	4.0	1.4	2.5
China	na	9.1	10.1	8.3
India	3.0	5.8	5.5	7.1
Brazil	8.6	1.6	2.5	4.1
Russia	na	0.6	-4.8	2.5

Source: IMF, *International Financial Statistics Yearbook* and *Oxford Economic Forecasting*

Growth

Having determined the size of the market the next question relates to its growth. This is one of the oldest questions in economics and there are many theories about why some economies grow faster than others. The answer is likely to be a complex mix of political, social, geographical and economic factors.

The World Bank has given much thought to this issue and some explanations are given in their report[1] on Asia's remarkable growth up to 1997. In this report they attributed rapid growth to a combination of policies that were pro-growth. These included encouraging high levels of investment (drawing on high domestic savings), improving the workforce skills through providing universal primary and better secondary education, welcoming new technology and foreign direct investment, keeping price distortions in check and spurring competitiveness by following an export-led strategy. The Asian crisis of 1997 is, however, a timely reminder that growth is not fully understood, though the impressive recovery since then suggests that many of the factors set out in the World Bank's analysis are still relevant.

At a more practical level, growth forecasts are readily available from independent forecasters. These forecasts tend to be either extrapolations of previous trends or based on econometric models (which are also, of course, based heavily on past relationships). They usually show the trend rather than the economic cycle. Table 9.4 shows forecasts for a number of the largest economies compared to the past.

Note that it is the GDP forecasts that are shown. Over the long term these will tend to be roughly matched by growth in private consumption (typically 60-70% of GDP). Where they do not, it will be necessary to build in a trend.

These forecasts represent one scenario but we have already suggested that the future is uncertain. Both the International Monetary Fund (IMF) and the Organisation for Economic Cooperation and Development (OECD) drew attention in 1999 and early 2000 to the risks of overheating in the USA, with consequent risks for other closely linked regions of the world. Box 9.2 shows such a scenario and its expected impact on other OECD regions.

The analysis so far has focused on the demand side – whether there is a market and how fast it is growing. It is now time to turn to the supply side to ask how it can be profitably served.

Supplying the market profitably

This issue breaks down naturally into two sub-issues:

1 *The East Asian Miracle: Economic Growth and Public Policy.* World Bank, 1993

Box 9.2

A Boom-bust scenario for the USA

At the end of 1999 the OECD referred to a boom-bust scenario as one of the risks to the world economy. In this scenario, rapid growth in the US economy leads to accelerating inflation. The Fed[1] raises interest rates rapidly to slow the economy, causing the $ to rise but then the stock market to fall. Consumers, who have been spending more than they earn on the back of a booming stock exchange, suddenly decide they need to save to reduce debt. Investment is also cut as capital becomes much harder to raise. As a result the economy goes into recession. The Fed then cuts interest rates to restore growth.

Other OECD countries benefit in the short term from the rise in US demand for imports and the higher $ but then suffer as the US economy slows.
The impact on growth estimated by the OECD is shown in the following table, comparing the Boom-bust scenario to their baseline projection:

GDP Growth (%)		2000	2001	2002	2003
USA	Base scenario	3.1	2.3	2.0	3.0
	Boom-bust	4.1	1.5	-0.2	3.2
Japan	Base scenario	1.4	1.2	2.1	2.2
	Boom-bust	2.3	1.3	0.9	2.0
Euro11	Base scenario	2.8	2.8	2.6	2.5
	Boom-bust	3.1	2.8	1.8	2.2

1. Fed = Federal Reserve Bank

Source: OECD, *Economic Outlook*, December 1999

1. Is it possible to make profits in the country?
2. Is it possible to remit profits to the home country for the benefit of shareholders?

The first question will depend on operating conditions in the country. These cover many factors such as:

- the availability and cost of raw materials and packaging;
- manufacturing costs, in particularly wage rates (and productivity), interest rates, land costs;
- the costs of delivering products to customers through the distribution chain;
- expected revenues, which in turn depend on market share and price charged;
- different tax treatment of profits;
- local regulations; it is particularly important to take into consideration any government-imposed price or wage/employment rules and import/export controls;
- exchange rates; important if imports or exports are significant.

Understanding and quantifying these factors is a major exercise in its own right and beyond the scope of this chapter.

One further issue, however, is worth mentioning – the choice between building a factory or supplying the market with imports. In addition to the factors mentioned earlier, this decision will need to take into account

Figure 9.1 *Real exchange rate and the balance of trade in the UK*

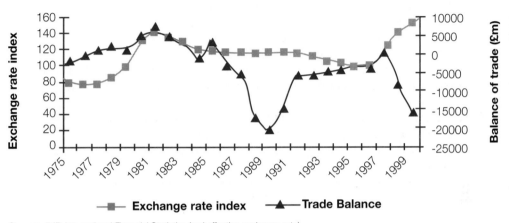

Sources: IMF, *International Financial Statistics* (real effective exchange rate)
NS, *Economic Trends Annual Supplement* (for balance of trade in goods and services)

other economic and political issues. On the economic side the cost of importing (e.g. transport costs, tariffs and the possibility of exchange rate movements) has to be weighed against the cost of local manufacture. Economies of scale in manufacturing can be important in this calculation. If the market is small it may be cheaper to supply the market from a factory abroad operating at a very high level of output and very low unit cost. Political factors will include the risk of expropriation (currently very small) or local business conditions. In some countries, criminal activity, legal uncertainty and the arbitrary application of taxes make local manufacture difficult.

Exchange rates

We will focus on just one factor that affects both the ability to make money, to remit it and even whether to make the investment in the first place. The issue is the exchange rate. This can often be the crucial factor determining the profitability of an investment. It can also affect the timing of an investment. A major devaluation of a currency can make assets in

that country suddenly appear cheap. Recent devaluations in Asia, Russia and Brazil are good examples.

Unfortunately, forecasting exchange rates is a very uncertain business. According to many, a "random walk" assumption is as good a predictor as any model. This means that assuming the exchange rate will move around its current value is as good a way of predicting the rate as any other method. While this may be true, at least in the short term, it is sometimes possible to make a judgment about the longer-term direction of the real exchange rate.

Several factors are generally thought to influence exchange rates. The first is competitiveness as reflected by a country's balance of trade in goods and services. Figure 9.1 shows how the UK balance of trade in goods and services changed over the last 25 years and compares this with the real effective exchange rate. A rise in the exchange rate means that British goods and services are less competitive, all other things being equal.

Figure 9.1 shows that there seems to be some relationship between the real exchange rate and the balance of trade in goods and services, albeit with a lag. The surge in the £ in 1979/81 is followed by a sharp deterioration in the trade balance in 1982-4 as a large swathe of manufacturing was rendered uncompetitive. Most recently, the rise in the £ since 1996 has been followed by a rapid deterioration in the trade balance in 1998/9. The relationship between these two variables broke down, however, during the boom at the end of the 1980s as strong domestic demand sucked in imports. It is clear, therefore, that there are additional influences at work.

Capital flows are another important factor determining exchange rates. If people are bringing money into Britain from abroad this will, other things being equal, cause the £ to rise. This could happen for several reasons. UK interest rates could be higher than foreign interest rates. As long as people expect this difference to outweigh the risk of devaluation it makes sense to bring money into the country to take advantage of the higher interest rates. Figure 9.2 shows UK short-term interest rates relative to Germany over the past 25 years, once again with the real effective exchange rate.

UK interest rates were 11 percentage points higher than German rates in 1979 and that was

followed by a surge in the £ in 1980 and 1981. The sharp fall in UK relative rates in 1991 and 1992 was echoed by a fall in the £ in 1993-5. However, it is again clear that the explanation provided by interest rate differentials is not very good on its own.

Capital flows can also take the form of portfolio or direct investment. If there are attractive opportunities to invest on the London Stock Exchange or build factories (e.g. to take advantage of British membership of the European Union) foreign individuals and companies will bring their money to the UK.

A good recent example of this concerns the $. A very large and rapidly growing current account deficit (equivalent to 4% of GDP) would normally have prompted a fall in the $ to correct it. The tidal wave of investment into the USA in 1999 and into 2000 kept the $ very strong. Conversely, the Euro was very weak since its launch in January 1999, despite the fact that the Eurozone was running a current account surplus. Continental Europeans were investing in US because it was seen to be a more open and flexible economy where financial returns and economic growth were higher.

From this discussion of the theory, it is clear that exchange rate forecasting is a very

Figure 9.2 *Real Exchange Rates and Interest Rate Differentials*

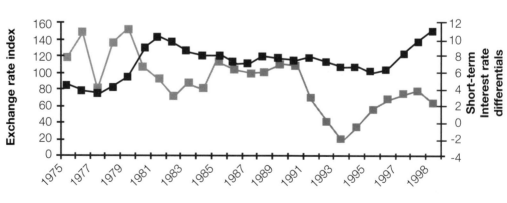

Source: NS, *Financial Statistics*

Table 9.5 *Household spending patterns*

	Share of Total Spending (%)			
	1975	1985	1994	1999
Goods	53.8	46.6	40.9	39.5
– Food at home	21.4	16.6	13.0	11.6
Services	15.8	17.7	24.6	25.9
– Food out of home	3.4	3.6	4.8	5.2
Housing/Fuel/Light	18.6	22.2	20.9	19.6
Motoring	11.2	13.0	12.8	14.7
Miscellaneous	0.6	0.4	0.8	0.3
Total	100	100	100	100

Source: NS, *Family Expenditure Survey*

inexact science. Adding in the actions of governments, which may have many motives in trying to manipulate exchange rates (ranging from legitimate economic goals such as control of inflation to less worthy motives such as giving 'insiders' access to opportunities to profit from a controlled rate), trying to forecast seems a lost cause. However, the rewards and risk can be so large that economists will keep trying.

A MICRO ECONOMIC EXAMPLE

The macro economic issues covered so far are a prelude to considering how to assess individual market opportunities. The micro economic issues are as wide-ranging. They cover how to assess a market's size and growth, the whole subject of industrial economics, market share modelling, the impact of the Internet and many others. This section will focus on how to use economic data to look at just one of these areas – how to assess market size and growth.

Market definition

The first, and probably most important issue, is to define the market. At first sight this may seem straightforward. Markets are the goods and services that people buy e.g. cars,

haircuts, ice creams. At a more fundamental level, however, what we buy is a means to satisfying deeper needs. We buy cars for a wide range of motives, including such diverse reasons as the desire for mobility or to impress our neighbours. We have a haircut because our hair gets in our eyes or because we feel the need to be pampered. We buy ice creams for nourishment or refreshment.

Official statistics provide an essential starting point to understand what is going on. In Britain, the annual *Family Expenditure Surveys* carried out by National Statistics are a very rich source of information about what British households buy (see chapter 4 for more details of the Family Expenditure Survey). Table 9.5 shows how spending patterns have changed over the past 25 years.

This shows a striking trend away from goods towards services and motoring. A good example is the contrast between the sharply falling share of spending on food eaten at home (21.4% to 11.6%) and an increasing share of spending on food eaten out of home (3.4% to 5.2%). Leisure services have also grown rapidly in recent years. These trends are exactly what we would expect to find. Having satisfied basic needs, people spend incremental income on luxuries.

The same trends are seen in other countries.

Table 9.6 *Household expenditure by income decile, 1998/9, (£ per week)*

	D1	D2	D3	D4	D5	D6	D7	D8	D9	D10
Average weekly spending per person (£)	86	77	94	107	122	144	144	161	180	252
Food	24.7	33.1	39.2	44.9	50.2	57.0	66.0	74.6	85.2	104.7
Tea	0.4	0.5	0.6	0.5	0.5	0.5	0.5	0.5	0.6	0.6
Coffee	0.3	0.4	0.4	0.6	0.6	0.7	0.8	0.7	0.8	1.0
Tobacco	3.7	4.3	5.4	5.9	6.8	7.1	7.6	6.3	6.0	5.1
Holidays abroad	1.0	2.1	3.5	3.6	5.2	6.8	13.0	16.3	17.4	34.0

Source: NS, Family Expenditure Survey

Over the 20 years 1975-95 in Europe spending on health, recreation and leisure has grown faster than average, while spending on food, beverages, tobacco, clothing and furniture has grown more slowly.

Although the Family Expenditure Surveys are in great detail they only provide a starting point for market definition. They need to be supported by market research about underlying needs. This is particularly important for understanding the likely market size for products and services which do not already exist. It is often very difficult to make a business case for investing in a totally new product or service as there is no track record.

Income

Table 9.5 shows that spending patterns have changed over time as the average level of incomes has grown, suggesting income is one of the determinants of market size and growth. This is confirmed when we look at a cross section of spending across income levels in a single year. Table 9.6 picks out some expenditure items from the British Family Expenditure Survey 1998/9. Expenditure by families is divided into ten groups or deciles (D1 to D10) by ascending income levels.

From these figures we can see that the effect of income varies considerably. Spending on tea rises from the lowest decile to the 3rd decile but then levels off. Coffee consumption increases more with income but also shows

signs of levelling off by the 7th decile. Tobacco consumption actually falls after the 7th decile. Spending on foreign holidays shows no sign of levelling off though we would expect, at some stage, that it would do so as diminishing returns set in.

These trends can be used to understand and estimate market size and growth in countries where good household spending surveys exist. In many developing countries, such information does not exist but an alternative method based on international comparison can be used. Figure 9.3 shows estimated market size for beer (measured by litres per head) plotted against average income (measured by GNP per head at Purchasing Power Parity exchange rates) for a number of countries in 1998.

This shows that beer consumption is very low in the poorest countries but tends to rise with income. However, this relationship is by no means precise. Some of the outliers in Figure 9.3 have been named to show how these differences can stimulate a search for an explanation. Singapore, which has an income per head of about $28,600, consumes 12 litres a head while China has an average consumption of 10 litres despite the fact that its average income is just over 10% of the Singapore level. On the other hand, beer consumption is very high in some Latin America countries such as Venezuela and Mexico. There are many factors which can

Figure 9.3 *Beer consumption and income*

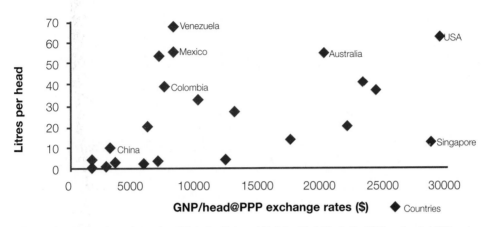

Source: Euromonitor, Market sizes – International Marketing Data and Statistics World Bank, (for GNP per head at PPP exchange rates)

explain these differences. Prices, competition and distribution will vary. Local habits and attitudes will be different, particularly towards alcohol. The basic relationship between income and consumption will, however, provide a good starting point.

The analysis in Figure 9.3 is at an aggregate level, using the average income per head for each country. We know, however, that incomes are not equally distributed. Table 9.7, from the World Bank, *World Development Report*, shows how incomes are distributed across quintiles for a sample of countries. Quintiles divide the population into five equal groups in ascending order of income.

The range is enormous. In India the richest 20% of the population earn over 4 times the lowest 20% but in Brazil the richest 20% earn over 25 times the poorest 20%.

Brazil's income distribution is applied to Brazil's 1998 income at PPP exchange rates in Table 9.8.

The average purchasing power of $6,575 actually hides the fact that there are 33 million people in Brazil with average purchasing power of $21,121, roughly the same as the average British figure. Disaggregating in this way gives a much better estimate of the potential market size in Brazil for different types of commodities.

Table 9.7 *Income distribution by quintile*

% of Total Income	Q1	Q2	Q3	Q4	Q5	Total	Q5/Q1
UK	7.1	12.8	17.2	23.1	39.8	100	5.6
USA	4.8	10.5	16.0	23.5	45.2	100	9.4
India	9.2	13.0	16.8	21.7	39.3	100	4.3
Indonesia	8.0	11.3	15.1	20.8	44.8	100	5.6
China	5.5	9.8	14.9	22.3	47.5	100	8.6
Brazil	2.5	5.7	9.9	17.7	64.2	100	25.7

Source: World Bank website: http://www.worldbank.org/wdr/2000/pdfs/engtable5.pdf

Table 9.8 *Brazil's GDP per head by quintile*

	Q1	Q2	Q3	Q4	Q5	Total
GDP ($m)	27	62	107	192	697	1085
Population (m)	33	33	33	33	33	165
GDP/head ($)	818	1879	3242	5818	21121	6575

Source: World Bank website, op cit

Demographics

Consumption will also depend on demographic factors such as age and family structure. Again in the UK we are fortunate to be able to draw on the Family Expenditure Surveys As this source has already been used at some length only one example is given. Table 9.9 shows the effect of age on consumption.

Age has a clear influence on spending patterns. As people grow old, food and leisure services account for an increasing proportion of their expenditure but motoring, alcohol, tobacco, clothing and footwear play a much smaller part.

CONCLUDING REMARKS

This chapter has tried to give some indication of how economic data from British and international sources can help a multinational company to make strategic and tactical decisions. It has only scratched the surface and it certainly has not answered all of the questions raised at the beginning of the chapter. But it should illustrate that, in many of the most important decisions that a company faces, a proper knowledge and use of the available statistics is fundamental.

Table 9.9 *The effect of age on consumption*

(%)	Percentage of average household expenditure by age of head of household				
	Under 30	30 – 49	50 – 64	65 – 74	75+
Housing	20	18	13	13	16
Food & non-alcoholic drinks	15	16	16	18	21
Motoring	13	15	17	13	8
Leisure services	9	11	13	16	11
Alcohol, tobacco, clothes & footwear	14	12	12	10	8

Source: NS, *Family Expenditure Survey*

10 Exports, Imports and Exchange Rates

Jean Mangan, Principal Lecturer, Staffordshire University Business School
Ian Jackson, Senior Lecturer, Staffordshire University Business School

FOCUS QUESTIONS

- How can firms use data on exports, imports, exchange rates and competitiveness?
- How can a firm examine its performance in relation to aggregate trends in exports and imports?
- What data allow firms to monitor trends in different product groups and foreign markets?

- How can a firm set about measuring import penetration and export performance?
- What is the likely effect of exchange rate changes on trade?
- What is competitiveness and how is it likely to affect export sales?

USING INTERNATIONAL TRADE AND EXCHANGE RATE DATA

The central aim of the chapter is to illustrate the use of *National Statistics (NS)* data sources on imports, exports and exchange rates for analysing trade flows and establishing benchmarks for assessing success in international markets.

Domestic firms export goods and services and face competition from imports. The factors that determine the demand for exports and imports are, in essence, the same as those for any good, namely price, income, the prices of close substitutes and complements, tastes, population and the distribution of income. However, these factors are complicated in the international trade setting. Price, both of the good itself and of close substitutes and complements, is affected by the exchange rate. Both the volume and value of exports and imports have to be considered. Profitability is affected by changes in domestic costs relative to those of foreign competitors. Demand is not only affected by changes in domestic income, but also by changes in the incomes of trading partners. However, the various influences can be complex. A high growth rate of income in a country to which a firm exports could either increase demand, or reduce it according to the nature of the product in question. High domestic demand may lower exports if firms switch sales to the home market, whereas low domestic demand may force firms to be more aggressive in export markets. Competition from other firms is also likely to be more intense in the international setting. The supply of exports and imports will also be affected by the higher risk to firms involved in these markets from such things as exchange rate variability, political uncertainties and increased possibilities of default on payments.

Factors influencing Export and Import Demand   Box 10.1

General Factors

- Price
- Income
- Prices of close substitutes
- Price of complements
- Tastes
- Population
- Distribution of income

Trade Complications

- Exchange rate
- Income at home and abroad
- Domestic and foreign costs
- More intense competition
- Increased risk
- Regulations, tariffs and quotas
- Relative population sizes

To compensate for higher levels of risk, firms may look for higher returns in foreign markets than they conventionally expect in the domestic one.

Given differences in the effects of these factors, individual companies face different opportunities for export growth and threats of import penetration according to the goods or services they provide. For example, a company supplying IT software may be operating in a market that has been expanding worldwide, while a clothing manufacturer could have been facing intense international competition, particularly from the Far East, with high and growing levels of import penetration into the UK market.

In order to understand how the overall international trading environment is affecting a particular sector it is important to examine recent statistics. Such data can help companies to appraise their own performance and develop appropriate market responses. Some of the important questions for firms to consider are:

- Is the export market or import penetration for my products expanding or contracting, both in the short term and long term? Are the changes due to factors affecting all similar producers, such as income and exchange rates?

- Have other UK producers of similar products been more or less successful at exporting or competing against importers than my company? Are there particular

circumstances affecting my firm's performance?

- Are there any product lines or geographical areas that which we should be expanding into or withdrawing from given recent trends in exports and imports?

- Is the trend in profits the same as the trend in sales for exports, or are profit margins changing? Have our changes in prices and profits been in line with those for other UK exporters?

- Are profit margins on domestic sales being reduced because of competition from foreign imports?

- Have exchange rate changes affected the competitiveness of our industry?

When using official data as part of its investigation of these questions, it is useful for a company to establish benchmarks for comparison. This involves identifying suitable data series against which they can compare their performance, either in general or for some particular product. Good benchmarks are ones that behave in the same way as a firm's trade flows, if the firm is performing in an average way. It is clear, therefore, that companies providing IT software will need to assess their performance against a different background from a clothing manufacturer. Having identified a relevant series, firms can investigate why their benchmark series are moving in a particular way and why they are experiencing a different trend from the benchmark.

In considering which data series are appropriate there are two complementary approaches:

1. Identify data series that are closely related to the company's product lines. Use of detailed data at the product level may give a good benchmark for comparison. In the UK, export and import data for goods is available on a detailed basis, for example import and export figures are available for the manufacture of wallpaper and of photographic chemical material. However, for some purposes a more overall measure may be useful or more appropriate. In strategic considerations of market and product development, firms may need initially to take a wider view.

2. Examine past data for related published series that closely track the company's position. Care must be taken with this approach. A poor relationship does not necessarily imply a poor benchmark, but may simply reflect that past performance of the company was not the same as the benchmark. For instance, a company may find that a particular product code in the official data is showing an expansion of exports, while its own exports remain constant. This may be due to particular features of its own product or brand, or to poor export marketing by the company. Such lack of correlation needs to be investigated, but it does not necessarily justify the immediate dismissal of a series being used as a benchmark. Recent poor performance of the benchmark could have been the result of new factors at work in the market. Conversely, a good past relationship may not indicate a good benchmark. The past relationship may not continue into the future or may have been purely a matter of chance.

The following sections of this chapter consider the types of official data series that may be of use as benchmarks and for evaluating the firm's performance. Two broad areas are considered. The first is how to investigate the trends in overseas trade, including the product and geographical breakdown of imports and exports. The second concerns how to investigate changes in the exchange rate and competitiveness.

NATIONAL TRENDS IN EXPORTS AND IMPORTS

Companies need to be able to assess whether their own product area is performing well or poorly in export markets in comparison with general national trends. They also need to be able to establish whether the rise in import penetration for their product is a particular problem in their industry or part of an expansion in overall trade.

In the second half of the twentieth century there was a great expansion in international trade. The General Agreement on Tariffs and Trade (GATT) led to a significant liberalisation of multinational trade. Another factor in trade expansion has been the increased speed and reduced costs of transport and communications. Figure 10.1 shows the resulting growth of the volume of UK exports. The index shows the large increase in trade, with exports of goods increasing in volume more than six fold since the end of the 1950s.

Figure 10.1 *UK exports of goods, volume index 1959=100*

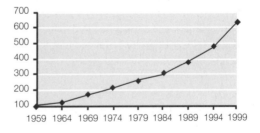

Source: NS, *Economic Trends*

Table 10.1 *Volume of UK exports and imports of goods, 1995=100*

Year	Exports	Imports
1995	100.0	100.0
1996	107.7	109.1
1997	116.5	119.0
1998	118.0	129.1
1999	120.6	137.8

Source: NS, Monthly Digest of Statistics

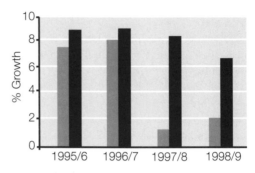

Figure 10.2 *Volume of UK exports and imports, growth rates (%)*

Source: NS, *Monthly Digest of Statistics*

In UK international trade statistics imports are valued c.i.f, that is including the cost of carriage, insurance and freight while exports are f.o.b., that is free on board (excluding the cost of carriage, insurance and freight). In some aggregate data published by *National Statistics*, including that in Table 10.1, this data is given on a Balance of Payments basis which both adjusts the import figure to remove the carriage, insurance and freight and adjusts European Union imports and exports to take account of estimated under-recording.

The growth of both the exports and imports of goods in recent years is shown as an index in Table 10.1 and as annual percentage changes in Figure 10.2. There was rapid growth between 1995 and 1997 with the volume standing nearly 17% higher in 1997 than in 1995 for exports, and 19% higher for imports. In 1998 and 1999 exports grew relatively slowly, but imports continued to expand rapidly. Assessed against this background, a manufacturing firm that, for instance, had a 5% increase in its export volume over the 5 years 1995/99 has expanded its exports by less than a quarter of the UK average.

DIFFERENT PRODUCTS AND OVERSEAS MARKETS

UK export and import data for goods is available at a disaggregated level (i.e. broken down into sub-categories) using two different classification systems:

1. The *Monthly Review of External Trade* gives data by the Standard International Trade Classification (SITC) of the United Nations. The data is in a two-way analysis showing figures for areas and countries on the one hand and commodity divisions and sections of the SITC on the other.

2. *Trade by Industry – Business Monitor MQ 10* gives exports and imports grouped by the 1992 Standard Industrial Classification down to the four digit code and is available quarterly. This is illustrated by the example in Table 10.2 which shows the aggregate category 'other non-metal mineral products' (26 is the 2 digit code), the subgroup 'glass

Table 10.2 *Exports by SIC (1992) classification, 1999 Q3, £ million*

	SIC Group	£ million
Manufacture of other non-metal mineral products	26	442
Manufacture of glass and glass products	26.1	132
Manufacture of glass fibres	26.14	33

Source: NS, *MQ10 Overseas Trade in Goods Analysed in Terms of Industries*

Table 10.3 *Exports by the financial services sector, £ million*

	1994 £m	1998 £m	% Change
Monetary financial services (banks)	1588	2526	59
Fund Managers	390	500	28
Money Market Brokers	130	225	73
Securities Dealers	1467	2388	63
Baltic exchange	262	297	13
Other	473	382	19
Financial Services Total	**4310**	**6318**	**47**

Source: NS, *UK Balance of Payments*, The Pink Book

and glass products' (26.1 is the 3 digit code) and the further subdivision 'glass fibres' (26.14 is the 4 digit code).

The data is available from *National Statistics* in both paper and electronic form.

Data on overseas trade in services are available from the Overseas Trade in Services surveys (OTIS), which are conducted quarterly with the largest businesses and elsewhere on an annual basis. The recording is of the value of services excluding trade expenses such as the cost of services purchased abroad. The example of financial services is given in Table 10.3. The largest export earnings are from monetary financial services, while the largest growth over this period was in the services provided by money market brokers. As you can see from Table 10.3, the growth rates varied considerably within the sector.

Data series for exports and imports are generally available in value terms but, for some series, volume terms are available (Tables 10.2 and 10.3 are in value terms while 10.1 is in volume terms). These are the same as the 'current price' and 'constant price' data discussed in Chapter 3. Linking these two series is the implicit price deflator, the change in which measures the price inflation of the series. All these types of series may be of interest to companies. Use of data for comparison of trends will both depend on the availability of published series, the data the firm has available internally and the use to

which it is to be put.

A firm may wish to compare their volume of a particular good exported with the volume series containing that category of export. The graph below presents exports of commercial vehicles in thousands, showing a rise in sales abroad to 1996 and a decline since 1996. In 1999 the volume of sales had fallen to lower than in 1995.

Most company data are likely to be in value terms. Certainly this will be so if the company is considering the performance of a group of products, for example a pottery manufacturer considering its ceramic tableware exports rather than the exports of a particular pattern of cup, saucer or plate.

As examples of the use of benchmarks for comparison using value data, consider two particular products that illustrate differing trends, ceramic tableware and cement. Figure 10.4 illustrates the trend exports of these

Figure 10.3 *Commercial vehicle exports*

Thousands

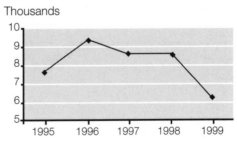

Source: NS, *Economic Trends*

Figure 10.4 *Exports by industry, current prices f.o.b. (1994 = 100)*

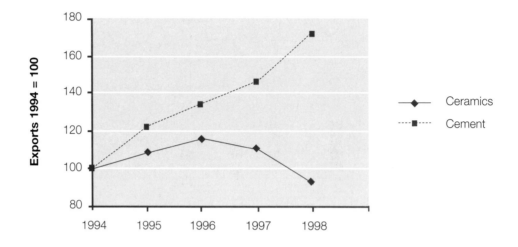

Source: NS, MQ 10 Overseas Trade Analysed in Terms of Industries

products in current prices, but indexed on 1994. The data have been indexed to allow a quick comparison of trends and is given annually to avoid the complication of seasonal variations. The first series for ceramic household goods shows a steady increase to 1996 and since then a fall to below the original level. The second series, for cement, shows increasing export sales throughout the period.

It can be useful to examine both the price and the volume series. An increase in the value of exports (or of imports) can be caused by changes in both the quantity of commodities traded and their price. What is happening to profit margins is important to the firm, and they may well want to compare their position to what is happening to other UK companies in their product area. If export values are being maintained by a reduction in the profit margin, this may be indicated by an increase in export volumes and a reduction in the price index. As an example, Table 10.4 gives the value of exports (in £ millions), the volume and price indices for chemicals. The value of exports barely changed between 1996 and 1998, but the volume index clearly shows an increase. The price index shows that the increased volume has been achieved by lowering prices. This may be due to a fall in costs or because of a reduction in profit margins. The connected areas of exchange rates and measures of competitiveness and

Table 10.4 *Exports of Chemicals*

	£ million	Volume index 1995=100	Price index 1995=100
1996	22194	105	102
1997	21883	111	94
1998	22141	117	92

Source: NS, UK Balance of Payments, The Pink Book

Figure 10.5 *Percentage change in UK exports of goods to the Americas and Africa*

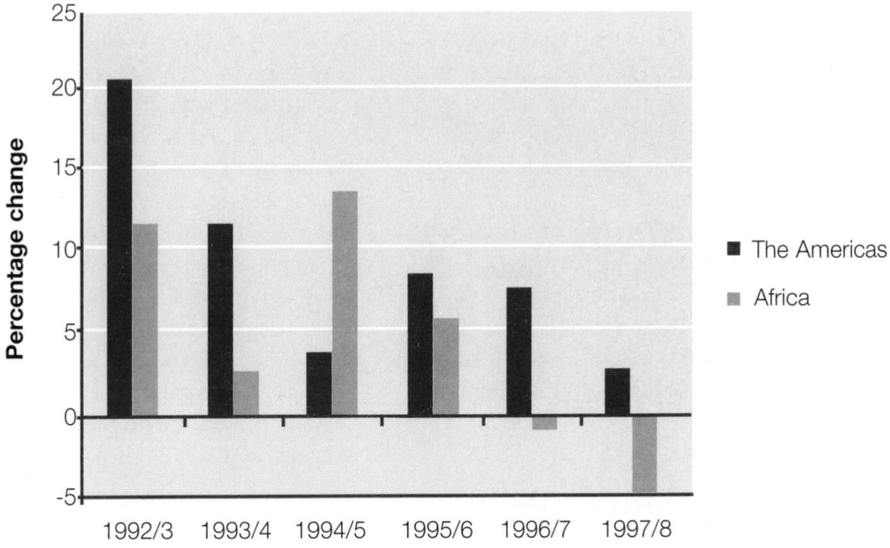

Source: NS, *UK Balance of Payments*, The Pink Book

profitability are covered later in this chapter.

Companies may also want to compare their performance in different geographical markets. This may be to assess whether their performance is in line with trends in a particular market, or to identify markets that have grown more quickly or slowly than average as part of an overall assessment of their export strategy. Data are available on an individual country basis and by various aggregates, down to product level.

Figure 10.5 shows that the growth of exports of goods was generally much stronger to the Americas than Africa over the period

1992 to 1998 - with an overall increase of seventy two percent, compared to thirty one percent. There was, however, considerable year-to-year fluctuation, with African trade growing more strongly than the Americas in 1994/5.

The growth rates may vary considerably within these areas and percentage changes do not show the absolute importance of the two areas as a large percentage change may be on a small base value. These points are illustrated for the Americas case. The trade growth varied between countries as illustrated in Table 10.5. Brazilian trade showed a 244% growth over

Table 10.5 *Levels and changes in trade in goods with countries in the Americas*

	1992	1998	% Change
Brazil	270	929	244
Canada	1637	2178	33
Mexico	302	544	80
USA	12640	21702	72
Other	1350	2530	87

Source: NS, *UK Balance of Payments*, The Pink Book

the period (compared to the average of 72%) and had overtaken Mexico as the third largest export market in the Americas. However, at £929 million in 1998 Brazilian trade was still very small compared to the £21,702 million with the USA. The figures presented here are for overall sales of goods to these continents and countries. Similar figures are available disaggregated by product.

Having identified the trend in a particular country or area, this can be further investigated. Is there, for example, a link between trade and income trends? Chapter 9, 'Using Economic Data: a multinational perspective' explains how to pursue such an investigation.

IMPORT PENETRATION AND EXPORT SALES RATIOS

Import penetration and export sales ratios published by *National Statistics* provide useful indicators of the UK's relative trade performance. Four main ratios are published, with industries grouped according to the 1992 Standard Industrial Classification (SIC).

These include two measures of import penetration:

Ratio 1:   imports as a percentage of home demand

Ratio 2:   imports as a percentage of (home demand plus exports)

Here home demand is total manufacturers sales plus imports minus exports.

Ratio 1 is the most commonly quoted measure of import penetration. However, at the start of this chapter it was noted that there had been a large growth in both UK exports and imports over recent decades. In general, import penetration levels have been increasing and the figures need interpreting against this background. If exports have also been increasing by approximately the same amount, the change in Ratio 1 may not imply a problem for domestic producers. Ratio 2 is an attempt to deal with this problem. Exports are added to the denominator, which means, for instance, that if exports are increasing the ratio will be reduced, other things being constant.

There are also two ratios that measure export sales:

Ratio 3:   exports as a percentage of total manufacturers' sales

Ratio 4:   exports as a percentage of (total manufacturers' sales plus imports)

Here total manufacturers' sales are home demand minus imports plus exports.

Ratio 3 is the common measure of the export sales ratio for UK producers. However, the same problem exists with interpreting this as with Ratio 1, that is any change in the ratio must be seen in relation to a general increase in trade. Ratio 4 is the equivalent of ratio 2. Imports are added to the denominator, which means that if imports are increasing the ratio will be reduced, other things being constant.

This information may be used to help a firm judge its position in the market. Take for

---

Table 10.6 *Import penetration and export sales ratios for medical, precision and optical instruments, watches and clocks*

	Import Penetration		Export Sales	
	Ratio 1	**Ratio 2**	**Ratio 3**	**Ratio 4**
1994	72	41	73	43
1995	76	42	77	45
1996	79	44	80	45

Source: NS, *Monthly Digest of Statistics*

example, a company that has been facing a decline in sales on the home market. One reason for this may be increased import penetration. The example in Table 10.6 shows these ratios for the SIC category medical, precision and optical instruments, watches and clocks. Ratio 1 shows high and increasing import penetration in this category in the mid-1990s. However, firms need to be a little careful in interpreting this given the background considered earlier of an increase in world trade. As the other ratios show, this is an industry where the UK has a large and growing proportion of exports as well as imports. Ratio 2, which includes exports in the denominator, is considerably lower and shows a slower rate of increase. Ratio 3 illustrates the increase in exports directly, showing a high, and growing, export sales ratio. However, this measure by itself gives a too optimistic picture of the industry as can be seen from Ratio 4. Overall the picture to be gained is that the proportion of both exports and imports in the industry is high and growing over this period. Given this evidence the problem for the firm may not simply be with home sales. It should be considering its home and export sales together. Are its export sales increasing in line with the benchmark indicators for the product area?

THE IMPACT OF EXCHANGE RATE CHANGES

The exchange rate is defined as the quantity of foreign currency required to purchase a single unit of domestic currency. An exchange rate of £1: $2 means that $2 dollars are needed to purchase £1 or conversely £0.5 (or 50p) is needed to purchase $1. That is, an exchange rate is simply the price of one currency expressed in terms of another currency.

A fall in the exchange rate is called **depreciation** and a rise in the exchange rate is called an **appreciation**.

The demand for a domestic currency arises in part from the foreign demand for our exports and domestic assets. An increase in foreign income will tend to increase the demand for exports. The supply of a domestic currency arises in part from imports and UK residents' purchases of overseas assets. An increase in domestic income will tend increase the demand for imports, which is measured by the **marginal propensity to import** (that is, the fraction of each extra £ of National Income which domestic residents spend on additional imports). Changes in interest rates will also have an impact on the situation, because they alter the cost of capital and thereby the demand for the currency.

Imports and exports are often affected by variations in the exchange rate. For example, a rise in the exchange rate, other things being equal, will make exports relatively more expensive and imports relatively cheaper. As a consequence, exporters and companies facing import competition may face decreased sales volumes or reduced profit margins.

There are several ways by which exchange rates can be measured. The commonest ways to express the external value of a domestic currency are:

- Current or spot value (time specific value)
- Annual average (mean value)
- Year end or month end value (time specific value)
- Annual high and annual low (range of values)

Also, it is worth noting that there are different rates at which banks will buy and sell currencies. This is known as the spread. For example,

Bank buys £1:	Bank sells £1:
$1.8500	$1.8550

This means a firm will buy sterling from a bank at $1.8550 and sell sterling to a bank at $1.8500, where both rates are favourable to the bank. This is because a bank will sell sterling at a high dollar price and buy sterling a low dollar price.

Why is it important for firms to have an understanding of exchange rate changes?

1. To adjust prices, forecast quantities and quantify the income from exports.
2. To assess the cost of imports.
3. To assess the competitiveness of imports and adjust their domestic sales strategy.
4. To value foreign assets and liabilities.
5. To calculate the profitability of an investment project.

Exchange rates, and variables such as interest rates, affect international competitiveness. Hedging is an important way to overcome the uncertainty of currency and interest movements. Buying foreign currency in the futures or forward markets, ahead of the time when it is needed, can protect firms against adverse movements in exchange rates. This is known as hedging. Past information on forward rates is available in *National Statistics* publications, but for current futures or forwards rates commercial sources have to be consulted. Although hedging against exchange rate changes may reduce the risk involved in exchange rate fluctuations it is difficult to hedge fully against swings in competitiveness. Exchanging currencies always involves transaction cost because of commission charges and differences in buying and selling rates. As a result, a single currency, such as the euro, covering a large trading area can be appealing to importers and exporters alike, since it means that they do not need to worry about currency transactions when buying and selling

commodities in the rest of the single currency area. However, already in certain global industries, such as aerospace, most international transactions are in one currency, namely the US dollar. A UK aerospace company will generally import components from the Far East in $s and export to the USA also in $s, thus reducing the overall need to exchange currency and the risk of exchange rate movements. Similarly, the global price of oil is always in US $.

Exchange rates are notoriously difficult to predict and the construction of an exchange rate forecast is not considered here. However, analysis of past trends can help firms to evaluate what position they should take in exchange markets. *Economic Trends* and *Financial Statistics* provide useful sources of information on past movements in exchange rates. There is, however, a reporting lag and for up-to-date information this can be supplemented with on-line sources for recent and current spot prices.

Table 10.7 shows the relative movement of the UK domestic currency, since 1960. Sterling has depreciated against the German deutchmark, the US dollar and the Japanese yen, and fluctuated against the French franc. Information is also now available on the euro, as well as other European currencies.

The overall change in the £ exchange rate is measured by the Sterling exchange rate index, (ERI). The index is weighted by the importance of each of the other countries' currencies to UK trade in manufactures, based on 1989-91 flows. The current series was

Table 10.7 *Selected post-war UK exchange rates, average of daily rates.*

Country	1960	1970	1980	1990	1999
France (FF/£)	13.8	13.2	9.8	9.7	10.6*
Germany (DM/£)	11.7	8.7	4.23	2.88	3.14*
Japan (Y/£)	n/a	858	526	257	184
USA ($/£)	2.8	2.4	2.33	1.79	1.62

Source: NS, *Economic Trends* and * Barclays Bank, *Economic Review*

revised in January 1996 and has a base of 1990. The ERI index has risen from 83.2 in January 1996 to 108.4 in February 2000. A rise in the index indicates an appreciation of the £. This shows the huge loss in competitiveness faced by UK exporters in the late 1990s due the relative strength of sterling, especially against the euro.

An important factor affecting the exchange rate in the long run is the rate of domestic inflation relative to that of our competitors. If the UK exchange rate falls, but this is linked to higher domestic price and/or wage inflation, UK exporters gain in competitiveness from the fall in the exchange rate, but lose from an increase in their costs of production. **Purchasing Power Parity (PPP)** is where the exchange rate is such that the same expenditure can purchase the same basket of goods and services in two different countries. For example, consider the case of two countries A and B that at the beginning of the year are at Purchasing Power Parity, but country A is inflating at 10% whereas country B has an inflation of zero. In order to maintain Purchasing Power Parity the exchange rate of

A relative to B needs to depreciate by 10% over the year. If it does not fall by this amount, then the basket of goods will be relatively more expensive in country A compared to country B. As a result, Country A will have a decline in its international competitiveness.

In Table 10.8, the ratio of PPP for 1998 is shown using the UK as the index base (i.e. UK=100). This shows that Denmark was 17% more expensive than the UK, Italy the same with Spain, Greece and Portugal considerably less expensive. This is important for firms to know, in terms of deciding the pricing strategy of their exports and comparing the costs of imports from different overseas countries over time. This can be critical for firms in terms of market entry and sustaining a long term trading presence in any given country.

UK COMPETITIVENESS AND THE EFFECT ON EXPORT SALES

National Statistics provides other useful measures of international competitiveness which include:

- Relative export prices
- Relative wholesale prices
- Import price competitiveness
- Relative profitability of exports

Table 10.9 shows the export unit value for the UK and USA, that is the unit value index of

Table 10.8 *The ratio Purchasing Power Parity (PPP) of the major European currencies in 1998 (UK = 100)*

Country	Index
Denmark	117
Belgium	116
France	116
Holland	110
Germany	108
UK	**100**
Italy	100
Sweden	98
Republic of Ireland	89
Spain	79
Portugal	72
Greece	69

Source: World Bank, *World Development Indicators* (www.worldbank.org/data/databytopic/keyrefs.html)

Table 10.9 *Export unit value index*

Year	UK	USA
1993	97.8	102.3
1994	102.5	103.1
1995	113.1	106.3
1996	112.1	105.6
1997	111.7	107.6
1998	110.6	107.6

Source: NS, *Economic Trends*

Table 10.10 *Unit labour costs index*

Year	UK	USA
1993	90.5	103.1
1994	91.0	102.6
1995	95.5	101.4
1996	97.7	99.9
1997	105.6	98.9
1998	115.4	99.0

Source: NS, *Economic Trends*

exports of manufactured goods divided by a weighted average of competitors export unit value indices for manufacturers. This indicates that the unit value of exports rose both in the UK and USA between 1994 and 1997. This may be due to increased competitiveness or to exporting firms exiting low-value markets for high-value markets, where price competition may not be so fierce.

Table 10.10 shows the index of unit labour costs for the UK and USA. **Unit labour costs** is an index of labour cost per unit of output divided by a weighted average of competitors' unit labour costs. This measure, as well as having implications for the relative cost of exports and hence profitability, is important to firms who may have overseas operations or who are considering setting up overseas sites. Table 10.10 in particular shows how unit labour costs rose in the UK between 1994 and 1998, while the USA showed a decline over the same period, increasing the competitiveness of the USA.

National Statistics produces summary measures of relative export prices and relative unit labour costs, which give the UK relative to competitors, as well as an index of relative producer prices.

As well as prices, interest rates have an important influence on exchange rates, as previously mentioned. If UK interest rates are relatively high, then this acts as an incentive to hold wealth in sterling, which increases the demand for the currency and causes it to appreciate in value. As a result, exchange rates and interest rates are closely linked and any consideration of exchange rate movements should not be in isolation from the possible changes in interest rates. Interest rate changes are also important to firms who may have borrowed capital in order to fund an export drive or pay for imports.

Generally, in assessing the impact of exchange rates and other factors on the company performance, decision-makers need to examine a wide range of statistics. For example, consider the case of a UK exporter to Japan in the late 1990s, facing competition from a German producer. The exchange rate series to investigate is not just the rate of the £ sterling to the yen, but also the euro to the yen. Since the euro fell in value during this period the German producer would have become more competitive. The situation would also have been affected by the poor growth performance of the Far East economies in the late 1990s and thus data on economic growth in Japan would also be useful.

Data Appendix

A Guide to Data Sources for UK Business

National Statistics produces an extensive range of statistical publications for business and other users. We concentrate here on the publications that are valuable standard sources for a wide variety of business users. The data they contain are increasingly available free of charge from the National Statistics web site:http://www.statistics.gov.uk. Readers needing an up-to-date list are advised to write for a current catalogue or to visit the *National Statistics* web site.

The National Statistics Information and Library Service (NSILS)

NSILS runs libraries that are open to the public at Drummond Gate, Pimlico, London SW1 and Newport, South Wales, between 9 a.m. and 4.30 p.m. Full addresses and contact numbers are given below.

Research facilities

The London library has particularly good collections of statistics on population, health and social issues, and is in the process of building up a complete collection of all UK official statistical series. The library is also responsible for a shop and enquiry office, where you may view or purchase the latest official statistical publications, or seek information on the work of National Statistics.

The Newport Library has an extensive collection of economic and business statistics, but also takes major statistical series in other subject areas, such as employment, population, and agriculture.

Enquiry services

NSILS offers an enquiry service by telephone, letter, e mail and fax, which forms a gateway to all official statistics.

Simple queries are answered immediately. A reasonable amount of data will be supplied by post or fax, but due to the huge number of enquiries they receive, they are not able to carry out detailed research, or provide data over long time spans. NSILS does provide guidance on sources - printed and electronic - and also advises on the various charged bespoke research services offered by different parts of *National Statistics*.

Contacting NSILS

The Library
National Statistics
1 Drummond Gate
Pimlico
London
SW1V 2QQ The Library

The Library
National Statistics
Government Buildings
Cardiff Rd
Newport
NP10 8XG
South Wales

Tel: 0845 601 3034
Fax: 01633 652747
e-mail: info@statistics.gov.uk

For a wide range of free data and information consult the *National Statistics* web site at http://www.statistics.gov.uk.

Printed Publications from National Statistics

Most of the following publications can be ordered from The Stationery Office (TSO) bookshops around the UK. A full list of distributors and publications can be found on The Stationery Office web site: (http://www.the-stationery-office.co.uk), or obtained from the London TSO bookshop: 123 Kingsway, London, WC2B 6PQ (Tel: 020 7242 6393, Fax: 020 7242 6394, e-mail tso.london.bookshop@theso.co.uk).

We have not included in the following list the many highly specialised series covering individual sectors. For details of these and of customised data services contact the National Statistics Library and Information Service directly.

Monthly Digest of Statistics

A standard reference volume containing the latest monthly and quarterly data for a wide range of business, economic and social statistics. Also features a monthly economic and social update on the United Kingdom.
National Statistics Monthly £15 £150pa incl. Annual Supplement

Regional Trends

A reference publication for the statistical regions and local authorities of the UK. It provides a summary of demographic, social industrial and economic statistics, including comparisons with other regions of the European Union. For the availability of Regional Trends data in electronic format, telephone 020 7533 5796.
National Statistics Annual September 1999 £39.50

Regional Trends 1965-1995 CD-ROM

The first 30 editions of Regional Trends brought together in full on one CD-ROM to give a picture of how life in the regions has changed over this period.
National Statistics ad hoc £99 + VAT (£49 + VAT for public libraries and academia)

Product Sales And Trade

Data derived from the PRODCOM (Products of the European Community) survey collected from UK manufacturers by the Office for National Statistics. For some industries data on

UK production (manufacturers product sales) can be matched with exports and imports at product level, giving the balance of trade and net supply to the UK market. Data are shown in both value and volume terms together with average prices for all categories. Please ring the PRODCOM Helpline on 01633 813065 for further details.
National Statistics Quarterly and Annual

The UK Service Sector

Latest statistics on the service and distribution sectors. Contains a wide range of official statistics relating to numerous activities, based on VAT trade classification, of the service sector. Includes data on number of businesses, turnover, capital expenditure, employment and overseas trade.
National Statistics – contact 01633 813380 for details

UK Directory of Manufacturing Business CD-ROM

Contains the names, addresses and types of business for nearly 7,000 UK manufacturers. Ideal for business location analyses, mailing lists or files.
National Statistics ad hoc April £95 + VAT Tel: National Statistics Direct 01633 812078

Economic Trends

A monthly compendium of economic data, giving convenient access in one volume to a comprehensive range of key UK economic indicators. Economic Trends includes up to five years of data on the UK economic accounts, prices, the labour market, output/demand and selected financial indicators. Regular articles are also included providing data and commentary on economic developments in the UK regions, in the UK as a whole and internationally. The data can be downloaded free of charge from the National Statistics website **www.statistics.gov.uk**.
National Statistics Monthly £23.50 £380pa (includes 12 monthly editions, Annual Supplement, four quarterly editions of UK Economic Accounts and postage)

United Kingdom National Accounts – The Blue Book

The key annual publication for National Accounts statistics and the essential data source for anyone concerned with macro-economic policies and studies. Provides detailed estimates of national product, income and expenditure for the UK. With tables containing data for up to the last eighteen years, it covers value added for industry, full accounts by sector – including financial and non-financial corporations, central and local government and households and capital formation. Consistent with ESA 95. Since 1999 contains environmental accounts and European Union Statistics. The data can be downloaded free of charge from the National Statistics website **www. statistics.gov.uk**.
National Statistics Annual August £39.50

UK Economic Accounts

Brings together recently published data on national and financial accounts and the balance of payments. Consistent with the EU ESA95 and the IMF Balance of Payments manual. The data can be downloaded free of charge from **www.statistics.gov.uk**.
National Statistics Quarterly £26

United Kingdom Balance of Payments – The Pink Book

Detailed estimates of the UK Balance of Payments for the last eleven years, including estimates for the current account (trade in goods and services, income and current transfers) the capital account, the financial account and the international investment position. Consistent with the fifth edition of the IMF Balance of Payments Manual. Since 1999 includes a chapter on the geographic breakdown of the current account. The data can be downloaded free of charge from the National Statistics website **www.statistics.gov.uk**.
National Statistics Annual August £39.50

Consumer Trends

Full tables from the 'household consumption expenditure' dataset as used in Gross Domestic Product. Consumer's expenditure is broken down into over 110 detailed series at current and constant prices. There is commentary on quarterly figures, sections on concepts, methodology and data sources and summary tables with figures dating from 1963. In addition an article describes the overall economic environment within the consumer sector by pulling together the most important underlying factors. Data are consistent with ESA 95. The data can be downloaded free of charge from the National Statistics website **www. statistics.gov.uk**.
National Statistics Quarterly £45 or £140pa

Consumer Price Indices (MM23)

Provides detailed background information on the latest month's price indices, historical series and international indices. Contains the Retail Prices Index summary, recent movements, detailed figures for the latest month, internal purchasing power of the pound and pensioner indices. The data can be downloaded from **www.statistics.gov.uk**.
National Statistics Monthly £185

Economic Trends Annual Supplement

A useful companion volume of the monthly Economic Trend. It mirrors Economic Trends in content but the data extends back 30-40 years further – long runs of data are provided as far back as 1946. A useful Notes and Definitions section provides methodological guidance on the data. Data are consistent with ESA 95. The data can be downloaded free of charge from the National Statistics website **www.statistics.gov.uk**.
National Statistics Annual November £28.50

Monthly Review of External Trade Statistics (MM24)

Latest statistics on trade in goods classified accordingly to Standard International Trade Classification (SITC). Contains seasonally adjusted data on the value of trade in goods on

a balance of payments basis, analysed either by commodity or trading partner. Price indices and seasonally adjusted volume indices for commodity groups are also included. Consistent with the IMF Balance of Payments Manual (5th edition). The data can be downloaded free of charge from the National Statistics website **www.statistics.gov.uk**.
National Statistics Monthly £185pa

Retail Sales (SDM 28)

Detailed information on retail sales. Contains tables on the volume of retail sales at 1995 prices (seasonally adjusted), value of retail sales at current prices (not seasonally adjusted), volume of retail sales at 1995 prices (not seasonally adjusted), value of retail sales at current prices (not seasonally adjusted) and year-to-date value of retail sales at current prices (not seasonally adjusted). Helps monitor the latest high street trends and performance. Can be downloaded free of charge from the National Statistics website **www.statistics.gov.uk**
National Statistics Monthly £15 £110pa
Tel: National Statistics Direct 01633 812078

UK Trade in Goods Analysed in Terms of Industries (MQ10)

A breakdown of the value of imports and exports by industry on a balance of payments basis, enabling the identification of key export earning industries. The data can be downloaded free of charge from the National Statistics website **www.statistics.gov.uk** on both a balance of payments and overseas trade statistics basis.
National Statistics Quarterly £75pa

UK Trade In Services (UKA1)

Invaluable service sector data highlighting who are our major trading partners, which services are common to a number of industries and what is the geographical breakdown on services and industries.
National Statistics Annual February £25
Tel: National Statistics Direct 01633 812078

UK Trade Trends (New)

Trade in Goods statistical journal containing statistics with analysis and comment. Will feature regular data tables and articles on trade-related subjects.
Her Majesty's Customs and Excise Quarterly

Labour Market Trends

Presenting a wide range of information relating to the labour market. Contains a comprehensive selection of labour market statistics; earnings, employment, labour disputes, redundancies, Retail Price Index, government training and enterprise programmes, unemployment and vacancies. Each edition includes special features, ad hoc news items and topical analyses from the LFS and other sources.
National Statistics Monthly £9.50 £95pa (UK) £122pa (overseas)

New Earnings Survey
GB (Parts A – F) + UK

Average earnings statistics in Great Britain including gross weekly and hourly earnings and hours worked. Contains data by occupation, industry, age, sex, region and county plus small area data, collective agreements, manual/non-manual workers, full-time/part-time. The results also show the make-up of pay, overtime hours worked, public/private sector earnings and quartiles and deciles. Part A – Streamlined and Summary Analyses Description of the Survey; Part B – Analyses by Agreement; Part C – Analyses by Industry; Part D – Analyses by Occupation; Part E – Analyses by Region, County and Small Areas; Part F- Distribution of Hours; Joint Distributions of Earnings and Hours; Analyses of Earnings and Hours for Part-time Employees; Analyses of Earnings and Hours by Age Group. The UK Volume includes Northern Ireland data.
National Statistics Annual Single issue £25, Parts A-F -£120pa, £130pa incl. UK Volume
Tel: National Statistics Direct 01633 812078

Family Spending

A breakdown of household expenditure and income in the UK derived from the Family Expenditure Survey. Contains detailed analyses of expenditure on goods and services by household income, composition, size, type and location. The complete set of data from the report is also available on floppy disk as Excel spreadsheets from National Statistics Direct Tel: 01633 812078, price £45 including VAT.
National Statistics Annual £39.50

Living in Britain 1998

Wide-ranging report on UK society based on findings of the government's General Household Survey. Subjects include population characteristics, households, families, marriage, cohabitation, fertility and education.
National Statistics ad hoc £39.50

OBTAINING DATA ELECTRONICALLY USING StatBase

StatBase is the database element of the National Statistics website, **www.statistics.gov.uk**. It provides detailed descriptions of all UK Government data sources, all its statistical products and services, and the relevant contact points. It consists of four main elements:

1. **StatSearch** tells you what sort of statistics are available from each part of the government and gives you a range of details about each, e.g. how and when they were obtained, what subjects they cover, in what format they are produced, when, how and where a customer can get hold of them. You can search it using a 3-tier hierarchical searching system based on, for example, Themes (e.g. Commerce, Energy and Industry), Subjects within Themes (e.g. Distribution and Service Trades) or Topics within Subjects (e.g. Retail Sales).
   StatSearch includes detailed descriptions of all the statistical censuses, surveys, administrative systems, (Sources), and derived analyses, (Analyses), managed by *National Statistics*. It includes details of all press releases, publications, databases, CD-ROMs, and other services – described as Products – as well as the contacts for each. It also includes **Dataset Products** which contain details of all the Datasets available in the database. Datasets are a range of statistical tables created by the Government's departments and agencies. Most importantly this facility contains the contact for each dataset who can provide more specific figures if the dataset does not give you exactly what you require. There is also a link to **StatStore** for viewing a dataset.

2. **StatStore** contains the actual datasets referred to within **StatSearch** They can be accessed from a list in alphabetical order or selected via a two-tier hierarchical Theme and Subject search. They can either be 'cross sectional tables' (multi dimensional) or 'time series tables' where time is always one of the two dimensions. Datasets may be either viewed on the screen or down loaded to your own PC. All datasets are free.

3. **TimeZone** is designed to meet the needs of Economic and Socio-Economic Users. It allows you to access and download directly to your desktop PC, most of the individual time series. These are also made available in a similar National Statistics subscription service called **DataBank** This provides access to more than 55,000 time series, primarily macro-economic data, which are drawn from a variety of sources including other government departments and the Bank of England. This is a chargeable service.
   Like **DataBank**, the **TimeZone** service allows you to access the complete histories of most of the time-series published in *National Statistics* major economic publications, whether they be First Releases

or Compendia volumes such as Economic Trends. The major difference is that **TimeZone** allows you to pick and choose individual time-series from the whole range on offer. It also works in a hierarchical way giving you the choice of selecting a Release, then a Table within a Release, then a Series within a Table.

TimeZone is not a suitable option for everyone because it does not contain much explanatory information (**metadata**) about the statistics and relies on knowledge of the unique four-character codes used to identify different time-series. These codes can be found, however, in NS's main economic publications.

4. **TextSearch** is a facility which allows you to enter a string of text and then initiate either a quick search of just the titles and descriptions of each of the records held on **StatBase**, or an extended search which looks at a more extensive range of the information held for a record.

FINDING DATA IN StatBase

How, for example, can you find information about the 'Retail Prices Index', and see what is the current rate of inflation? There are 5 ways to find the RPI:

1. **Using TextSearch** - Type the initials RPI into the **TextSearch** box, choose Titles and Datasets, and then press 'Search'. Look at the dataset called 'Retail Price Index: index numbers of retail prices'. The inflation rate has the identification code 'CHAW'.

2. **Using SeriesSearch** -If you know it, type in the 4 character 'CSDB identifier' for the series you want. The inflation rate has the identification codes 'CHAW'. This will only search for timeseries datasets in **StatStore**. There is no equivalent search in **TimeZone**.

3. **Using StatStore** - Choose the 'Economy' Theme, and within that, choose the 'Costs', Prices and Inflation' Subject area and then

view all the relevant datasets of your choice. In this case 'Retail Price Index: index numbers of retail prices'.

4. **Using StatSearch** - Choose the 'Economy' Theme and Search, or within Economy select the 'Costs, Prices and Inflation' subject area and then Search and view all the relevant Sources, Analyses, Products, and Dataset Products which are listed on the screen. The drop down list of Dataset Products contains the links to the RPI dataset 'Retail Price Index: index numbers of retail prices'.

5. **Using TimeZone** – Choose the Release called 'MM23' Consumer Prices Index. Choose the Table 'Recent Movements in the RPI and HICP. The 4 character 'CSDB identifier' for the series 'CHAW' will be found in the table.

OTHER SOURCES OF DATA MENTIONED IN THE TEXT

Consensus Economics, *Consensus Forecasts* 12 monthly issues per year. Detailed coverage of the G-7 countries (United States, Japan, Germany, France, United Kingdom, Italy and Canada), the Netherlands, Norway, Spain, Sweden and Switzerland, featuring both individual and consensus (average) forecasts for 9-15 economic indicators each, and summary forecasts of a range of other countries. Address: Consensus Economics Inc., 53 Upper Brook Street, London, W1Y 2LT. Tel: 0207 491 3211. (Price £370). Internet: **www.consensuseconomics.com**

European Commission, *European Economy* This periodical publication includes a Data Annex of harmonised long-term macroeconomic series for the economies of the EU, USA and Japan. Address: Office for Official Publications of the European Community, L-2985, Luxembourg. Also from The Stationery Office. Price Euro 112.

International Monetary Fund, *International Financial Statistics*
This monthly publication is a standard source of international statistics on all aspects of international and domestic finance. It reports, for most countries of the world data on exchange rates, international liquidity, international banking, money and banking, interest rates, prices, production, international transactions, government accounts, and national accounts. Information is presented in country tables and in tables of area and world aggregates. Address: Publication Services, Catalog Orders, 700 19th Street, N.W. Washington, D.C. 20431, U.S.A.. Telephone: (202) 623-7430. E-mail: **publications@imf.org** Price of single copies $30.

London Business School,
The Risk Measurement Service is a quarterly publication designed for use by investment professionals and corporate executives. It contains risk measures and other key data for some 2,300 British shares, estimated using the London Share Price Database. Price: £375. Address: London Business School, Regent's Park, London NW1 4SA. Tel: 020 7262 5050. Internet address: **www.london.edu/ifa/services/services.html**

National Institute of Economic and Social Research, *National Institute Economic Review*. Each edition includes detailed forecasts of both the UK and World economies, commentary, comprehensive statistical appendix and special articles by Institute researchers and external authors. Address: 2 Dean Trench Street, Smith Square, London SW1P 3HE, UK. Tel: +44 (0) 20 7222 7665 (**www.niesr.ac.uk**) Price: Annual Subscriptions £105.00 UK & EU; £115.00 outside EU. Single issues £27.50 UK & EU.

Organisation for Economic Cooperation and Development (OECD), *Economic Outlook* Projections for OECD countries of output, employment, prices and current balances over the coming two years. Summary statistics and projections are included for developments in

non-member countries, in particular in Central and Eastern Europe as well as in selected Asian and Latin American economies. There is a general assessment of the macro-economic situation in a global context. Also 60-70 pages of data on Demand and Output, Wages, Costs and Inflation, Labour Force, Employment and Unemployment, Business Sector, Saving, Fiscal Balances and Public Indebtedness, Interest Rates and Exchange Rates, External Trade and Payments. Address: 2, rue André Pascal, 75775 Paris Cedex 16, France. Orders by fax: 33 (0) 1 49 10 42 76. E-mail: sales@oecd.org Online ordering: www.oecd.org/publications/ Price: £58.

Society of Motor Manufacturers and Traders Limited, *The Motor Industry Monthly Statistical Review*
Comprehensive data on retail sales of private and commercial vehicles. Address: Forbes House, Halkin Street, London, SW1X 7DS. Tel 0171 2357000. Price £30.

The British Phonographic Industry Limited, *BPI Statistical Handbook*
Source of data on the market for recorded music. Address: 25 Savile Row, London W1X 1AA. Tel 0207 2874422. Internet: **www.bpi.co.uk.**

World Bank, *World Development Indicators*
This annual book and CD-ROM includes data on 210 countries. It contains more than 80 tables and 600 indicators for the most recent observations, with a comparison for earlier decades, the WDI has become an invaluable source to those in the private sector who analyse business opportunities in developing countries and emerging markets. A sub-set of the WDI Data is contained in the annual *World Development Report* of the World Bank. Address: P.O. Box 960, Herndon, VA 20172-0960, USA. Tel: 1-800-645-7247 or 703-661-1580. E-mail: **books@worldbank.org**. Price: Book $60, CD-ROM $275. Free data on the Internet: **www.worldbank.org/data/databytopic/key refs.html.**

Index

Absolute difference   46
Accounting ratios   5
Accumulation accounts (National accounts)   24
Additivity   31
Administrative systems   34
Age distribution and consumption   138
Age distribution of population   63
Aggregate demand, composition   103
Aggregating data   36
Annual chainlinking   31-2
Appreciation   99, 147
Auto Regressive Integrated Moving Average
   (ARIMA)   37
Average cost pricing   77-80
Average earnings index   71
Averages   64
Balance of payments   22, 26
Balance of trade   133
Balance sheets (National accounts)   24
Bar graphs   44-5
Base index   43
Base index graph   45
Base weighted index   28-9
Base year   30
Basic prices   25, 116
Behavioural relationship   123
Behavioural segmentation   56
Benchmarks   140-5
Beta values   103
Boom-bust scenario   132
Capital Asset Pricing Model   102-3
Capital consumption   25
Capital flows   134
Carriage, insurance and freight (c.i.f.)   142
Causal relationships   90
Central tendency   64
Chain linking   31, 71
Checks and balances   24
Company accounts   19
Company information   12
Company sales index   18
Compensation of employees   23
Competing goods and demand   92
Competitiveness, international   148
Competitiveness, measurement   17
Composite commodities   40
Constant growth series   48
Constant prices   26, 28-30, 41, 88, 93, 121
Consumer expenditure   23, 88

Consumer expenditure, seasonal trend   90
Consumer goods   6
Consumer prices, calculation   89
Consumer spending, effects of   101
Consumption   104
Consumption and income   90
Consumption and relative price   90
Corporate Services Price Indices (CSPIs)   31, 34
Corporations   23
Cost   5
Cost index, weighted   75, 77
Cost trends   74
Crosschecking   24
Cross-price elasticity of demand   92
Cross-sectional data   57
Current account of the balance of payments   109
Current accounts (National accounts)   24
Current expenditure   41
Current prices   26, 28, 30, 41, 88, 121
Current weights, calculation   44
Cycles   49-50
Cyclical unemployment   106
Data processing   36
Deciles   58
Deflation   29, 76
Demand   87-97
Demand data   88
Demand estimation   82
Demand function   91-93
Demand models   92
Demand projections   16
Demographic segmentation   56
Demographics   138
Department of the Environment, Transport and the
   Regions   17
Depreciation   25, 117, 127, 147
Derived data   13
Disposable income   42
Disproportionate stratified sampling   63
Distribution   8
Distributive transactions   23
Dummy variables   93
Dynamic analysis   69-78
Earnings index, creating   70
Economic Accounts   22
Economic forecasting   122
Economic growth   101-2
Economic transactions   23
Economy, definition   22

Elasticity of demand   93
Employment   122
Endogenous variables   122-3
Equivalised post-tax income   60
Euro   99
European System of Accounts   113
Excel spreadsheet, regression procedure   94
Exchange rate   99, 109-11, 129-30, 147-8, 133-4, 139-50
Exogenous factors   54
Exogenous variables   122-3
Expenditure approach (GDP)   24, 30, 114
Expenditure by income decile   136
Exponential smoothing   53
Export demand   140
Export sales ratios   146-7
Exports   23, 104, 139-50
External factors   54
External information   5
External trade statistics   6
Extrapolation   11
Factors of production   6
Family Expenditure Survey   32, 136
Federal Reserve Bank   132
Final Expenditure Price Index (FEPI)   31, 34
Financial assets   23
Financial corporations   117
Financial Intermediation Services Indirectly Measured (FISIM)   117
Financial liability   23
Financial services sector   143
Financial transactions   23
First Release of National Statistics   36-7
Fixed capital formation   23
Fixed costs   81
Food processing   18
Forecasting   11, 53-4
Forecasting, economic   122
Forecasting, using regression analysis   96
Forward market   148
Free on board (f.o.b.)   142
Frequency of time-series data   48
Frictional unemployment   106
Futures market   148
GDP   104
GDP at market prices   25, 116
GDP in current and constant prices   27
General Agreement on Tariffs and Trade (GATT)   141
General government   117
Geographical segmentation   56
Globalisation   7
GNP per head   136
Government   23
Government consumption expenditure   23
Government spending   104
Graphs, cross-sectional   64

Graphs, time-series   44
Gross and net values   117
Gross Domestic Product (GDP)   23, 25, 114, 117
Gross National Disposable Income (GNDI)   117
Gross National Income (GNI)   117
Gross National Product   26
Growth rates   46
Growth, economic   131
Harmonised Index of Consumer Prices (HICP)   26, 31, 33, 76
Harmonised System of statistics   6
Hedging   148
Household consumption expenditure   23, 42-3
Household spending patterns   135
Households   23, 117
Identity   123
Implicit price   88
Import demand   140
Import penetration   146-7
Imports   104, 139-50
Income   136
Income approach (GDP)   30, 114
Income deciles, and expenditure   136
Income distribution   60-1, 137
Income elasticity of demand   91
Income method (GDP)   24
Index number, construction   27-9
Index of Consumer Prices (ICP)   34
Index of Government Prices (IGP)   34
Index of Investment Prices (IIP)   34
Index of output   44
Index of production   11
Index of productivity   73
Indirect taxes   114
Inferior good   91, 102
Inflation rate   22, 108
Inflation and interest rates   107
Inflation, measures of   31
In-house data   39
Input PPIs   33
Interest rate differential   134
Interest rates   99, 107, 132
Internal information   5
International investment   128-135
Interviews   64
Investment   104
Labour costs   114
Labour Force Survey   34
Labour productivity   72
Laspeyre's index   28-9, 32-3
Law of demand   91
Line graphs   44-5
Logarithmic series   46-7
Long-term changes   51-2
Macroeconomic data   7, 113
Macroeconomic environment   99-111
Management accounts   5

Marginal cost pricing 80-5
Marginal propensity to import 147
Marginal revenue 81
Market 5
Market exchange rates 130
Market prices 25
Market research 6
Market segmentation 9, 10, 55-6
Market segmentation, international 130
Market share 12, 17
Market size 8-9, 128, 135-8
Market structure 9, 14
Market trends 11, 15
Marketing 8
Markets 55
Mean 66
Median 66
Minimum wage 99
Mixed incomes 114
Mode 66
Monetary Policy Committee, Bank of England 123
Monitoring 8
Moving annual totals 7
Moving averages 52-3
Multinational strategy 128
Multiple regression analysis 93
National Accounts 22, 113
National Income 26
National Statistics (Office for National Statistics)
     21-2
Natural rate of unemployment 106
Net Domestic Product (NDP) 25
Net lending/borrowing or companies 26
Net property income from abroad 26
Nominal and real values 120
Nominal expenditure 40
Nominal interest rate 108
Nominal prices 93
Non-financial corporations 117
Non-profit institutions serving households (NPISH)
     117
Normal good 91
Numeraire 40
Official statistics, role of 12-13, 39
Operating environment 100
Operating surplus 23, 114
Ordinary least squares 52
Output approach (GDP) 23, 114
Output PPIs 33
Panel studies 6
Percentage change 46
Performance evaluation 8
Periodicity of time-series data 48
Pie chart 32, 66
Planning 7
Postal surveys 64-5
Press Release of National Statistics 36-7

Price elasticity of demand 91
Price indices 31
Prices and quantities 120-2
Primary data collection 62
Producer Price Index (PPI) 26, 31, 33, 74, 77
Production 8
Production or output approach (GDP) 30
Production statistics 6
Profit calculation 84
Profit margin 77
Profitability 102
Profits 5
Proportional stratified sampling 63
Psychographic segmentation 56
Publication of official data 36
Purchasing Power Parity (PPP) 129-30, 149
Quality of data 37
Random sample 62
Real exchange rate 133-4
Real expenditure 41
Real index of unit costs 76
Real interest rate 108
Real price 89, 93
Rebasing an index 30
Regional characteristics 10
Regression analysis 93, 95
Regression line 51
Relative magnitudes, measurement 42
Relative prices 89
Relative weights 44
Rereferencing data 31
Research and development 8
Rest of the world 23
Retail audits 6
Retail Prices Index (RPI) 26, 31,-2, 75, 122
Revaluation 29
Revenue 5
RPIX and RPIY 32, 76
Sales costs 10-11
Sample error 36
Sample selection 35
Sampling 62
Saving ratio 26
Scatter graph 90
Seasonal adjustment 37, 42
Seasonal dummy variables 93
Seasonal variations 49
Sector characteristics 6
Sectoral accounts 117-20
Ships' manifest data 7
Shocks 49-50
Short-term changes 51-2
Simple base index 43
Size of customer 10
Size of market estimation 13
Spot exchange rate 147
Standard Industrial Classification (SIC) 1992 24,

33, 142, 146
Static analysis 69, 78-85
Statistical surveys 34
Statistics of Trade Act 1948 19
Sterling exchange rate index 110, 148
Straight-line fitting 52
Strategic planning 7
Stratified sampling 63
Structural changes 50
Structural unemployment 106
Structure of economy 31
Subsidies 25, 114
Substitutes 92
Superior goods 102
Survey data 34-5
Survey design 64
Survey forms 35
Systematic sampling 63
Taxes on expenditure 25
Technical and economic change function (TECF) 16
Time-series data 39
Total cost 84
Total revenue 84

Totals, physical quantities 40
Tradable sector 111
Trade association data 39-40
Trade balance 22
Transactions 23
Transactions in products 23
Transfer payments 116
Trends 49-50
Turnover 5
Uncertainty and forecast errors 124
Unemployment 105, 122
Unit labour costs 150
Unit wage costs 73
Updating, Production data 13
User industries 9
Value added 116
Variable costs 81
Volume extrapolation 29
Volume of output 26
Wage inflation 105
Weighted index of costs 75

Index to Statistical Sources

Annual Business Survey   34
Barclays Bank Economic Review   148
Business Statistics Data analysis Service   38
Census of Production   18
Consensus Forecasts   127-9
Consumer Price Indices (MM23)   32
Economic Outlook, OECD   132
Economic Trends   33, 34, 37, 38, 71, 73, 74, 76,
     88,103, 104, 107, 109, 141, 143, 148, 149
Economic Trends Annual Supplement   133
Employment Report, Annual   14
ESRC Data Archive   38
European Economy   102, 105
Family Expenditure Survey   32, 57, 59, 135, 136,
     138
Family Spending   58, 59
Financial Statistics   109, 148
General Household Survey   57, 59
Index of Production   17
Inter-Company Comparisons (ICC)   19
Interdepartmental Business Register   19
International Financial Statistics, IMF   128, 129,
     131
International Marketing Data and Statistics,
     Euromonitor   137
Labour Force Survey   34
Labour Market Trends   71
Living in Britain   59
London Business School   103
Market profile   17
Monthly Digest of Statistics   27, 31, 41, 42, 71, 76,
     88, 142
Monthly Review of External Trade   142

Motor Industry Monthly Statistical Review   40
National Accounts Blue Book   30
National Food Survey   57
National Institute Economic Review   124-5
National Statistics Information and Library Service
     (NSILS)   38
Overseas Trade Analysed in Terms of Industries
     MQ10   142, 144
Oxford Economic Forecasting   130
PRODCOM, UK Product Report   6, 11, 13, 17, 88
Regional Trends   60, 61, 62, 63
Retail Sales Inquiry   34
RPI Technical Manual   32
Size Analysis of UK Business, PA1003   15
Social Trends   60
Statbase   38
Trade by Industry – Business Monitor MQ10   142
Trade partners   145
UK Balance of Payments, The Pink Book   38, 143-5
UK Economic Accounts   38
UK National Accounts   38, 115, 119, 121
World Development Indicators, World Bank   130
World Development Report, World Bank   137, 149

Internet sites
http://dawww.essex.ac.uk   38
http://www.statistics.gov.uk   22, 38, 88
http://www.worldbank.org/data/databytopic/keyref
     s.html   130, 149
http://www.worldbank.org/wdr/2000/pdfs/engtable
     5.pdf   137